Designing Curriculum for TESOL

Designing Curriculum for TESOL

Key Concepts and International Practices

Darío Luis Banegas

BLOOMSBURY ACADEMIC
LONDON · NEW YORK · OXFORD · NEW DELHI · SYDNEY

BLOOMSBURY ACADEMIC
Bloomsbury Publishing Plc, 50 Bedford Square, London, WC1B 3DP, UK
Bloomsbury Publishing Inc, 1359 Broadway, New York, NY 10018, USA
Bloomsbury Publishing Ireland, 29 Earlsfort Terrace, Dublin 2, D02 AY28, Ireland

BLOOMSBURY, BLOOMSBURY ACADEMIC and the Diana logo are trademarks of Bloomsbury
Publishing Plc

First published in Great Britain 2026

Cover design: Megan Wilson
Cover image © Eugene Mymrin via Getty Images

A catalogue record for this book is available from the British Library.

A catalogue record for this book is available from the Library of Congress.

ISBN: HB: 978-1-350-50330-4
         PB: 978-1-350-50331-1
         ePDF: 978-1-350-50333-5
         eBook: 978-1-350-50332-8

Typeset by Integra Software Services Pvt. Ltd.
Printed and bound in Great Britain

For product safety-related questions, contact productsafety@bloomsbury.com

To find out more about our authors and books, visit www.bloomsbury.com
and sign up for our newsletters.

Contents

Figures

Tables

On the Author

Darío Luis Banegas is Senior Lecturer in Language Education at the Moray House School of Education and Sport, University of Edinburgh, UK. He leads a course on second language teaching curriculum and is Director of Postgraduate Research. Darío is co-convener of the Language Curriculum Special Interest Group with the British Association of Applied Linguistics. His main areas of interest are: curriculum development, socially just initial language teacher education, content and language integrated learning and action research. He has delivered talks worldwide, and has (co)edited volumes with Bloomsbury, Routledge, Springer, Multilingual Matters and Palgrave.

Preface

Introduction

Hello! Hola! Every time I write for publication, I remind myself of The Devil's Dictionary (Bierce, 1911) entry for *publish*: 'to become the fundamental element in a cone of critics'. Writing is such an act! And you, dear reader, will be one of those critics.

Perhaps you are an undergrad or postgrad student, or a tutor, or a researcher, or something else and you are here because you need to work on something connected to TESOL and curriculum development. I should say that I have written this textbook having my master's students and myself as a tutor in mind. At the University of Edinburgh, I have led a core course called Second Language Teaching Curriculum for a number of years in the MSc TESOL programme. The pages that follow are the result of my teaching and learning with more than 250 students every year. I have had so much fun teaching the course that I thought of turning the lectures and workshops into a textbook.

I would like to thank all my students, colleagues and friends, who, in one way or another, have contributed to this textbook. Special thanks go to Bloomsbury for trusting me once again. I dedicate this book to my sister, Alejandra, who taught me to read and write in Spanish before I started my formal education.

How to Use This Textbook

You can use the textbook in any way you wish. Although, there is a certain logic to it. Let me address two aspects: the chapter titles and the order of the chapters. You may notice that every chapter starts with a question. This is because when I was teaching, I could hear myself repeating those questions a few times. Therefore, I found myself thinking about the TESOL curriculum around questions enabled me to refine my thinking, reflect and decide on what I wanted to include and how. Questions usually trigger answers. In this case, these questions have triggered answers the length of a chapter.

In terms of the order of the chapters, I wished the book to go from what is more visible and concrete to what appears to be more abstract and complex. Also, the book adopts an ecological perspective (Chapter 1), which includes micro, meso and macro aspects. Hence, Chapters 1–3 address the very essentials of the TESOL curriculum: what it means (Chapter 1), who brings it to life (Chapter 2) and what it contains (Chapters 3). I see these topics as micro aspects of the TESOL curriculum. As we know, a curriculum is often enacted in an institution. To me, evaluating the curriculum (Chapter 4) and carrying out possible changes (Chapter 5) is a more concerted enterprise that involves several actors. To me, these two aspects are at a meso level. Both micro and meso aspects respond to wider issues which we may not see at first, but they are embedded in any curriculum decisions. These are macro aspects because they respond to sociopolitical dynamics. Therefore, the book moves on to discuss key issues such as politics (Chapter 6), decolonization (Chapter 7) and identity (Chapter 8). Finally, I thought that I needed a chapter which would enable potential users (e.g. master's students) to bring micro, meso and macro aspects together by carrying out research on a TESOL curriculum. This is when I decided to include a chapter on different forms of research (Chapter 9). Despite this order, I recognize that some of you may just read the first three chapters, or you can start with the chapters addressing broader aspects such as ideology. Or you can use it as a reference book, dipping in and out. Or you can also use it to keep a door partly open ☺

The textbook contains several QR codes to facilitate access to different articles and sites. It also features a digital space I have called *TESOLand* so that people can share some of their answers to the activities included in each chapter.

Darío

Abbreviations

AI	Artificial Intelligence
AR	Action Research
BBC	British Broadcasting Corporation
BICS	Basic Interpersonal Communication Skills
BRAZTESOL	Brazilian Association of Teachers of English to Speakers of Other Languages
CALP	Cognitive Academic Language Proficiency
CELTA	Certificate in English Language Teaching to Adults
CLIL	Content and Language Integrated Learning
CLT	Communicative Language Teaching
CV	Curriculum Vitae
CPD	Continuing Professional Development
CSE	Comprehensive Sexuality Education
EAP	English for Academic Purposes
EAs	Extracurricular Activities
EFL	English as a Foreign Language
ELF	English as a Lingua Franca
EME	English-Medium Education
EMI	English-Medium Instruction
ERIC	Education Resources Information Center
ESD	Education for Sustainable Development
ESL	English as a Second Language
ESOL	English to Speakers of Other Languages
ESP	English for Specific Purposes
FoI	Funds of Identity
GenAI	Generative Artificial Intelligence
ICA	Intercultural Awareness
ILO(s)	Intended Learning Outcome(s)
IRE	International Relations English
JALT	Japanese Association for Language Teaching
LCs	Language Centres
LGBTQ+	Lesbian, Gay, Bisexual, Transgender, Queer and More
MEXT	Ministry of Education, Culture, Sports, Science and Technology
MoE	Ministry of Education
MSc	Master's of Science

NES	Native English Speaker
NHS	National Health Service
NMS	New Mexican School
PBL	Problem-Based Learning
PDF	Portable Document Format
PRISMA	Preferred Reporting Items for Systematic Reviews and Meta-Analyses
QR	Quick Response
RP	Received Pronunciation
SDG	Sustainable Development Goal(s)
SEP	Secretariat of Public Education
SFL	Systemic Functional Linguistics
TBL	Task-Based Learning
TESOL	Teaching English to Speakers of Other Languages
UNESCO	United Nations Educational, Scientific and Cultural Organization
US	United States

Chapter 1
What's the TESOL Curriculum?

Summary

The aim of this chapter is to introduce the complex construct of *curriculum*. The chapter adopts an ecological view that particularly underscores the importance of the *enacted curriculum*, i.e. the curriculum that teachers and learners co-create in the classroom. Drawing on the works of influential scholars in the language curriculum, such as Graves, Macalister, Nation, and Richards, the chapter describes a roadmap for curriculum design, types of curriculum (e.g. expected, taught, assessed, hidden), parts, dimensions and processes. It invites learners to discuss the role that Artificial Intelligence can play in process design.

1.1 Warm-Up

When you think of the word *curriculum*, you may think of a curriculum vitae (CV). If you do an online search, you will find a plethora of templates and tips on how to create an effective and appealing CV. But my question for you is: If you were to explain to a child what a CV is, what would you say? You can use Figure 1.1 to write your thoughts.

If I were you, I would tell the child that a CV is a written summary of someone's career, education, qualifications and skills. As we know, an effectively designed, 'good' CV will help you secure a job interview. But what do we mean by 'a good CV'? Based on your knowledge, experiences and understanding, what makes a CV 'good'? You can use Figure 1.2 to write your ideas.

Again, I would say that what makes a CV 'good' is its clarity and pertinence. This is achieved by highlighting what is really relevant to the job you are applying for. It is also

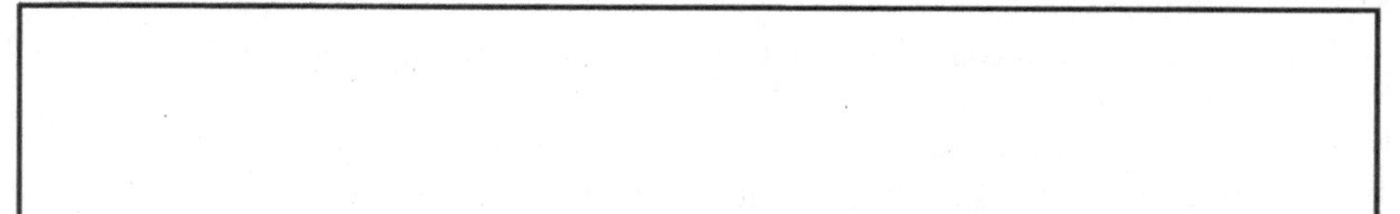

Figure 1.1 Box for your definition of curriculum vitae

Figure 1.2 Box
for characteristics
of a 'good' CV

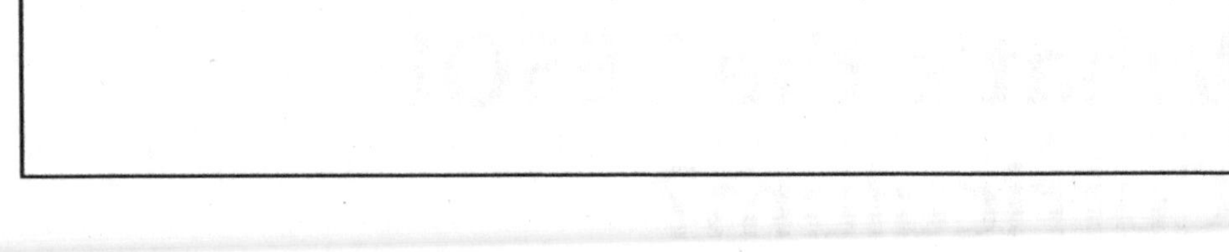

achieved by arranging your education, qualifications, experiences and so on in a logical and helpful manner. This is where you can draw parallels between a CV and the understanding of *curriculum* in education. Both share a common feature: organization. This is because in Latin, the word *curriculum* means 'course'. Hence, a CV could be understood as someone's life course, whereas in education, this refers to a course of studies.

With varying degrees of difference, education in general, and the teaching of English to speakers of other languages (TESOL) provision in particular, is an organized endeavour. For example, in your own context, there might be a Ministry of Education or an institution/ office of some sort that establishes how education should be organized, planned and delivered. There might be laws, regulations or policies that determine or suggest how the educational system should be run. For example, in Argentina, there was a Ministry of Education at the national level, and its role was to suggest how to organize and run the educational system, both public and private. There is also a National Law of Education (Congreso de la Nación Argentina, 2006b), which states in Chapter II, Article 87 that the teaching of a 'foreign language' is mandatory in primary and secondary education. It is worth noting that the law does not determine what language this is. In practice, this is almost always English, and, to a lesser extent, other named languages such as Portuguese, French, Italian or German, among others.

With this in mind, I would like you to complete Activity 1.1. The aim of this activity is to raise your awareness of how the educational system is organized in your own context.

Activity 1.1 Understanding the Educational System in Your Country

Answer these questions. You can then share them with a peer to compare and contrast contextual circumstances.

    a. Is there a role, such as minister/secretary of education? If the answer is 'yes', who is this person?
    b. Is there a law of education? Are there policies that regulate educational provision?
    c. Is education mandatory?
    d. Do high-level laws/policies say anything about language teaching?
    e. What institutions are in charge of preparing future teachers?

1.2 Programme, Course and Syllabus

Perhaps your answers to Activity 1.1 may have allowed you to identify broad organizational aspects of education in your country. With that in mind, I would like to introduce three key concepts related to curriculum: programme, course and syllabus (Table 1.1). These concepts are important in the understanding and shaping of how education is often arranged. However, do bear in mind that these concepts may change from country to country or from language to language. It might be helpful to refresh your own understanding of these terms in the languages that you usually use for professional purposes.

Figure 1.3 is my attempt at showing how the concepts defined in Table 1.1 may be part of a curriculum. Depending on contextual circumstances, the national, university or school curriculum may be the broadest educational organizer. That curriculum may include one or several programmes. Each programme may have its own curriculum, which would most likely consist of one or more courses. In turn, each course may have its own syllabus. Teachers may use a coursebook to support themselves with course delivery, but they can use a coursebook together with other resources/materials (e.g. YouTube videos, articles, picture books, teacher-made worksheets, apps, virtual environments)

Programme	This is usually the structure of a degree (e.g. master's in TESOL) or level of education (e.g. secondary), and it may contain several courses offered by a particular school, institution or department.
Course	This is usually a teaching/learning experience that occurs over a period of time with a specific goal. *Course* is usually found in higher education, but equivalents could be *subject* in secondary education. For example, you can complete an English for specific purposes (ESP) course at university or have English as a mandatory subject in your schooling.
Syllabus	This is usually understood as a plan for what is to be learnt in a particular course. It often includes the course aims, content, assessment and key references.
Coursebook	This refers to a textbook produced by a global or local publisher, an institution or an individual. This is one resource among many others that language teachers/learners can use to support their teaching/learning. Coursebooks may be specifically designed to match a certain curriculum. More often, coursebook series which are labelled as 'global' (i.e. they are meant to be used by people across different contexts) have their own rationale and structure. Thus, we can say that the series is a curriculum in itself, and the different levels/coursebooks in the series may be considered courses with their corresponding syllabus. This will be the content page.

Table 1.1
Definitions of Programme, Course, Syllabus and Coursebook

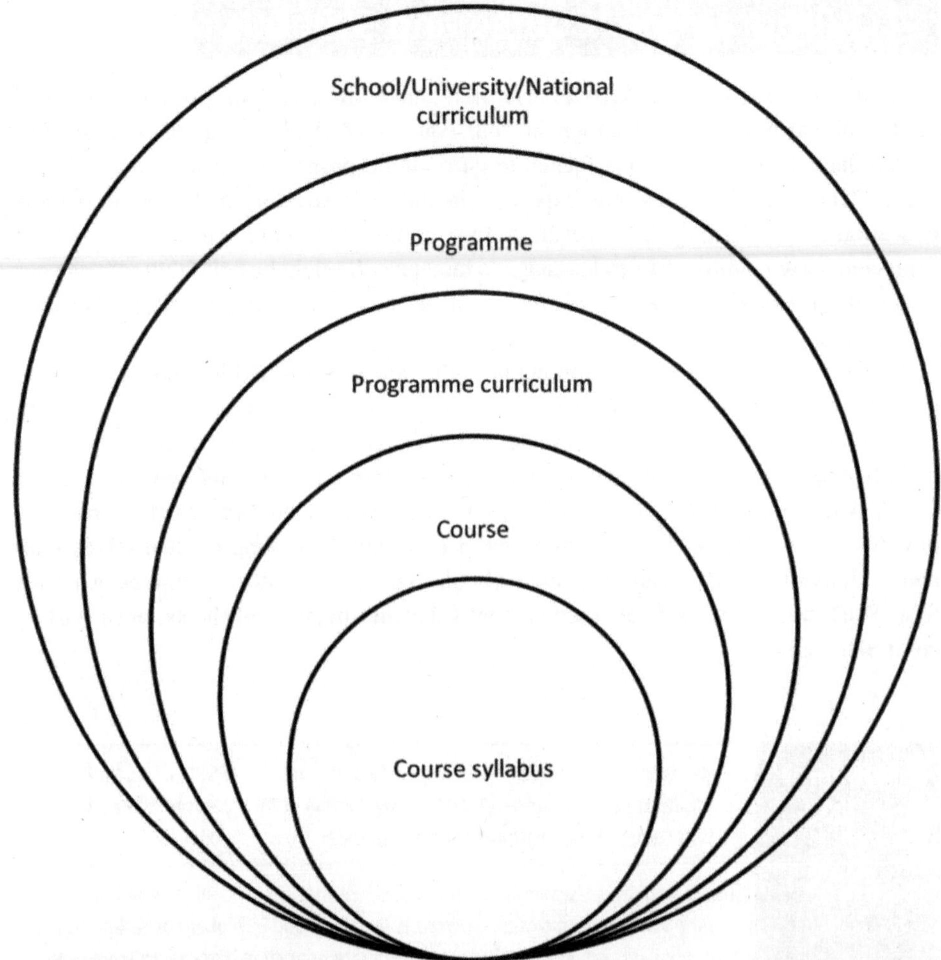

To show you an example, let me share with you details about the master's of science (MSc) TESOL programme at the University of Edinburgh delivered in 2024–2025. The programme curriculum, which they called handbook, was a 35-page document with information about: (1) teaching and support staff, (2) programme aims, (3) programme outline, (4) teaching and learning, (5) support for learners, (6) communication, (7) school visits and (8) a glossary of key terms. For the purposes of this warm-up, Vignette 1.1 concentrates on the programme outline.

I hope that the example offered in Vignette 1.1 has given you a hint of what a curriculum includes. With what has been discussed so far, I would like to draw your attention to Activity 1.2. The aim of this activity is to help you retrospectively examine previous courses you have completed.

<table>
<tr><td>Vignette
1.1</td><td></td></tr>
</table>

MSc TESOL (University of Edinburgh)

According to the MSc TESOL handbook, in 2024–2025 the programme consisted of four core courses, two option courses and a dissertation (Table 1.2).

Table 1.2 University of Edinburgh MSc TESOL Programme 2024–2025

Semester 1 (Sep–Dec)	Semester 2 (Jan–Apr)	Semester 3 (May–Aug)
Core: *TESOL Methodology* (20 credits) *Second Language Teaching Curriculum* (20 credits) *Language and the Learner* (20 credits) *Research Methods 1: Sources of Knowledge* (10 credits)	Core: *Research Methods 2: Conceptualizing Research* (10 credits) Option courses: You need to select two courses from a menu (each course is worth 20 credits)	Dissertation (60 credits)

Each of these courses has its own organization, and this is outlined in their syllabus. For example, the TESOL Methodology course syllabus (you can find it online) includes a summary of the main topics and teaching approach used, a breakdown of the contents included, entry requirements, course delivery information (e.g. start and end dates, number of hours, activities such as lectures and workshops) and information about summative assessment and feedback.

Activity 1.2 Looking at a Past Course You Are Familiar With

Think about an English language learning course you took, or a current course, and try to complete these sentences using the prompts in square brackets. Feel free to tweak the sentences so that they are contextually meaningful to you.

1. The name of the course was...
2. I completed the course in... [place] in... [time period].
3. The aim of the course was to...
4. The course was directed towards learners who... [What were the learners' characteristics? Did they need to have a certain level of English before taking the course?]
5. The course included contents such as... [topics]
6. The course was taught by... [role/name]
7. In terms of teaching approaches and activities, the course included...
8. The course was assessed by means of...

1.3 Defining the Curriculum

As you may be aware, the term *curriculum* is a potent construct to understand and structure the complex processes of teaching and learning. The construct has been defined from different perspectives over time as these respond to different theories of education and broader ideologies, and ways of conceiving the act of teaching (Ashbee, 2021; Schiro, 2012). As Kelly (2009) has rightly noted, there is a plethora of definitions. Hence, I would like you to be critical of the definitions you find in this section as well as elsewhere and understand them in their context of production, i.e. where they come from (this does not just refer to geographical location, but also conceptually and politically speaking) and time of publication. You can have a look at the titles included in Section 1.8 if you would like to know more about curriculum theory in general.

From all the definitions available, I have selected a few which come from the area of language teaching. Professor Kathleen Graves is a world-known expert in the field of the language curriculum, and her 2008 definition was situated within a social-contextual perspective, i.e. a perspective that recognizes all the people and the setting in/for/with whom/which a curriculum is developed. Her definition was:

> A curriculum is the processes and products of planning, teaching and evaluating a course of study or related courses [...]. Curriculum involves planning what is to be taught/learned, implementing it and evaluating it.
>
> (Graves, 2008, p. 147)

According to this definition, there are processes as well as products. These two words indicate that a curriculum responds to temporal circumstances, i.e. it begins at some point, and this refers to its planning, and those processes that occur over a certain period of time (e.g. a school year, a term) lead to products. In this case, products include what learners have learnt, the new knowledge they have constructed and have been able to demonstrate through exams, and hopefully, beyond the context of schooling. After all, we do not (or should not?) teach English (or any other area of knowledge) only for the purposes of learners passing exams. While it is true that, from an instrumental and short-term perspective, learners need to pass exams to obtain a certificate, the main goal is that learners are enabled to use English for different purposes (e.g. interactional) in different contexts so that English can become a meaningful mediating tool to construct experiences and knowledges.

Another helpful definition of curriculum has been put forward by Professor Jack Richards. You can find videos of his talks on YouTube. In 2013, he explained that the term curriculum refers to

> the overall plan or design for a course and how the content for a course is transformed into a blueprint for teaching and learning which enables the desired learning outcomes to be achieved. [...] Once content has been selected, it then needs to be organized into teachable and learnable units as well as arranged in a rational sequence. The result is a syllabus.
>
> (Richards, 2013, p. 6)

You may note that the Graves (2008) definition and the Richards (2013) definition agree on planning as a key feature of what a curriculum is. Richards (2013) mentions other elements such as content, learning outcomes and sequence. (We will discuss these elements in Chapter 3.) He also highlights that whatever is planned needs to be developed in such a way that is *teachable and learnable*. In other words, it has to be pedagogically possible. This view reminds me of Chevallard's (1985) notion of didactic transposition, a concept that has not found much traction in Anglo-Saxon education, but it has informed French and Latin American education. In rather simple terms, didactic transposition refers to the transformations that scholarly knowledge or a language, in our case, undergoes from its production to its selection, planning and teaching in a given course of studies (Chevallard & Bosch, 2014). In the case of TESOL, this might explain why we break down English into interconnected teachable units such as grammar (e.g. tenses, prepositions, word classes), vocabulary, pronunciation and mediation skills (listening, reading, speaking and writing). It may also explain why the teaching of English often involves teaching one specific variety (e.g. British English), register (e.g. formal) or set of functions (e.g. describing) which are deemed as more regular (or dominant) than others.

The idea of what is teachable and learnable may also be understood from a perspective that sees the curriculum as a site of constraints as well as possibilities. According to Young (2014), while a curriculum does put a limit, at least on paper, on what is taught and learnt (we can't just possibly learn it all at school, otherwise a school day would be almost twenty-four hours!), it 'make[s] some things possible to learn that most of us would find impossible to learn without them' (p. 7). The possibility of learning resides in the rationale behind and actual content selection and sequencing as well as the educational and pedagogical principles and learning outcomes that give life to a curriculum. Vignette 1.2 is an example of a TESOL curriculum from China. You can take this opportunity to find the curriculum in your area/country/school/university. This may be available, for example, in the Ministry of Education website or other official sites. Bear in mind that it may be written in the official language(s) of your country.

So far, we have highlighted that planning is a core feature of a curriculum because it seeks to allow organized implementation. Along these lines, Graves reconsidered her 2008 definition (Graves, 2016) and proposed that the actual implementation of the curriculum deserves more attention. Therefore, in her 2016 publication, she states that:

> a curriculum is the dynamic interplay of three interconnected processes: planning, enacting and evaluating. In this view, a curriculum is not just a design for learning, it is also the learning itself; it is both the plan and the enactment. The enacted curriculum is what happens in the classroom among learners and the teacher.
>
> (Graves, 2016, p. 80)

While planning still plays a pivotal role, her definition recognizes that what has been planned and included in what we may call *the official curriculum* (i.e. the curriculum you would find printed or as a PDF document on an official website) may not be what actually happens in practice, which is often the case. This is what she means by enactment: the actual teaching and learning practices that occur in a classroom. This emphasis on what teachers actually do is rooted in Graves' (2008) view that there has been (or there

<table>
<tr><td>**Vignette 1.2**</td><td>**Compulsory Education English in China (2022), by Yupei Wei**</td></tr>
</table>

In most Chinese public schools, English classes start from Grade 3 to Grade 6 in primary school (four years) and then continue in secondary school (three years) and high school (three years). Primary school and secondary school levels comprise the compulsory education stage. English class is one of the compulsory courses from primary school to university stage.

The aims of English language teaching and learning change according to grades in different stages. For each grade in the compulsory education stage and high school, developing language skills, cultural awareness, quality of thinking and learning strategies are the main focus of the English Curriculum Standards. The specific requirements of these four skills will gradually increase according to different grades in each stage. Language skills have been prioritized among these skills.

The content in English classes is structured in 8–9 units per English textbook for each semester in public primary schools. Topics to frame such content include: festivals, transportation, foods, cities and countries around the world, foreign literature, travel and daily conversations in textbooks. Each unit in English textbooks mainly covers grammar, vocabulary and pronunciation. Although mediation skills are also covered, listening and speaking skills have always been paid less attention. Cultural awareness, quality of thinking and learning strategies are less discussed in the textbooks.

In terms of teaching approaches, the suggestions are extremely general and only refer to communication and drilling in their broadest sense in the English Curriculum Standards. Although the Standards provides examples of teaching, these examples seldom become real cases in practice in English class. As for assessment types, these include performance in the classroom and examinations after each unit and the whole textbook used each semester in an academic year.

Useful links:

English language teaching textbooks across the stages: http://www.dzkbw.com/books/all-yingyu/

Compulsory Education English Curriculum Standards (2022): W020220420582349487953.pdf (moe.gov.cn)

should be) a shift from seeing curriculum development through a specialist approach to designing a curriculum through a socially enacted, context-sensitive approach. To illustrate this (desired) change, let me share with you Vignettes 1.3 and 1.4 based on my first-hand knowledge and own experience as a curriculum developer in Argentina. Please note that both cases only refer to the planning stage of curriculum development – what we may call curriculum design. You can also benefit from the activities accompanying the two cases.

I must say that Vignette 1.3 paints a rather negative picture of the specialist approach, as it may raise some questions: Who qualifies as a 'specialist' to design a curriculum? Who provides/should provide feedback? To what extent should consultation be involved? What levels of consultation should there be? Who would these potential consultants be? In some cases, the specialist is someone with (a) expertise in additional language teaching achieved through postgraduate degrees (a master's and/or a PhD in, for example, education, language teaching, applied linguistics, TESOL) and (b) teaching/teacher education experience in the context for which the curriculum is for. However, I am aware of cases around the world where a government may hire a specialist based elsewhere (e.g. an academic based in the UK) to design the TESOL curriculum. In the best of cases, this international specialist may work together with a group of local specialists to gain contextual insights.

Based on the discussion held so far, here is my attempt at defining the TESOL curriculum: *I understand the TESOL curriculum as a powerful and dynamic organizing context-sensitive educational tool that seeks to orient, structure and support teachers' construction of meaningful language learning events for learners in a given context*. Note that this definition could be applicable to the total curriculum or any other subject of the curriculum. Now, you can do Activity 1.5.

Activity 1.5 may have helped you notice that there seems to be a lot packed into my definition. Now, let me unpack the content words included in it:

<table>
<tr><td>Vignette
1.3</td><td>

The Specialist Approach to TESOL Curriculum Design

</td></tr>
</table>

Argentina is divided into several provinces. While there is a National Ministry of Education, each province has its own Ministry of Education. This is because the budget is decided and funded by each provincial government. In 2002, a provincial Ministry of Education commissioned the design of a new curriculum for secondary education. To this effect, it brought together one expert/specialist from each school subject the new curriculum would have. In the case of English, one experienced TESOL teacher educator wrote the section on English. She had plenty of experience as a teacher of English in the private sector, and to a lesser extent in the state sector of the province for which the curriculum was for. She worked on her own and set out the aims, content, teaching approach and assessment criteria. In line with developments at the time and macro-agreements at national level, she decided that the aim of teaching English in secondary schools was to enable learners to engage in transactional and interactional exchanges through the additional language. The contents for the six years of secondary education were organized into six levels, one per each year, and it was broken down into language functions (e.g. narrating, suggesting, expressing opinions), grammar (e.g. passive voice), vocabulary (e.g. countries and nationalities), pronunciation, and oral (speaking and listening) and written skills (reading and writing). When her deadline approached, she submitted the English curriculum to the relevant authorities, who then submitted it to the National Ministry of Education for feedback. The specialist revised the curriculum in light of the feedback received and submitted it again to the provincial Ministry of Education. The curriculum was almost automatically accepted and then included in the 2003 total curriculum (i.e. a curriculum that includes all school subjects for a certain context/system of education). It was implemented between 2003 and 2012.

Activity 1.3 On Vignette 1.3

Read Vignette 1.3 (again) and choose the best option for each of the statements below. In some cases, more than one option is possible. Think of a reason to justify each choice. (Answers and justifications in Chapter 10.)

1. The specialist had ___________ autonomy in the design of the curriculum.

   a. little   **b.** a great deal of   **c.** no

2. It seems that the specialist did not ____________ ELT stakeholders as she worked on the curriculum.

   a. have conversations with   **b.** collect feedback from
   c. share drafts of the curriculum with

3. The provincial Ministry of Education appeared to ____________ the curriculum design.

   a. have exercised strict control over   **b.** have supported the specialist with
   c. have detached itself from

Why powerful? It is powerful because it can have a tremendous impact on an educational system and society at large and on what learners learn in a formal context. It sets what is to be learnt and how (and what is not to be learnt… at least formally). It is also powerful because it can transform society to make it more (or unfortunately less) equitable and inclusive.

Why dynamic? Although there is an officially published version, a curriculum is not set in stone. There is a dynamic and complex relationship between the curriculum and those who use it. This dynamism captures the fluctuations between the planned curriculum and the enacted curriculum.

<table>
<tr><td>**Vignette 1.4**</td><td># The Socially Enacted Approach to TESOL Curriculum Design</td></tr>
</table>

In 2007, I was tasked with supporting TESOL teachers with the implementation of the TESOL curriculum briefly described in Vignette 1.3. My intervention led to a new TESOL curriculum for secondary education in 2012. Use either Figure 1.4 or 1.5 to access an article (Banegas, 2011) that describes that journey.

Figure 1.4 QR code to access Banegas (2011)

Figure 1.5 QR code to access a free version of Banegas (2011) (sign-up may be required)

From this article, you may wish to focus on Sections 1, 3, 4, 7 and 8. The sections are not numbered in the versions shared, but I trust you can identify them if you take the Introduction as Section 1 and so on.

Activity 1.4 On Vignette 1.4

1. Go over the Banegas (2011) article featured in Vignette 1.4. Individually or with your peers, think (and discuss)

   a. the ways in which this case study illustrates a socially enacted approach to the TESOL curriculum.
   b. differences and similarities between Vignettes 1.3 and 1.4.
   c. benefits and challenges of the specialist approach and the socially enacted approach to the TESOL curriculum.

2. Create a concept map that summarizes the ideas expressed in (1) above. You can share them with the world using Figure 1.6.

Figure 1.6 QR code access to TESOLand

Activity 1.5 Comparing Definitions

Go back to the definitions of curriculum provided by Graves (2008), Richards (2013), Graves (2016) and my definition included on page 8. What commonalities and differences can you notice? You can use Table 1.3 to help you.

Table 1.3 Comparing Definitions

	Graves (2008)	Richards (2013)	Graves (2016)	Banegas (this chapter)
Similarities				
Differences				

Why organizing? It shows what is to be taught and how. There is often some kind of logic behind the selection of the whats, hows and whys of TESOL education. These elements are also logically sequenced.

Why context-sensitive? It is designed for a specific setting (e.g. a country, a region, a school), people, needs and time, and therefore, it should respond to the needs and affordances identified in that environment.

Why orient? It includes general and specific goals. It can be understood as a compass that provides a sense of individual (a teacher and their learners) as well as collective (a school and their teachers and learners) direction.

Why structure? It provides a framework for educational and institutional coherence and cohesion. It can be metaphorically seen as a map that helps understand and enhance quality TESOL provision. A curriculum provides the larger picture, a sensible whole.

Why support teachers? It is a tool that teachers can use to improve their TESOL teaching practice. It shows them what their learners are expected to learn. Teachers can make changes to it as they enact the curriculum. A curriculum has teachers and educational authorities (e.g. school principal, programme coordinator) as its primary readership.

Why meaningful language learning events? The teaching of English needs to have a societal purpose. A language is a living organism that we use to construct meanings either with others or when we language thoughts, states and events individually.

While it may be agreed that a curriculum can be a helpful tool, Graves (2023) acknowledges that there are limits to what it can do, and hence discusses two fallacies (i.e. misleading claims, statements that look argumentatively sound but they are not) that I have condensed in Table 1.4.

With the aim of capturing the practice-related aspects of the discussion so far, you can now complete Activity 1.6.

Table 1.4 Curriculum Fallacies According to Graves (2023)

Fallacy	What Makes it Misleading?
'A good curriculum is the foundation for effective teaching and learning' (Graves, 2023, p. 199).	A curriculum, understood as a document, is just a tool, a framework. It is not effective on its own. A curriculum may be in principle written in a clear, cogent and helpful manner, but it does not guarantee that what the printed document says is what learners will experience in the classroom. Here we see the difference between the official curriculum that is *intended* or expected to happen, and the *enacted* curriculum. For example, think about your own experience as a learner of English. The curriculum (or the coursebook) may have been great, but did that automatically make your learning experience meaningful?
'When teachers faithfully follow a curriculum as designed, they will produce consistent learning results' (Graves, 2023, p. 199).	Teachers are not passive implementers of a curriculum. They are neither robots nor technicians that only do what they are told. While I recognize that there may be highly top-down educational systems with prescriptive curricula, this does not guarantee that every teacher will be doing exactly the same. It's just preposterous! There is also an incorrect assumption that curriculum development is a linear process, i.e. that the curriculum will directly translate into effective teaching, that will in turn translate in consistent learning. If this were the case, we would have extremely homogenous systems where every teacher and learner thrive. Think about this: Is this what you experienced when you learnt English at school?

Activity 1.6 On Definitions and Fallacies

Based on the definitions included in this section and the fallacies condensed in Table 1.4, address these questions:

1. Individually, what is a curriculum for you? How would you define the *TESOL curriculum*? What should it do? Do you agree or disagree with the fallacies discussed in Table 1.4? Do you know what expectations teachers may have of the TESOL curriculum in your context? Give yourself some time to think about these questions, and note down any key ideas.
2. Get together with other peers. Nominate someone to keep a record of what is discussed (Note: you will return to these notes later). Share with them your answers to (1) above.

1.4 A Roadmap

So far, we have discussed what a curriculum is. Nevertheless, a curriculum is part of an even larger picture: curriculum development. This is what Graves (2016) means by planning, enacting and learning, or Richards' (2013) reference to transforming the curriculum into doable teaching and learning. This takes me to Figure 1.7, which is my attempt at outlining some possible stages or steps in curriculum development. While Figure 1.7 shows a sequence of events, this does not mean that it is a linear process. More often than not, steps could develop in tandem, or there is a need to go a step back to ensure consistency, clarity or a stronger sense of direction. In this proposed sequence, I also endorse Graves' (2008) social-contextual perspective, as it is of paramount importance to develop a language curriculum that is situated in the context for which it is intended, and that it involves the relevant stakeholders in that context. I should also highlight that this proposed roadmap may be lengthy, and, in my experience, it may take at least a couple of years. Last, the enactment of this roadmap could benefit from the use of artificial intelligence (GenAI) (Karataş et al., 2025). As you read each stage, make a note of how GenAI can assist, enhance and accelerate TESOL curriculum development.

Let us look at Figure 1.7 in more detail:

Exploration: This stage refers to having informal conversations with relevant stakeholders, such as policymakers, TESOL teachers, teacher educators and TESOL programme coordinators, to understand what they expect from a TESOL curriculum. This could be done through emails or a casual conversation. This may allow TESOL curriculum developers to have a feel of stakeholders' experiences with a past or current TESOL curriculum and how (or whether) they use it. Possible questions to ask: What do you think

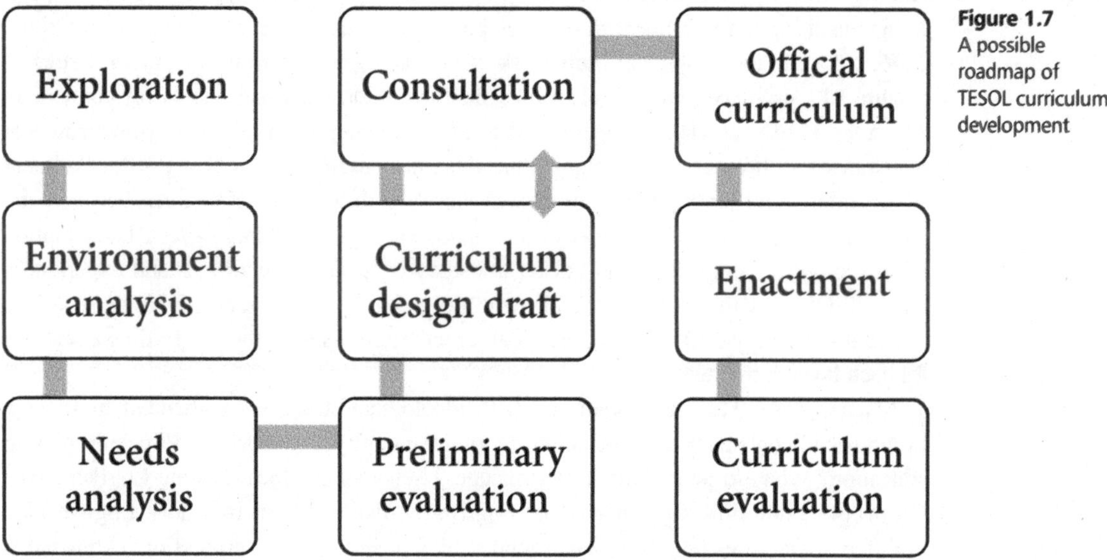

Figure 1.7
A possible roadmap of TESOL curriculum development

of the current curriculum? Have you found it helpful? What do you like about it? In what areas is there room for improvement? If you were to sell it to another context, what would you highlight? How do you use it? When do you use it? Why should English be included in the curriculum? How do people use English in your context? These questions may prompt stakeholders to evaluate the TESOL curriculum, but in this case, curriculum developers will be collecting impressions that can be used more strategically in the next step. Let me add that this stage also refers to those who will lead the design of a new curriculum. So, if you are one of them, what are your own goals with this new curriculum? What is driving you to engage in developing a new TESOL curriculum? What would you like it to be like? What's your own understanding of curriculum development and TESOL? What are you bringing to the table? What might you need help with? Who could support you?

Environment analysis: As suggested above, the exploration stage seeks to collect impressionistic views. It is like a quick survey of landscape experiences and perceptions. Such mapping can help calibrate the environment stage, which seeks to provide information about the views and roles of English as well as details about its users, primarily learners. It also includes those who will use the curriculum: teachers and other educational actors (programme leaders, head teachers, etc.). For this analysis, I suggest taking an ecological perspective. This perspective can in fact inform the whole roadmap put forward in Figure 1.7, but in my experience, it may be conducive to start small, and from there the process can be more comprehensively addressed.

What do I mean by an ecological perspective? According to Bronfenbrenner (1979), ecology is a way of understanding the set of embedded and interconnected systems present in human development, paying attention to process, person, context, space (place) and time. From this perspective, ecology allows for an organic description of the environment from micro to macro contextual layers. Bronfenbrenner's (1979) model of ecological theory has been employed, for example, to represent the semiotics, (inter)actions and developments in language learning (van Lier, 2004, 2011), or 'the multilayered complexity of L2 learning' for a transdisciplinary framework of second language acquisition (The Douglas Fir Group, 2016, p. 24). In the ecological framework of language curriculum development, I suggest (Figure 1.8), each concentric circle represents three interrelated subsystems or contexts in which the TESOL curriculum operates. A fourth subsystem is represented by an arrow that penetrates the three circles to signify the dynamic environmental changes/development which may occur over time. The broken lines symbolize the interstices between the subsystems; that is, the possibilities of interaction among the different layers. The adoption of an ecological perspective can bolster the study of working conditions and experiences with TESOL since these influence and are influenced by the environment in different layers.

What does Figure 1.8 entail in practical terms? Here, I suggest a few guiding questions for each layer/subsystem:

Macrosystem: This subsystem refers to ideological structures embedded in society. In the social context of the curriculum (e.g. city, country), what value do people give to education? What do people think of languages? What status does learning English have? Do people value different varieties of English/Englishes? What role does English play in different activities (e.g. business, social media, hospitality, the professions, knowledge

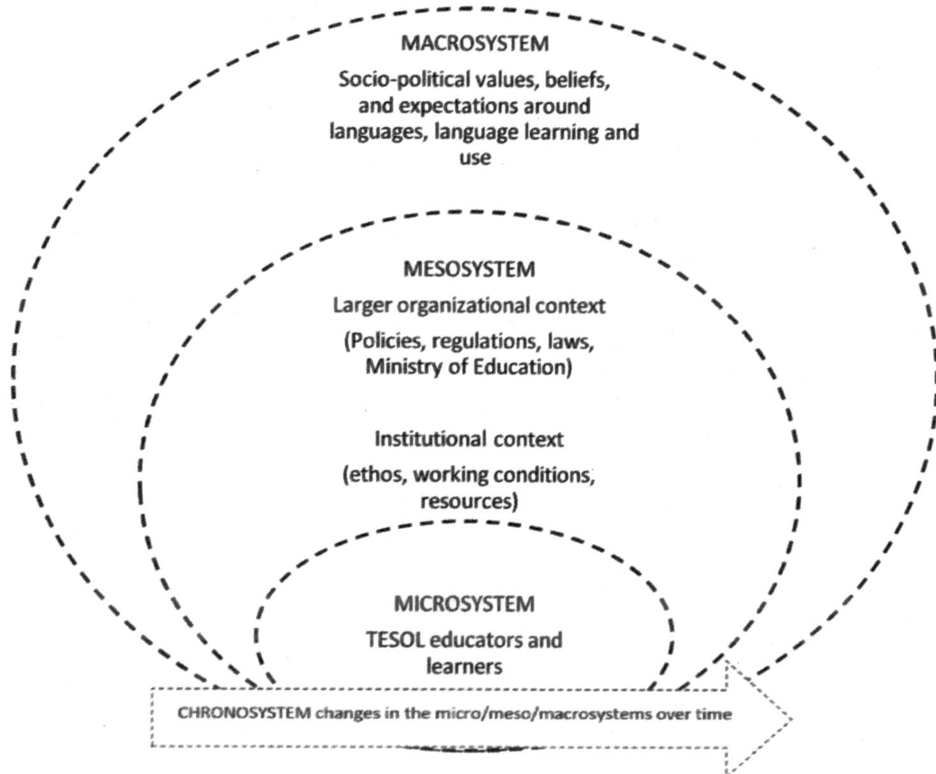

Figure 1.8
An ecological framework of the TESOL curriculum

creation and dissemination, entertainment)? Should everyone have the right to learn English according to those in power? Who agrees/disagrees with them?

Mesosystem: This subsystem includes national/regional/local as well as specific educational institutions. Questions to understand this layer could be: Are there official languages by law? Is there a law of education? Does the law say anything about the teaching of additional languages? Are there national/regional policies about how formal education should be organized? Is there a national/regional curriculum that stipulates the number of teaching hours allocated to English or any other language? How are teachers of English prepared? Is there a shortage of teachers of English? Is English part of the core curriculum? Is it compulsory or optional across the educational system? Are there national exams for learners learning English?

At institutional level, some possible questions are: What type of institution is it (e.g. state, private, bilingual)? What are the institution's ethos, values, mission, etc.? Where is the institution geographically located? What is its reputation? Are some teaching approaches preferred over others? Are TESOL educators permanent or under a contract? Are they full- or part-time? Does the institution have any explicit (or hidden) requirements to employ a teacher of English (e.g. some institutions sadly still prefer 'native speakers' of English with or without TESOL qualifications)? Who funds their salaries? Can they take annual leave? Are they expected to work during annual leave? How many teaching periods are allocated to the teaching of English? How are these distributed? Can they take place on any day and time in the timetable? Are there TESOL leaders/programme coordinators? What does administrative work involve, and who does it? Are there teaching assistants? Could the institutions hire assistants? Could learners be regrouped according to English language proficiency for the TESOL lessons? What teaching resources are available? If teachers need physical or digital materials (e.g. an app, a paid website, photocopies), will the institution provide them? Are teachers expected to use coursebooks? Can they select the coursebooks? Who buys the coursebooks (learners' families, The MoE, The school)? Are there institutional exams (entry exams, diagnostic exams, end of year exams)? Are learners prepared to take international exams (e.g. Cambridge ESOL exams, Trinity exams)? Where does learning take place? Who changes classrooms, the teachers and/or the learners? What are the classrooms like? Is it OK for TESOL lessons to take place in different spaces (e.g. school library, corridors, computer lab, school yard)? Could lessons be in-person, hybrid, online? How many learners are there per class? Can they work in groups? Is there an online platform/campus TESOL teachers can use? Can teachers use digital spaces (e.g. Padlet) for educational purposes? If the teachers would like to purchase a subscription to digital tools (e.g. Canva), who would fund it? If teachers would like to take a course to further develop their teaching skills, will it be paid for by the institution? Can they take paid leave? Will it be officially recognized/encouraged? If the institution expects teachers to keep themselves abreast of new developments in the field, who is in charge of addressing these expectations? As you may note, the list of questions could be endless, but it is important that curriculum developers are aware of the possibilities and constraints they may encounter (a T table with strengths and constraints, and how to address the latter could be a good start) since these will be influential in the success of the TESOL curriculum.

Microsystem: This subsystem refers to the primary users of the TESOL curriculum, i.e. teachers and learners. Some initial questions: Who are the TESOL teachers? What's their background? What's the job profile? What is their teaching experience? Do they usually take part in continuing professional development (CPD) opportunities (e.g. short courses, a master's degree)? What are their views on TESOL? What (de)motivates them? Are they members of any professional association (e.g. TESOL International, BRAZTESOL in Brazil, JALT in Japan)? Who are the learners? What's their profile (age, etc.)? What's their background? What are their learning experiences? What (de)motivates them?

Chronosystem: This subsystem refers to the interactions and concomitant changes that occur within and across the micro, meso and macrosystems over time. Some initial questions to understand this subsystem could be: Do stakeholders' views and experiences with a TESOL curriculum change after each year of its implementation? What factors affect or change the TESOL curriculum over time? Does continuous curriculum enactment and evaluation help students, teachers and institutions develop over a given period of time?

Needs analysis: As Macalister and Nation (2020) suggest, for a TESOL curriculum to be context-responsive, it should be based on what curriculum users and beneficiaries need. This type of analysis is more people-oriented as it includes learners, teachers and even learners' carers. To gather information about what is needed, surveys, focus groups and individual as well as group interviews could be utilized. Also, feedback from previous school years, and learners' academic achievements and overall performance can be good

Activity 1.7 Carrying Out Needs Analysis

Imagine that you have been asked to co-develop a new TESOL curriculum for an organization that provides English language learning lessons to refugees in the UK. Design one or two instruments (e.g. a focus group interview and a survey) that will help you conduct needs analysis in preparation for the design of the TESOL curriculum.

indicators of what has been accomplished and what needs to be done. Regarding teachers, it is vital to understand what needs have been identified in relation to their own teaching practices. In other words, what do they need to make the TESOL curriculum successful? What CPD could be offered to them? Would it work to put in place a mentoring scheme? Who would run it? How? Will this be institutionally supported? Equally important, what are the teachers good at? What/How do they particularly enjoy teaching? And as for learners, what do they want from learning English? What will they use English for? What have they achieved so far? What are they good at? What do they need support with? What do they seem to lack to achieve their goals? Do they wish (or need to) pass certain exams to get a job, obtain a qualification, secure a visa or be offered a place at a university course?

Before we move forward, you can work in a small group or on your own to complete Activity 1.7.

Preliminary evaluation: The information gathered from the initial exploration, environment analysis and needs analysis should allow curriculum developers to make some initial, informed decisions about the TESOL curriculum to be designed. For example, if you were to actually implement the instruments designed in Activity 1.7, you may gather that on the one hand, teachers will need to be familiarized with less formal ways of teaching since teaching refugees may be very different from teaching international postgraduate learners on a pre-sessional TESOL course in higher education. On the other hand, the learners who receive English language learning lessons may primarily need English to understand regulations, rights, processes, 'legalese' (i.e. legal English), as well as English to participate in social and community life while they wait for a decision on their status. They may also need English to apply for jobs, register with the NHS general practice and so on. These answers will certainly have an impact on the aims, content, the overall shape and operational side (budget, number of teachers, duration and frequency of lessons, etc.) of the curriculum.

Curriculum design draft: This stage refers to the discussion and drafting of the curriculum. Initial questions for this stage could be: What are the aims? What philosophical, educational and language teaching principles will inform the curriculum? What information should the curriculum contain? How can this information be effectively organized? (We will come back to this aspect in Chapter 3.) Who will be the intended users? How long should it be? How should it be available? In what language(s) will it be written? This stage may take some time, as it is not easy to distil the complexity of the TESOL curriculum into coherent,

<table>
<tr><td>Vignette 1.5</td><td><h2>On Drafting a Curriculum</h2></td></tr>
</table>

In 2018, I was employed as a consultant to join a group of five academics to design an English for academic purposes (EAP) programme for a university in Ecuador. By the time I became part of the working group, they had already gathered data about the environment and conducted a needs analysis by means of online surveys and an analysis of learners' coursework from past and current EAP courses. Based on the evaluation of the data gathered, we agreed that the curriculum would be rooted in a combination of systemic functional linguistics, genre-based pedagogies and corpus linguistics and would aim at developing learners' written and oral academic language skills. We agreed that the new EAP programme would consist of six one-term courses which would combine in-person and online delivery. There would be placement tests, achievement exams and so on. We agreed that the official curriculum, i.e. the curriculum as a document, would have teachers and programme coordinators as the primary audience, and that it would be written in Spanish (dominant language in Ecuador) as the curriculum should be inclusive of other relevant stakeholders and staff within the university. We also agreed that our first draft of the curriculum would include: (a) a summary of the needs and environment analysis as a way to justify our context-responsive decisions, (b) the aims of the programme and aims of each course, (c) a table with the overall contents of each course, (d) a section on the programme pedagogical framework (i.e. a quick summary of systemic functional linguistics, genre-based pedagogies and corpus linguistics) together with sample activities, suggestions for materials selection, adaption, creation, suggestions for feedback, (e) guidance on testing and assessment, including criteria, sample rubrics, sample tests, and (f) a section on further reading. The write-up of the first draft, which was accompanied by online meetings monthly, took us about six months to complete.

cohesive writing. For example, look at Vignette 1.5 to enhance your understanding of what this process might look like in practice.

Consultation: This is a vital step, as it can provide curriculum developers with key insights regarding clarity, coherence and pertinence. In a nutshell, this step refers to circulating a drafted curriculum among relevant stakeholders (e.g. teachers, line managers, policy makers, ministerial authorities) with the aim of gathering feedback. There are different ways of obtaining comments. Here are some options:

A circulating the draft among teachers and TESOL programme leaders with a set of questions.

B holding a small meeting with teachers and other stakeholders where the curriculum developers give a brief presentation about the core elements of the proposed curriculum (e.g. aims, contents, teaching approaches, materials). The presentation is followed by asking those attending to discuss some questions in small groups, and then they can report back. On this option, it is important that the curriculum developers remain open to different forms of comments (even some that could 'hurt' a bit). In any case, follow-up questions could be asked so that those providing feedback and suggestions offer examples or their rationale. However, this should not escalate into a situation in which the curriculum developers feel they need to 'defend' their ideas, as it may place them in an uncomfortably defensive position that may prove of little value.

C inviting/contracting an experienced TESOL educator (e.g. teacher educators, academics, textbook authors) as a consultant to provide written feedback on the draft. Sometimes, institutions may choose a consultant from their own context to work together with someone who is based elsewhere or may be unfamiliar with the context. This does not mean that they are looking for objectivity (which may

Activity 1.8 Finding Examples

Go online and find examples of TESOL curricula or TESOL syllabi in your context or from other settings. If they are from your own context, note that they may be written in the dominant/official language of your country/region. Also, note that sometimes the curriculum to teach English is contained within a more general curriculum, such as the curriculum for secondary education.

Browse your examples. What are they like? What do they include? How are they organized? Who are the authors? When were they published? What aspects of them do you find interesting/unique/puzzling?

be really, really,… really hard to achieve in education); they may be interested in a 'fresh pair of eyes' who has other experiences, views and perspectives.

When curricular developers share their draft either in paper or in digital formats (a PDF file), it is of vital importance that they include a watermark to indicate that this is a *draft*.

The feedback collected in writing and/or through notes during a meeting/focus group is to be used to go back to the drafted curriculum and introduce a few changes to enhance its quality. It goes without saying that this process does not mean that all feedback will need to be integrated into the revised curriculum. Curriculum developers will make informed decisions about what to consider and what to disregard. If you go back to Figure 1.7 you will notice there is a small double-ended arrow between curriculum design draft and consultation. This is because, as you may have noted, designing a curriculum is a highly processual activity. Therefore, there may be several drafted versions and opportunities for consultation before a final version is produced.

Official curriculum: This stage refers to the process of curriculum developers writing the final version of the curriculum. This could be considered the official or published version and the one that will be formally recognized, made public and adopted. The official curriculum is sometimes made available on an institution's website or, for example, a Ministry of Education.

Enactment: This step refers to the implementation of the official curriculum. As you can imagine, this step could develop over a long period of time, or at least one school/academic year/term. During this stage, all actors involved in the TESOL curriculum will experience the alignments, differences and tensions between the official curriculum and what teachers and learners do as part of their teaching and learning experience.

Curriculum evaluation: This last step is a vital part of curriculum development as it seeks to collect information about the ways in which the curriculum has responded to demands, needs and aims identified and articulated in previous steps of the process. This step could happen alongside enactment. See Chapter 4 for a fully fledged discussion of this phase.

Activity 1.9 Informing the TESOL Curriculum

Imagine that you are part of a team that has been asked to design a new English for Specific Purposes (ESP) curriculum for an educational organization in your context. The curriculum will serve to provide ESP for people working in tourism, community management and finance. The team has initially decided to follow the roadmap presented in Figure 1.7. The team has also agreed that, together with gaining feedback and views from the relevant stakeholders, they would like to inform their decisions on the relevant literature (e.g. books, edited volumes, journal articles) and TESOL curricula from other contexts as they navigate the roadmap. With this scenario in mind, your task is to make a list of relevant literature that could help you and the team build a strong rationale for the new TESOL curriculum.

Example:

Needs analysis: Ahmed, K., Ali, S., & Khan, A. (2023). 'ESP Needs Analysis of Productive Skills: A Case Study of Engineering Learners'. *Pakistan Languages and Humanities Review, 7*(3), 800–812. https://doi.org/10.47205/plhr.2023(7-III)69

1.5 Official Curriculum Approaches

As noted in the roadmap in Figure 1.7, the development of the TESOL curriculum entails making some executive, creative and procedural decisions in terms of how to envision and organize the curriculum. As discussed above, Young (2014) understands that a curriculum is an organizer of teaching and learning, but in that organizing, some things are included, and some others are left out; some things are made possible to learn, and some others are constrained.

Richards (2013) puts forward three core elements to determine what is included (and what is left out):

- Content: this element refers to what learners are expected to learn. This could include, for example, vocabulary, grammar, pronunciation, speaking development and learning skills. We may also see this element as the input.

- Methodologies: this element refers to how the content is to be delivered. We can think of it as the pedagogical approach(es) (e.g. task-based learning), methodologies and strategies that will characterize teaching.

- Outcomes: this element refers to the products or outputs of teaching and learning. These are usually associated with learning outcomes, i.e. what learners are expected to have achieved by the end of a course.

Based on those elements, some possible scenarios emerge in front of us as approaches to TESOL curriculum design. I will describe three, but my aim is that as you read them, you think about other approaches which can be used.

1 Content-driven curriculum: This approach takes the element of content as its starting point. In this regard, what is to be taught determines the processes, which in turn determine the outcomes. For example, a school may decide that they would like to focus on allowing learners to use English to discuss social issues in different contexts, and therefore, they propose topics such as inclusion, bullying, wellbeing, enjoying nature and from there they decide the grammar, vocabulary, mediation skills and so on. Or they may decide that grammar should be the driving element, and so the rest of the curriculum is constructed around it.

2 Methodology-driven curriculum: This approach prioritizes the teaching process, i.e. the pedagogical aspect, which includes the teaching approaches, methodologies and strategies available to TESOL educators. For example, a Ministry of Education may decide that the teaching of English in primary education will follow task-based learning or TBL (Ellis, 2003; Willis & Willis, 2013). Thus, content and learning outcomes are oriented towards TBL. This type of curriculum can also be found in institutions that wish to innovate and adopt one particular approach, for example content and language integrated learning (CLIL) (Coyle et al., 2010; Banegas & Zappa-Hollman, 2023), as a way to enhance bilingual education, or if they wish to give technology-enhanced language learning a pivotal role in supporting English language provision.

3 Outcome-driven approach: This approach is goal-oriented; therefore, based on the learning outcomes to be achieved by the end of a course, the content and methodologies are developed. According to Richards (2013), this can be called *backward design* because what is to happen by the end of a course influences what happens before, in other words, what leads to those outcomes. For example, if you are an EAP tutor and the main learning outcome is that your higher education learners are able to write an academic essay and deliver a professional presentation by the end of the course, then those two outcomes will influence the content to teach and the methodologies you will use to enable the learners to achieve those outcomes.

Based on these three approaches, you can now read Vignette 1.6, which is a practical example of one of them, and complete Activity 1.10.

<table>
<tr><td>

Vignette 1.6

</td><td>

On Konttinen (2022)

</td></tr>
</table>

At a university in Finland, Konttinen sought to understand how English-medium education (EME) teachers translated the curriculum into meaningful teaching and learning opportunities, as she noted that EME teachers seem to lack professional preparation for EME. With this aim, she concentrated on EME curriculum implementation and had two guiding research questions: '(1) Which aspects guide the implementation of the curriculum in English-medium master's programs? (2) How should these aspects be addressed in EME teacher training?' (Konttinen, 2022, pp. 382–383).

To this effect, she interviewed four teachers. The interviews also included the participants completing a task out loud (think-aloud protocol) to gain more insights into their informed practices and pedagogical decisions. The findings revealed that the teachers' practices were teacher-oriented, with a heavy emphasis on content and activities, which left little margin for a learning/learner-centred approach. In light of these findings, the author suggests:

> Designing a curriculum and putting it into action should always start from the desired learning outcomes and results, which understandably ought to be at the core of all education. Then the process should move on to the evidence needed to determine whether these outcomes have been achieved. Finally, entire programmes and individual teachers can move on to planning the relevant and appropriate instruction modes and learning experience […]. (Konttinen, 2022, p. 383)
>
> On a more practical level, EME teacher training could entail sessions or even an entire module, which would have the backward design at its core, i.e. during the training EME teachers could look at their own courses, or even entire programmes, and revise them with the help of the backward design. EME teacher training could introduce the three parts of the design (i.e. setting the desired learning outcomes, determining the needed evidence and designing appropriate instruction modes and learning experiences) in the right order and it would thus inherently force the participants to stick to this order. In this way, learning and its outcomes would become the first step, and the pitfalls of becoming too teaching-centred or content-driven could perhaps be better avoided in this facilitated designing done as part of the training. (Konttinen, 2022, p. 389)

In other words, she suggests that the EME teacher education curriculum should be outcome-driven, and from there content and methodologies are agreed on and implemented as a potent way of supporting teachers to engage in learning-centred education.

Activity 1.10 On Approaches to Curriculum Design

Imagine that you have been hired to develop a new TESOL curriculum for a private bilingual school in your region. The school heads have established that by the end of the primary and secondary school levels, all learners will sit for an international exam of English. Which kind of approach (content/methodology/outcome-driven?) would you prioritize for the development of the new TESOL curriculum?

1.6 Curriculum Types

I would like to close the content side of this chapter by drawing your attention to different curriculum types. So far, we have mentioned the total curriculum and the enacted curriculum and discussed the official curriculum a bit more. However, there are other types as well. Please note that all these are interwoven and are part of the broad ecology of curriculum development. You can find more details about types of curricula with particular reference to language teaching in Graves (2016). Table 1.5 provides a summary, but I do encourage you to do an online search to find more about them if you wish. It should be noted that while the total and official curriculum are found in paper as text, the other types of curricula included in Table 1.5 represent observable behaviour and attitudes.

Table 1.5
Curriculum Types

Type	Definition	Example
Total curriculum	The overall curriculum of a country/city/region/school for a year or level of education, or programme. It is 'total' because it includes all the subjects, disciplines or courses that learners take in order to graduate. This formal curriculum could be found online or printed and it may be written in the dominant language of a country.	In Uruguay, the total curriculum of a secondary school includes all the subjects that learners will take throughout secondary education. The curriculum includes general objectives, etc., and then a section for each of the subjects for each year. English as a foreign language will have its own section with aims, content, methodologies, etc. In other words, the TESOL curriculum is embedded in a larger, hence *total* curriculum.
Official/expected curriculum	The formal and written curriculum that teachers are expected to follow or be guided by. It is similar to the total curriculum in the sense that it can cover a whole education system or course, or it can be for a subject in particular. Differently put, the total/subject and official curriculum is also the expected one and it is set as the norm.	
Taught curriculum	This is the curriculum that teachers teach. The curriculum is seen from teachers' perspective, and it captures the particularities, tensions and opportunities that teachers may encounter at the seams of the official curriculum, their context and learners' needs.	As a teacher of English, the official curriculum or my syllabus may include six units for a whole year, but this year I only have managed to teach five of those units because I have spent more time supporting my learners' speaking skills and recapping on contents from last year. I also included a project that was not part of the official curriculum because I wanted to explore project-based teaching, a methodology that was marginally suggested in the official curriculum. This shows the difference between the expected curriculum (six units) and the taught curriculum (five units, support on speaking, project-based learning).
Learnt curriculum	This is what and how learners learn and manage to exhibit in different situations. The curriculum is observed from learners' perspective.	As a teacher, I may have taught my university learners twenty different connectors to make their writing cohesive; however, they usually remember four or six of them and use them effectively in their essays.

Type	Definition	Example
Enacted curriculum	This is the curriculum that is constructed in action between teachers and learners. It can be seen as the combination of the taught and learnt curriculum, and it gives relevance to what teachers and learners do in the context of the classroom (physical and/or digital)	In response to learners' demotivation, a group of teachers of English decide to ask their learners for topics and activities they would like to do to learn English, some of which may not be included in the official curriculum. For a full example, see Banegas and Velázquez (2014).
Assessed curriculum	This is the knowledge which learners exhibit in (oral/written) exams/tests/quizzes.	Learners could obtain a high grade in an exam because they have memorized rules and understood the mechanics of the exam, but a week later, they may not remember what they studied. On the other hand, a test may provide a partial picture of what a learner may do in English. A multiple-choice test may give information on form (e.g. grammar rules of past tenses) but may not capture a learner's ability to narrate a story using past tenses.
Hidden curriculum	This is what learners experience and 'learn' through activities such as wearing a uniform, or standing up when the teacher enters the classroom, etc. It is also implied to learners by teachers' comments and feedback, or what is reinforced or left out in terms of topics, sources of input or activities. This is not only about what happens in the classroom, but also what may happen at a meso-level (the institution).	The teacher only allows learners to use English, which may give learners the impression that English is better than other languages. The hidden curriculum could be happening when a coursebook may include several speaking activities, but in these activities, learners are usually placed as employees rather than employers, which may give the idea that the curriculum is preparing them for the former, not the latter.

1.7 Bringing It All Together

This section contains a set of activities aimed at recapping as well as extending some of the concepts discussed in the chapter.

Activity 1.11

In Activity 1.4, you were invited to upload your concept map onto TESOLand (a dedicated Padlet for this book). Go back to TESOLand and choose three or four concept maps uploaded by other people who completed the activity. What similarities and differences can you note? How do their concept maps compare to yours in relation to the understanding of the socially-enacted curriculum?

Activity 1.12

In Activity 1.6, you noted a few thoughts on your definition of curriculum and your views on two fallacies discussed by Graves (2023). Based on the knowledge you have developed by the end of this chapter, would you change your definition and views of curriculum development in any way? If you are/not changing your views, what is your rationale?

Activity 1.13

In the chapter, we have discussed a roadmap for curriculum development (Figure 1.7), which includes the drafting of a curriculum. With the advent of Artificial Intelligence (AI), the act of drafting a TESOL curriculum could be accelerated and ostensibly improved. Read a blog available by scanning Figure 1.9 and discuss these questions:

1. How could you use the case study included in the blog to create a TESOL curriculum or syllabus for your own context?
2. Go over the blog again and be critical about it. For example, does it offer evidence to support the claims made? Does it cite published research? Are there any other aspects of the blog that you find questionable?
3. Do an online search and identify published articles that have investigated (TESOL) curriculum development generated by AI. What can you take away from them?

Figure 1.9 QR code to access reading material

Activity 1.14

This activity consists of two parts.

Part 1. Without looking at anything, make a mind map of what you have learnt in this chapter.

Part 2. Go over your notes and the different sections of this chapter. Turn the mind map into a concept map that can help you establish relationships among the concepts addressed in the chapter.

1.8 Further Reading

Below, I list a few titles on curriculum theory, development and practice. These come from the wider field of education, as well as language teaching. In addition, you may also want to take a look at books and articles published in your own context and in languages other than English. This is important as they may enable you to diversify your theoretical framework.

- Paraskeva, J. M. (2011). *Conflicts in curriculum theory: Challenging hegemonic epistemologies*. Palgrave.
- Pinar, W. F. (2019). *What is curriculum theory?* (3rd ed.). Routledge.
- Richards, J. (2017). *Curriculum development in language teaching* (2nd ed.). Cambridge University Press.

I am also including two other books with different foci. Also note that they are not only related to TESOL but to the teaching of other languages, which is absolutely fine, as there are many commonalities across the teaching of different languages.

- Connor, J. (2017). *Addressing special educational needs and disability in the curriculum: Modern foreign languages* (2nd ed.). Routledge.
- van Lier, L. (2014). *Interaction in the language curriculum: Awareness, autonomy and authenticity*. Routledge.

If you have access to any of them, consider these questions:

A Who is the author? What can you find out about them?

B Take a quick look at the table of contents. What topics does it include? Do you find any of the topics particularly appealing? Why?

C Does the book seem to include different perspectives on curriculum theory?

D Would you recommend the title to a colleague? Why (not)?

Chapter 2
Who Enacts the TESOL Curriculum?

Summary

The aim of this chapter is to raise awareness of *the human element* in curriculum design for TESOL. Maintaining the ecological perspective introduced in Chapter 1, this chapter discusses the roles that learners and teachers, as well as other socio-educational actors, play in curriculum design and enactment. The chapter pays attention to the importance assigned to age in structuring learners' schooling. Regarding teachers, the chapter reflects on some of the links between teacher preparation (pre-service) and development (in-service) and curriculum development.

2.1 Warm-Up

In Chapter 1, we introduced some of the basic concepts behind the TESOL curriculum, which could be defined as a pedagogical tool designed to organize the teaching of English as a foreign/second/additional language in a given context (institutional/local/regional/national/transnational). In Figure 1.7 in Chapter 1, I proposed a roadmap. While there are several actors involved in the roadmap, such as programme leaders or parents/carers in the needs analysis stage, or policymakers and academic experts in the consultation stage, teachers and learners are at the heart of the enactment and evaluation stages as they bring the curriculum to life, so to speak. As we explained in Chapter 1, teachers and learners can be placed in the microsystem of the ecology of the TESOL curriculum.

I firmly believe that it is important not to lose sight of the human element in the TESOL curriculum. Just like any policy, a curriculum should be at the service of people, not the other way around. Let us remind ourselves that the primary actors and beneficiaries of a curriculum are teachers and learners because the curriculum is expected to organize, guide and support the teaching and learning experiences they will navigate together. That said, being the primary actors in curriculum enactment comes with great responsibility and roles.

Activity 2.1 On Roles and Responsibilities

Think about a TESOL course/class/programme from your context. What roles does the teacher have? What roles do learners have? Use Figures 2.1 and 2.2 to record your thoughts. You can add more circles.

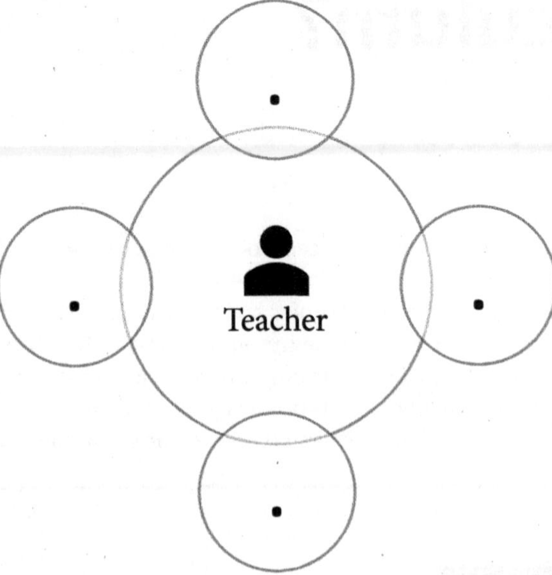

Figure 2.1 Teacher's roles

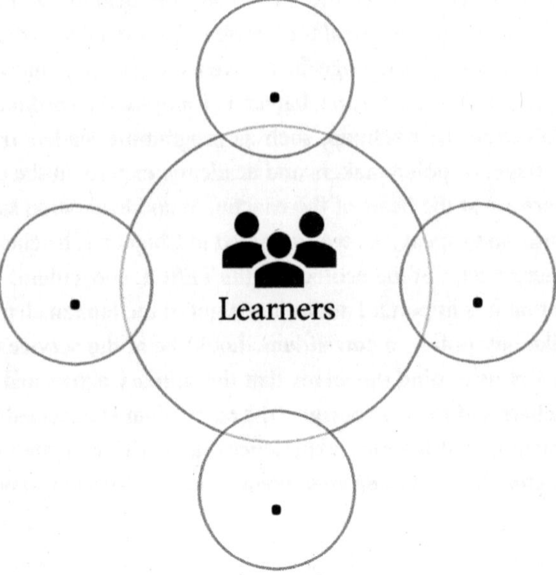

Figure 2.2 Learners' roles

2.2 Learners

It is often concurred that learners' lives should be an integral part of the curriculum (Banegas & Velázquez, 2014). This means that their experiences, needs, wants, etc., should inform the different aspects and elements that characterize a curriculum. This is what we usually term the *learner-centred curriculum* (Nunan, 1988). Placing learners at the centre of a curriculum draws from key concepts developed by John Dewey. Vignette 2.1 provides a summary of his notion of the spiralling curriculum.

Vignette 2.1

Dewey's Spiralling Curriculum, by Luis S. Villacañas de Castro

'Education is by its nature an endless circle or spiral,' Dewey (1929, pp. 76–77) wrote in *The Sources of a Science of Education*, a short essay published in 1929. As the title of his work conveys, for Dewey *science* was one of the two key axes – the other was *art* – around which teachers could maximize learners' growth. Throughout his extensive oeuvre, Dewey saw artistic and scientific inquiry as the two main conduits for human beings to interact intelligently – not destructively – with their environment. By channeling their actions through art and science, individuals and communities would be able to expand their options for future transformation and control. These two conduits allowed individuals to 'enlarge the range of action, and this enlargement in turn confers upon our desires greater insight and foresight, and makes choice more intelligent. There is a circle,' Dewey (2008d/1928, p. 104) claimed, 'but an enlarging circle, or, if you please, a widening spiral.'

No wonder, then, that art and science figured also at the core of his educational programme, as the two main activities that should structure school life. As Mayhew and Edwards' (1936) account of Dewey's Laboratory School made clear, it was through *occupations* – Dewey's (2008a/1900, pp. 12–13) original pedagogical units – that the 'practical activities in the school [were turned into] allies of art and centers of science and history.' As likely inspired by prehistorical renditions in sand or clay, by children's play, instances of informal learning occurring in the household or the workplace, or by the new house-building techniques of industrial society, occupations afforded instances of growth in history that the teachers in the Laboratory School sought to expand and enrich by imbedding the perspectives of art and science into them.

By envisioning education thusly, Dewey avoided the dualism that plagues educational thought to this day, namely: children's interests versus the curriculum, *children-* versus *curriculum-centred* pedagogies. Through occupations, Dewey favoured neither the acritical affirmation of learners' interests and experiences, nor a blind race towards the attainment of decontextualized, curricular objectives. Neither did he come to regard that education was about bridging the gap that separated the child from the curriculum – to paraphrase one of his early masterpieces (Dewey, 2008b/1902) – as third space pedagogical orientations seem to suggest. Dewey came to believe that education was nothing if not a spiral, a process that lent continuity to, but also expanded and improved, the range and breadth of learners' original experiences. Rather than creating a transition between the children's and the curricular realities, **the spiral form suggested that education was about learners expanding their experiences and family cultures at school**, instead of replacing them – no matter how gradually – with academic forms of thought. By so placing the focus on expanding and enriching, Dewey bestowed an open-ended quality to the educational process, which accordingly went beyond curricular knowledge and competencies. 'The educational process has no end beyond itself; it is its own end; [...] it is one of continual reorganising, reconstructing, and transforming,' Dewey (2008c/1916, p. 54) concluded. For him, the curriculum never was the aim of education, but rather a flexible and experimental means to sustain but at the same time enrich learners' preexisting impulses, experiences and cultures – the only conceivable aim of education in societies that are worthy of being called democratic.

> ## Activity 2.2 Visualizing the Spiralling Curriculum
>
> Imagine that for a meeting at a/the school where you work, you would like to explain to parents why and how their children are important in the school's TESOL curriculum. You have decided to make a visual representation of Dewey's notion of the spiralling curriculum.
>
> For the visual representation, you could use any kind of technology (e.g. paper and pencils, PowerPoint).
>
> If possible, share your visual representation with a peer and discuss any similarities and differences.
>
> Additionally, if you are in a class, you could do a bit of role play. Ask your peers to be the parents, and you are the teacher talking them through your visual representation.

Now the question is, how could we translate the spiralling curriculum into practice for the teaching and learning of English? How could a TESOL curriculum enable learners to harness their experiences and family cultures and expand on them as Vignette 2.1 explains? Here I list a few ideas based on my experience as a curriculum developer and teacher of English:

- Design a curriculum which is based on current theories and understanding of how learners learn. For example, if you are developing a TESOL curriculum for very young learners, then it is essential that the educational/pedagogical principles informing the curriculum respond to how children learn. For example, Pinter's (2011) book on children learning second languages or Bland's (2015) edited volume are must-reads. You can still look for updated publications from your own context, or in languages other than English.

- Develop a curriculum or syllabus which is topic-based; the topics should ideally come from a needs analysis exercise about learners' interests. For example, if learners are interested in pets, a unit of the course could be about describing their pets, narrating an event which involves their pets, discussing why pets could support people's wellbeing, start a campaign to raise awareness of adopting an animal (as opposed to buying one). The rest of the content of the curriculum/syllabus, such as language systems (e.g. syntax, lexis, pronunciation) and mediation skills (e.g. reading, speaking), is to be decided, organized and sequenced according to such topics.

- Design activities which are learning- as well as learner-centred, i.e. give learners agency and participation about how the activities could be completed. This idea could be based on the notion of problem-based learning (Ansarian & Teoh, 2018), which allows learners to work on a real-world case/scenario/issue using their knowledge, experiences, etc. For example, at the end of every unit, learners are given a situation/problem to solve (e.g. the need to advertise their city/town/region to attract tourism). Learners should be allowed to work in groups or individually.

- Include end-of-unit or end-of-course student-led projects in which they set out what *they* would like to investigate (e.g. local activists in their town, water preservation) using English. This could be a conducive opportunity to explore inquiry-based learning (Pedaste et al., 2015). Just remember that in this approach, the process of inquiry is paramount, so learners, for example, could be asked to make a presentation/video/report in which they describe the steps they took in completing the project.

Developing a spiralling curriculum for the teaching of English has the power to enhance the inherent relationship between language learning and learners' identity and affective factors such as motivation, engagement and autonomy, among others. Why is this? The short answer is that when the TESOL curriculum is based on learners' interests, identities and contexts, they will be enthused to learn the language and invest in their learning because they can see meaning in learning English as they see themselves represented in the learning process. The long answer? See Dörnyei and Ushioda (2021) or Lamb et al. (2019).

On the topic of motivation and the spiralling curriculum, Activity 2.3 may help you see what the relationship of these two constructs may look like in practice. Although the article by Banegas and Lowe (2021) does not explicitly refer to the spiralling curriculum, you may see why the experience reported could be considered a good example of it.

Activity 2.3 Learner Motivation and the Enacted Spiralling Curriculum

Use Figure 2.3 to access an article by Banegas and Lowe (2021).

Figure 2.3 QR code access to Banegas and Lowe (2021)

1. Read Section 2 of the article. According to the literature reviewed on creative writing, would you say that supporting learners' creative writing could be a form of practising the spiralling curriculum?
2. Read the beginning of Section 3 and Section 3.2 in particular. According to what is described, what features did the enacted curriculum have because of the creative writing initiative?
3. Read Sections 4.1 and 4.2. Pay particular attention to Extracts 3, 6, 7, 10, 11, 12 and 13. According to what the learners said, in what ways did the initiative and the enacted curriculum consider the learners' interests, etc.? What aspects of the initiative were welcomed by the learners?
4. According to the overall experience reported in the article, how did the enacted ELT curriculum develop features in line with the spiralling curriculum?
5. Do you think that teachers in your context could carry out a similar initiative? Why (not)?

Vignette 2.2 **On Entry Requirements**

In 2024, the Intensive English Programme offered by the English Language Centre, Michigan State University (MSU) in the USA stated that Intensive English learners included: (1) 'individuals who are not seeking a degree at MSU, but who want to improve their English skills', and (2) 'already enrolled, degree-seeking international learners at MSU who need to improve their English language skills before beginning academic coursework'.

In the application requirements, learners were also asked to take an online English screening test, i.e. a test to measure the applicant's English language proficiency. The requirements explain that:

> A score of 9, 10, or 11 may be eligible for the lowest level English language course offered by the ELC. However, we cannot guarantee that, with standard effort and attendance, you can be successful at this level. Learners who are not able to pass all classes in a level are required to repeat the same level in a subsequent semester. Please be mindful of this information in continuing to pursue admission to the ELC.

They also say that

> [a] score of 8 or below means we do not have a class to accommodate your current level of English language proficiency. We recommend that you continue to study English at another institution and welcome you to look into our program again in the future.

With their application, international learners must also submit a copy of their valid passport visa page plus other legal documents.
Source: https://elc.msu.edu/core-programs/intensive-english-program/ (Accessed 1 October 2024)

You may have noted that Dewey's spiralling curriculum has children in mind. However, when we talk about learners/students, we should be aware that they could be of any age. While mandatory education is often associated with very young (kindergarten), young (primary) and teenage (secondary) learners, other age groups are part of the 'learners' category, such as babies, young adults and adults. It is absolutely crucial to understand who the learners of a curriculum are/will be, as many of the decisions to be made respond to or are influenced by a comprehensive understanding of their lived experiences, needs and wants, etc. Who our learners are may determine vital aspects of curriculum development and enactment, such as expected profile and entry requirements. Read Vignette 2.2 for an example.

Vignette 2.2 illustrates that the MSU Intensive English Programme curriculum has been designed for people who are not necessarily higher education learners. This decision could be interpreted as a sign of inclusion, as it means that non-higher education individuals, for example, senior members of a town, could sign up. However, the programme is not for everyone when it comes to English language proficiency. I believe that this should not be seen as an exclusionary policy. I would say that it responds to constraints such as human resources (e.g. not enough teachers), space (e.g. not enough classrooms) and budgetary limitations. It may also respond to the overall goals and priorities of the programme such as offering more support to learners with an advanced level of English proficiency.

In contexts of societal multilingualism, i.e. communities where different languages are spoken, it is equally important to recognize learners' cultural and linguistic capital. For example, in the USA and the UK, immigrant learners are usually labelled as *English language learners* or *English-as-an-additional-language learners*. What do these terms emphasize? I would say that they stress that learners need to develop their English language proficiency because they are in an educational system in which formal education and a wide range of social activities are mediated through English. So, in this respect, the goal is clear. I would also say, notwithstanding, that the label may have a deficit perspective. In other words, learners are identified by what they lack. Some would say this is unavoidable since these learners need to operate in an educational system and society which is primarily English-speaking. In fact, we may even say this is an inclusive practice. While it is fine to concentrate on what learners need to successfully negotiate learning in English as the language of instruction, the term may be erasing other aspects of the learners' identities. Therefore, there could be some exclusionary undertones. In response to this issue, Kanno et al. (2024) remind us that terms such as *emergent bilingual* and *multilingual learner* could become a more inclusive alternative. Nevertheless, the authors call for the careful consideration of how learners are (mis)labelled, represented, and, in some cases, systemically minoritized or even racialized in the curriculum.

What we have discussed so far comes to show that a curriculum, whether it is for the teaching of English in particular, or for teaching across all school subjects, needs to be positioned in such a way that all efforts, decisions, processes and outcomes have learners not just in mind, but actively involved. In other words, we need to allow learners to become curriculum developers on their own right.

2.3 On Learners' Age

In most educational systems around the world, age seems to be the defining criterion for the organization of learning in terms of grades/years and even what contents or skills are appropriate for one age and not another. For example, Table 2.1 shows how the UK National Curriculum (2024) is organized into blocks of years, where age 5 is the compulsory school age.

Regulations go even further since the year a child goes into depends on when their birthday is:

> Your child must start full-time education once they reach compulsory school age. This is on 31 December, 31 March or 31 August following their fifth birthday – whichever comes first. If your child's fifth birthday is on one of those dates then they reach compulsory school age on that date. For example, if your child reaches compulsory school age on 31 March, they must start full-time education at the beginning of the next term (summer term that year).
>
> (UK Government, 2024)

Why do education systems seem to be fixated with age? You may think that the organization of schooling according to the age-class tandem may be linked to development psychology and stages of cognitive development (e.g. Ludlow & Gutierrez, 2014; Pillemer & White, 2005). However, the answer seems to be more complex. According to Caruso (2023), the long-standing practice of age grading or grouping responds to governments and bureaucrats' understanding of schooling as a social system through which governmentality must be exercised; hence, the need to direct human development and conduct through orchestrated forms and techniques, one of them being a child developing knowledge with children of the same age. The governing of entire social groups, that is, individuals are not recognized, is attached to the notion of social promotion by which learners are required to

Child's age	Year	Key stage	Assessment
3–4		Early years	
4–5	Reception	Early years	Assessment of pupils' starting points in language, communication, literacy and maths and teacher assessments
5–6	Year 1	KS1	Phonics screening check
6–7	Year 2	KS1	National tests in English reading and maths. Teacher assessments in maths, science and English reading and writing
7–8	Year 3	KS2	
8–9	Year 4	KS2	Multiplication tables check
9–10	Year 5	KS2	
10–11	Year 6	KS2	National tests in English reading, maths and grammar, punctuation and spelling. Teacher assessments in English writing and science
11–12	Year 7	KS3	
12–13	Year 8	KS3	
13–14	Year 9	KS3	
14–15	Year 10	KS4	Some children take GCSE (General Certificate of Secondary Education) exams
15–16	Year 11	KS4	Most children take GCSEs or other national exams

achieve a set of academic standards at critical points in their schooling. This explains why learners in the UK must sit for national exams in Year 6 (age 10–11). I am sure something similar happens in your own context. You may want to either go back down memory lane and remember your own school years, and think about how old you were when you started kindergarten, primary or secondary education. Or you might want to think about any exams that learners must take by a certain age if, for example, they want to be *promoted* from primary to secondary schooling.

Now, when we think about learner age in TESOL, the perennial question is: Is earlier the better? To unpack this question, I will use an article by Spada (2015) in which she discusses second language acquisition research (SLA) and pedagogy. In that article, the author starts addressing the role of age in SLA and language teaching by saying:

One of the things that most people agree about when it comes to L2 learning is that early starters are likely to attain high levels of linguistic competence, often comparable to native speakers of the language, whereas late starters (adolescents or adults) are less likely to reach comparable levels. Late starters exhibit much greater variability in their levels of linguistic attainment and the majority of them would not be mistaken for native speakers of the language. Of course, there are exceptions to this, and several cases have been reported in the literature (Ioup et al. 1994; Birdsong 2006).

One explanation that has been offered for the differences between early and late starters is biological: that there is a critical period after which it is no longer possible to learn language in the same way or to achieve the same level of competence as someone who learns before that period (Scovel 1988; Long 1990; Singleton 2001); this has become known as the CRITICAL PERIOD HYPOTHESIS (CPH). In the literature, different views have been expressed as to the duration of this period, but, generally speaking, it ranges from two to fifteen years of age, depending on particular aspects of language (e.g. pronunciation, grammar). And the argument is that if language is not learned some time during this 'window(s) of opportunity', it will not be complete (Lenneberg 1967).

(Spada, 2015, pp. 72–73).

So, CPH may support the belief and practice of introducing the teaching of English earlier in formal education. For example, the first time I learnt English at school was when I started Year 1 in secondary education. So, I must have been 12 or 13 (it feels like a century ago!). However, in the same context, English is now a school subject as from Year 4 in primary education. That said, in private bilingual schools, English has always been there from the moment children start their formal education. However, Spada (2015) argues that SLA research has been misapplied since studies about rate of learning and ultimate attainment have been carried out in naturalistic settings, i.e. in contexts where learners are immersed in the L2 language in the natural environment. This is very different from contexts where English is not the dominant language. For example, a child learning English in Brazil, France or Vietnam might struggle as exposure to English could be limited, and sometimes only circumscribed to the English language classroom.

In relation to the age factor in L2 learning, Spada (2015, p. 74) says:

The most recent and arguably most extensive research to examine the age factor in relation to instructed L2 learning is that of Carmen Muñoz and her colleagues, who are investigating the learning of English as a foreign language (EFL) in schools in Spain. What is particularly valuable about this program of research is that the researchers have carried out longitudinal studies following the same children over several years in primary and secondary schools. They have observed (among other things) that the older EFL [English as a foreign language] learners progress faster than younger learners on a variety of oral and written tasks including oral fluency, vocabulary acquisition, morphological accuracy and writing (Muñoz 2006, 2011). They have also observed that younger learners catch up with older learners on oral tasks but not on written measures. Furthermore, the younger learners do not surpass the older learners over

<table>
<tr><td>Vignette
2.3</td><td>

English in Colombia, by Mario Molina

</td></tr>
</table>

In 2004, the Colombian Ministry of Education (MoE) developed the National Bilingual Program (NPB) 2004–2019. The NBP aimed to give learners the opportunity to reach a B1 proficiency level in English by the end of secondary school, and, thus, educate citizens who are able to communicate in English in order to insert the country into universal communication, global economy and cultural openness (MEN, 2006).

By 2006, the MoE, in cooperation with the British Council, issued the *Basic Standards for Foreign Language Competencies: English*, which outlines the target learners' proficiency levels for the different grades (e.g. A1 for 1st–3rd grades, A2 for 4th–7th grades and B1 for 8th–11th grades), and includes standards for each grade group in terms of receptive skills (listening and reading) and productive skills (writing, monologues and conversation). The proficiency levels are aligned with the Common European Framework of Reference for Languages (Council of Europe, 2020). The goal was that, by 2019, 100 per cent of high school graduates would have a B1 level; this, however, has not been achieved, especially in the public sector.

The document also offers recommendations to enhance student learning, specifically at the elementary school level. These encompass the implementation of an English across the curriculum model, in which the goals of the English class are aligned with those of other content areas, and the use of portfolios to promote student autonomy.

Additionally, learners can learn different content and have different hours of English instruction based on the type of school. For example, depending on their contextual realities, learners can use local or imported materials and be exposed to either a bicultural or intercultural approach. Also, while international bilingual schools must offer more than 50 per cent of their curriculum in the foreign language, the range in national schools (including most public schools) can be 10–15 hours or lower (MEN, 2018).

The British Council (2015) recommended the minimum number of hours of English per week: two hours for 1st–3rd grades, one hour and fifteen minutes for 4th–7th grades and one hour and forty-five minutes for 8th–11th grades. Nonetheless, issues such as big size classes and lack of practice outside of the classroom have not been considered (British Council, 2015). These factors may also have impeded the achievement of the B1 level set by the MoE, especially among public schools, whose performance in standardized English tests has been significantly lower than that of private schools during the past decade (LEE, 2023).

In 2016, the MoE, in collaboration with some renowned Colombian universities, issued two set of guidelines: *The English learning guidelines* (kinder to 5th grade) and *The suggested guidelines and pedagogical principles for English* (6th–11th grade). Both documents offer ideas on how to effectively help learners achieve their goals in English and, thus, make Colombia the most educated country in Latin America by 2025 (MEN, 2016a; MEN, 2016b). At the time of writing this vignette, the British Council Colombia is offering online English classes to secondary learners, young adults, and adults through the programme English without Borders (EwB). The programme, which is free and provides four hours of remote English instruction per week, attempts to help overcome some of the barriers that have historically affected English learning among Colombian citizens (British Council, 2023).

time, as has been observed in the research on age with natural L2 learners. That is, the older learners started out stronger and even though the younger learners improved along the way, the older learners maintained their advantage throughout.

The author moves on to conclude that learners who start learning English earlier do not necessarily outperform those who start later, particularly in settings where instructional time is limited (e.g. an hour a week) and exposure to the language is restricted to the school context. In those cases, what may be more advantageous is that the limited instructional time is compressed over a shorter period of time. In other words, it seems to be more beneficial for learners to have three hours of English in one year than one hour over three years. I know of a kindergarten in Argentina that used to offer five-year-olds one thirty-minute session of English per week during the whole school year, but later shifted to three thirty-minute sessions per week in the last term. Therefore, they chose intensity over time.

Under the light of Sections 2.2 and 2.3, I would like to draw your attention to Vignette 2.3 as it can help us make use of some of the concepts and issues discussed so far.

According to Vignette 2.3, the curriculum for TESOL in Colombia conflates age, class and social promotion since learners are expected to achieve a certain proficiency level by the end of a school year/age. It is interesting to note that social promotion in the learning of English is bound to the Common European Framework of Reference for Languages (CEFR) (Council of Europe, 2020). I say 'interesting' because of its transcontinental influence since the framework has been conceived for the teaching and learning of languages in the

> **Vignette 2.4**
>
> ## Change in the Foreign Language Curriculum for Primary Education in Türkiye, by Yasemin Kırkgöz
>
> In 2013, the Turkish Ministry of National Education introduced a major curriculum change in English language teaching (ELT). Known as the 4+4+4 system, education was restructured into three four-year segments covering primary, middle and high school levels. As a result, the start age for English language instruction was shifted from Grade 4 to Grade 2, around the age of seven, reflecting a commitment to enhancing language education from an early age. English is a compulsory school subject in Turkish schools. The ELT curriculum emphasized the development of oral-aural skills during Grades 2 through 4, prioritizing speaking and listening skills in alignment with the natural progression of language acquisition. The curriculum gives priority to the use of English in authentic, real-life contexts to create relevance in learners' daily lives and foster effective communication skills. English textbooks are designed according to the objectives of the curriculum. The content of each English textbook comprises ten units per academic year, and the Ministry of Education delivers the textbooks to learners free of charge.
>
> To examine teachers' perceptions on the primary ELT curriculum and their experiences in teaching English to younger learners, I administered a questionnaire to 245 teachers. The questionnaire was made available both electronically and in hard copy. It consisted of thirty-five items, and the quantitative data obtained from the Likert scale responses were complemented by qualitative data from open-ended questions. The findings revealed that teachers overwhelmingly held positive perceptions towards the lowering of the starting age for English learning, with 98 per cent of teachers expressing welcoming remarks for its introduction at around age seven, compared to the previous age of nine. Teachers highlighted two main reasons underlying their positive perceptions: the 'age factor' and 'curriculum content'. A prominent aspect of the new curriculum, as perceived by teachers, revolves around the age at which English learning begins. They recognized the significance of age in language acquisition and development, emphasizing the benefits of starting English instruction at a younger age. As for its content, all teachers expressed support for the objectives set forth by the current curriculum. Teachers welcomed the primary ELT curriculum's prioritization of listening and speaking skills in Grades 2 and 3, highlighting the importance of fostering learners' oral communication abilities in English. One significant challenge reported by teachers, particularly those used to teaching older learners, was the difficulty in adapting their teaching methods to the level of younger learners. While many recognized the value of introducing English at lower grades, they admitted struggling to tailor their instruction to suit the developmental needs of younger children. Lack of specific training or education geared towards teaching younger age groups compounded this challenge. As a result, teachers expressed frustration over having difficulty to effectively adjusting their teaching style to accommodate younger learners.

European continent, but it has been adopted, without any context-responsive adaptations, in other countries, such as Colombia, a country located in South America.

The vignette also mentions the number of hours allocated to the teaching of English, as well as the issues, such as class size, which may operate against the language proficiency goals set for each class. In relation to this barrier, I wonder whether English language education in Colombia could consider Spada's (2015) suggestion of doing the opposite of spreading English (too thin) throughout the entirety of primary education with just an hour or so a week. Perhaps, learners' language proficiency may be improved if the teaching of English were concentrated in three years, with more hours per week.

Let's look at a similar case from another country in Vignette 2.4:

As you may have noted, Vignette 2.4 seems to indicate that the lowering of the starting age to receive English language instruction, with a special focus on listening and speaking, may have responded to 'natural progression of language acquisition'. Later in the vignette, there is also mention of language acquisition and development. Such arguments may make you think of what Spada (2015) has raised in terms of decision makers equating language development in natural environments to second language learning in formal settings.

2.4 Teachers

My assumption is that if you are reading this textbook, it is because you are studying to become a teacher, or you are a teacher already and would like to deepen your knowledge

Activity 2.4 When and How Much? Let's Debate!

This activity is meant to be carried out with a group of students (like yourself?); however, if you are studying this chapter on your own, just feel free to come with arguments for both sides.

The aim of this activity is to develop arguments in favour of/against this statement from a fictional school: 'Dear parents, We believe that children should have contact with English from an earlier age. Currently, in Primary Grades 5–7, pupils have one lesson of English a week. We are happy to announce that as from next school year, Grade 1–7 pupils will have two periods of 40 minutes a week.'

Create two groups, one group will think of arguments in favour of the school's decision, while another group will think of arguments to oppose the decision. For the arguments, think about the issues raised by Spada (2015) as well as other organizational/structural/logistic/materials/teaching approaches/teacher development factors or impact on the whole curriculum (e.g. more hours of English may mean that pupils will have fewer hours of another school subject).

Each group can choose one representative to articulate their arguments in front of the class. At the end of the debate, everyone in the class can cast a vote.

of curriculum development, or you are teaching but do not have a teaching a degree, or you are doing a degree related to English language teaching but you are not interested in becoming a teacher yourself, or none of this is true and by some miracle and/or mystery you have come across this book. In any case, I am glad you are here.

As we discussed in Chapter 1, teachers play a pivotal role in the ecology of English language education. If they are part of a top-down approach to English language curriculum development, then it is only fair to say that on their shoulders they carry the weight of everyone's expectations, be these from parents, the institution, the government or society at large. If, on the other hand, they are part of a bottom-up, participatory approach, then they are co-responsible for the delineation of context-responsive, agentic and informed decisions. Therefore, while learners and their learning (of English) are the ultimate goal of a (language) curriculum; teachers are the primary actors since their job is to understand and translate an official curriculum into a world of possibilities and memorable experiences for learners.

Who becomes a teacher of English? What are their experiences? What are their motivations and expectations? How do they see themselves? How would they like to be seen? What do they know about curriculum development? How do these questions resonate with you?

As we have discussed in relation to our possible roadmap of TESOL curriculum development and in Activity 2.1, teachers of English can play pivotal roles. To support teachers, we also need to understand their trajectories, experiences and beliefs. In a master's course on second language teaching curriculum I have taught at the University of Edinburgh, I have asked my students (many of them teachers of English) to complete a survey (Figure 2.5). Feel free to complete it yourself.

Activity 2.5 Hello! This Is Me!

1. If you were to tell about yourself to other people who are teachers of English or studying to become one, what would you tell them? Think about this question and write a brief text of around fifty words.
2. If you are happy, post it on TESOLand to share it with the world! Use QR code 2.2 and locate the Chapter 2 section.

Figure 2.4 QR code access to TESOLand

A. How much does each statement represent your own experience?

	Not at all	A little	Some	A great deal
1. I have teaching experience.	O	O	O	O
2. I have experience in choosing my own teaching materials (e.g. a coursebook).	O	O	O	O
3. I have experience in creating my own syllabus to teach.	O	O	O	O
4. I have experience in collecting feedback to improve my teaching.	O	O	O	O
5. I am aware of curricula in my context.	O	O	O	O
6. I have experience in designing my own teaching materials.	O	O	O	O
7. I have experience in creating a new programme for teaching English	O	O	O	O
8. I have experience in choosing how to teach English	O	O	O	O
9. I have experience in designing my own tests/exams.	O	O	O	O
10. I have experience in including topics/content not found in the curriculum.	O	O	O	O

Figure 2.5 Extract from a survey

You may have noticed that most of the items in Figure 2.5 seek to capture teachers' experiences, i.e. what they have done in terms of enacting the TESOL curriculum and making decisions in terms of implementation. These decisions range from selecting a language teaching approach (Item 8) to designing their own syllabus (Item 3) and exams (Item 9).

We can also ask teachers of English about their beliefs and perceptions. In the same survey, I also asked my students about their views in relation to the curriculum for teaching English in their context (Figure 2.6). This time I am showing you the results, but you can of course answer the questions as well (just ignore Item 5). Figure 2.6 shows that the students, overall, had a positive view about the need to know about the TESOL curriculum and contribute to its development and change.

Figure 2.6 Survey extract with results

#	Field	Completely disagree	Somewhat disagree	Somewhat agree	Completely agree	Total
1	I want to work as a teacher in my context.	1.31% 3	7.42% 17	51.97% 119	39.30% 90	229
2	Teachers in my context can change the syllabus if they wish.	4.37% 10	27.51% 63	53.28% 122	14.85% 34	229
3	Teachers in my context can change the teaching material (e.g., they can choose a coursebook).	12.66% 29	21.40% 49	47.60% 109	18.34% 42	229
4	I believe that knowing about curriculum deveopment can help me become critical of curricula in my context.	1.31% 3	2.18% 5	30.13% 69	66.38% 152	229
5	I think that after this course I will be better prepared to make my own decisions about what/how to teach.	1.75% 4	0.44% 1	26.20% 60	71.62% 164	229
6	Teachers don't need to know about curriculum development. They just have to follow what's given to them.	78.60% 180	17.90% 41	3.06% 7	0.44% 1	229
7	I think that changes in the TESOL curriculum in my context can lead to changes in society.	0.87% 2	9.17% 21	62.88% 144	27.07% 62	229
8	I don't think I'll be able to contribute to social change in my context after this course by managing my own teaching	32.75% 75	48.47% 111	17.03% 39	1.75% 4	229
9	I feel that I'll be able to change teaching in my context to make it more accessible to everyone.	2.18% 5	9.61% 22	52.40% 120	35.81% 82	229
10	I don't want to make changes to the curriculum in my context even if I can.	55.90% 128	37.55% 86	5.24% 12	1.31% 3	229
11	I believe that knowing about curriculum development can help me manage my teaching for critical thinking development among my students.	1.31% 3	2.62% 6	29.26% 67	66.81% 153	229
12	Teachers in my context are asked to suggest changes to the curriculum	3.49% 8	24.45% 56	54.15% 124	17.90% 41	229

Activity 2.6 What Do You Think?

1. If you haven't, answer the survey questions found in Figures 2.5 and 2.6.
2. How do your answers compare to the students' answers in Figure 2.6?
3. In your view, what do you think you need to do in order to develop a more informed and participatory attitude towards curriculum development?

Why this attention to teachers? Teachers are fundamental designers in co-creating with their learners the enacted curriculum. This enactment can even signify that the curriculum is a living organism that is shaped in relation to changes in its ecology. This involves teachers in developing their own responsiveness to conceptualizing practice-oriented principles that impact what learners *do* and learn on a daily basis.

2.5 Teacher Preparation

Hopefully, your answer to the third question in Activity 2.6 confirms that English language teacher education is key in ensuring that the TESOL curriculum is designed, enacted and evaluated in ways that are ecologically situated and informed.

Teacher preparation usually refers to the formal education that someone completes to become a teacher. In the case of TESOL, we may talk about initial or pre-service English language teacher education or preparation to include higher education programmes at undergraduate (e.g. a bachelor's degree in TESOL) and postgraduate level (e.g. a master's degree in TESOL). Pre-service teacher education refers to undergraduate as well as postgraduate programmes that students complete before they have gained teaching experience. These students are often called student-teachers, future teachers or teachers to be. However, there are postgraduate programmes aimed at experienced/in-service English language teachers. There are also shorter courses such as certificates (e.g. Certificate in English Language Teaching to Adults or CELTA) or diplomas, but these do not have the same official recognition as undergraduate or postgraduate programmes. Different scholars (e.g. Diaz Maggioli, 2023; Nguyen, 2019; Zolin Vesz, 2024) agree that teacher preparation is absolutely crucial to offer learners English language learning experiences which are meaningful, context-responsive, inclusive and situated.

In terms of TESOL curriculum development, why is teacher preparation so important? Usually, English language teacher education programmes enable (future) teachers of English to develop professional knowledge and practice of language teaching approaches and methodologies, general pedagogy, teacher reflection, materials development, classroom management, development psychology, language use and (applied) linguistics, assessment, policy, theories of education and perspectives (e.g. sociocultural theory, critical pedagogy), and so on. As we will see in Chapter 3, knowledge about these issues is fundamental as they play a central role in informing how a TESOL curriculum could be designed, implemented and evaluated. In other words, curriculum design for TESOL draws from a wide range of subject areas (e.g. pedagogy, psychology, linguistics, management).

Sometimes, English language teacher education programmes also offer courses especially devoted to developing professional knowledge of the language curriculum and the interconnections between the micro, meso, macro and chronosystems of the ecology of the TESOL curriculum. For example, the University of Strathclyde offered a four-year BA Education and TESOL programme. In Semester 1, Year 2, there was a module/course called 'Placement and Curriculum'. According to the programme's website:

> This module allows students to spend 70 hours working with children and young
> people in a setting of the student's choice. Lectures and tutorials support learners
> to develop the skills required to participate fully in the organisation with which they
> choose to work and allow learners to explore issues that impact on the lives of children
> and young people.

This blurb seems to show that attention was given to the institution, which we would frame as part of the mesosystem of the ecology of the TESOL curriculum, combined with the enacted curriculum since the module included a practice/placement element.

Another example comes from Mexico. In a BA ELT programme offered by the Autonomous University of Mexico, there was a module called 'Curriculum Design' in Year 4. The module looked into aspects such as language teaching from a curricular perspective, types of curriculum, curriculum organization, materials and assessment, understanding the local curriculum and so on. In this case, emphasis was given to student-teachers familiarizing themselves with national/regional/institutional curricula and how the teaching of English is expected to develop according to the official curricula.

Master's programmes may also include content on curriculum development. In the MSc TESOL programme at the University of Edinburgh, there was a core module called 'Second Language Teaching Curriculum' in Term 1. The learning outcomes were: (1) analyse and evaluate the components of second language curricula and articulate the dynamic relationship between them; (2) understand, analyse and evaluate a curriculum from a social justice perspective; (3) demonstrate a critical understanding of (de)colonization in the context of second language teaching curricula, (4) provide a detailed and critical evaluation of the role of the teacher as agent of change in a particular curricular context and (5) present and lead during class discussions to critique relevant literature related to second language curricula and pedagogy. To achieve those outcomes, the module included the contents that this very textbook has. Differently put, this book is based on my experience as the leader of the module. I also taught a similar module when I was part of the MSc TESOL at the University of Strathclyde.

As a lecturer on the TESOL curriculum at both institutions, I have carried out research to examine the ways in which learners enrolled in the course benefit from it. Activity 2.7 is based on that research.

Activity 2.7 Curriculum Development and Professional Identity

In this activity, you will be working with an article about the impact of curriculum development on student-teachers' identity (Banegas, 2023b). This is an open-access article, which you can read online or download by using Figure 2.7.

Figure 2.7 QR code access to Banegas (2023b)

1. Read the introduction and conceptual framework. Which concepts discussed in these sections are known to you?
2. Read the first paragraph in the second subsection of the Conceptual Framework section again. Can you notice any differences between how the curriculum is defined and classified in the paragraph and in Chapter 1 of this book?
3. Who were the participants of this study?
4. According to the findings, the participants identified themselves as language learners, student-teachers, future teachers and curriculum developers. How do these identities relate to you? Do you feel represented by any of the participants' views? How do you see yourself? How would you like to see yourself in the future?
5. In general, did the student-teachers benefit from a module on the TESOL curriculum?

2.6 Teacher Development

Focusing on teacher development that foregrounds practitioner *ownership* of theoretical constructs is fundamental to practice-design and learning-by-design (Cope & Kalantzis, 2015).

Teacher development may support teachers in creating their theory of practice as they engage in the TESOL curriculum. According to Coyle and Meyer (2021):

> Theory of Practice begins with practitioners constructing their own vision of classroom learning identifying key tenets which matter to them, built on beliefs about practices both established and new, built on research and evidence in the field that challenge thinking … … documenting emergent principles, prioritising them and selecting a focus for development or enquiry as collaborative work that is ongoing.
>
> (p. 29)

Teachers theorizing practice stresses the position of viewing teaching as a lifelong learning activity since 'good teachers are always learning' (Murray, 2021, p. 229). Others will say it is a journey. Where does the journey begin? Formal teacher preparation by means of an undergraduate and/or postgraduate programme is usually the beginning of a journey. It is like a first formal step. What is the difference between that first step and the ones to follow, or the ones before? I would say that in that first step, you do not have a great degree of say as you are completing a programme which is pretty much established. In my experience, that first step provides you with foundational and introductory knowledge at the intersection of theory and practice.

Once you begin to learn the ropes of the profession, the next step is what we usually call continuing professional development (CPD) with the aim of keeping updated (Cirocki & Farrell, 2019). This may include bottom-up initiatives (e.g. joining a teacher association, taking short courses or one-off sessions on specific aspects related to English language teaching, carrying out your own research, pursuing postgraduate degrees), i.e. actions which respond to your own needs and wants as a professional. Bottom-up CPD may entail starting a mentee-mentor relationship with experienced teachers (Pérez Berbain et al., 2023). CPD may also comprise top-down initiatives. For example, as a teacher, I have been required by my employer to complete courses on inclusive practices, materials design or understanding of curriculum change in my teaching context. They are called top-down because these are not self-led or self-initiated. These derive from decisions made by your employer, whether this is a private institution, local council or the government. It is worth pointing out that there may be initiatives that sit between bottom-up and top-down approaches. For example, there may be an initiative organized by a Ministry of Education, but teachers enrol voluntarily (e.g. the implementation of a didactic ateneo [athenaum] as described in Banegas & Glatigny, 2021).

In a comprehensive volume on CPD of TESOL teachers, Cirocki et al. (2023, p. 5–6) summarize key attributes of effective CPD (Table 2.2).

As mentioned above, there are different CPD initiatives which teachers can become involved in, or generate themselves to support their understanding, enactment, evaluation and development of the TESOL curriculum. Vignette 2.5 provides examples of CPD activities.

Let me close this section by referring to the use of generative artificial intelligence (GenAI) as a potent force for professional development. AI tools may support teachers' growth and engagement with curriculum design as they can offer on-demand information, ideas, resources, pedagogical strategies, lesson plan and syllabus design drafts, and

Effective CPD is:	It is vital that practitioners attend CPD events that …
Ongoing	regularly offer them both formal and informal opportunities to learn.
Purposeful	have a practical and useful purpose.
Supported	enable them to be mentored by experienced colleagues from the same or other institutions.
Impactful	intrinsically motivate them to not only enact changes in teaching, but also enhance classroom learning.
Collaborative	engage them in group work and co-construction of new knowledge and understanding; learning is a cognitive process that takes place in a social context.
Needs-based	address their objective and subjective needs and respond to the challenges they face in their classrooms and educational institutions.
Theory-driven	are underpinned by explicit theoretical models/frameworks.
Evidence-based	are informed by the most important research to date.
Language enhancement oriented	promote intercultural communicative competence in the target language.
Job-embedded	focus on classroom practice whereby teachers and teacher educators learn by tackling real problems and arriving at practical solutions.
Context-specific	promote context-specific pedagogy; that is, teaching suitable for the context in which they work.
Reflective	encourage them to critically reflect on their practice by asking probing questions about their teaching experiences.
Sustainable	promote learning that not only lasts, but also encourages practitioners to critically analyse and understand the material being studied.
Evaluated	teach them to critically evaluate their pedagogical practice and perpetually seek feedback on the effectiveness of their teaching.

feedback, potentially enhancing the learning process for educators (Kartal, 2023; Niemi, 2024). As with everything that becomes innovative and popular, teachers need to remain vigilant and critical since the suggestions provided by GenAI are often decontextualized

Activity 2.8 Priorities!

Imagine that you are working at a private language school and your employers would like to organize some CPD based on the attributes put forward in Table 2.2 (Cirocki et al., 2023). They have asked you to select five characteristics from that table and rank them in order of importance (1 is the most important). Which five would you choose and how would you rank them? Give reasons.

1. _______________________ because _______________________ .

2. _______________________ because _______________________ .

3. _______________________ because _______________________ .

4. _______________________ because _______________________ .

5. _______________________ because _______________________ .

Vignette
2.5

On CPD Among English Language Teachers

To examine the practice and motivations behind CPD among English language teachers in Iran, Sadeghi and Richards (2021) carried out an interview-based study with twenty-four teachers. According to the findings, the teachers engaged in (1) consulting online sources (70 per cent), (2) watching educational videos (63 per cent), (3) reading books on English language teaching (57.5 per cent), (4) conducting classroom research (37 per cent), (5) joining discusnsion groups with colleagues (37 per cent), (6) attending workshops and conferences organized outside their institutions (8 per cent), (7) becoming members of support groups (8 per cent) and (8) reading professional journals (4 per cent).

   Among their motivations to engage in CPD, the participating teachers primarily mentioned instrumental reasons such as career promotion (e.g. from working in a language institute to working at a university), salary increase and, to a lesser extent, broadening their professional knowledge. Since the authors found that attending workshops and conferences was not really popular among the participants, they probed into this issue in the interviews. The teachers expressed scepticism with such options because, in their context, trainers were usually external to their context and therefore lacked, in their view, contextual and curricular understanding of TESOL in their settings. They also mentioned that they would like to attend more practice-oriented workshops.

or lack a deep understanding of the complex educational landscape. Therefore, the same attributes listed in Table 2.2 should be observed when merging GenAI and teacher professional development towards the many aspects of the TESOL curriculum.

Activity 2.9 On Your Own CPD

Think about your future professional self in three years from now. What types of CPD would you like to do to broaden your understanding of TESOL? How could these types contribute to your knowledge and practice of the TESOL curriculum?

2.7 Bringing It All Together

This section contains a set of activities aimed at recapping as well as extending some of the concepts discussed in the chapter.

Activity 2.10

Browse a TESOL curriculum for primary, secondary or higher education from your context and answer these questions (Note: Some of the questions may not always be applicable):

1. Does the curriculum say anything about learners? Are there any specific learners in mind?
2. Does it mention any entry requirements?
3. In terms of organization, does the curriculum perpetuate an age-class approach?
4. Does the curriculum mention anything about teachers' background/ preparation/professional development?

Activity 2.11

Copland et al. (2024) published a free-access report about teaching English to young learners around the world (Note: To download the report, go to the reference and just type in the report title on your search engine). Read the following extracts from the report and think about (and discuss with your peers) how they relate to some of the issues discussed in this chapter.

A 'The reasons for the early introduction of English have changed very little in the last ten years, perhaps unsurprisingly, and in some cases have been reinforced. The notion that earlier language learning in school contexts produces better results continues to hold sway, even though the evidence remains inconclusive at best (see, for example, Muñoz and Singleton, 2011; Singleton and Pfenninger, 2018). As a result, the last decade has seen three trends: a) more countries have introduced English as a compulsory subject at primary level; b) other countries have further lowered the age at which children start learning English; c) some countries have increased the number of hours of English a week.' (Copland et al., 2024, p. 11)

B 'One issue in the introduction of English or in the increase in the number of
hours concerns where space on the curriculum is found. English will inevitably
replace another subject and, according to Kirkpatrick (2012), that is often
a local language. Concerns about the impact of English on the survival of
local languages, as well as on children's literacy in their local languages,
has been raised in a number of contexts, for example, Thailand (Baker and
Jarunthawatchai, 2017).' (Copland et al., 2024, p. 11–12)

C 'The role that parents play both in influencing government policy and on
children's success in language learning has become the focus of more
attention. For example, Indonesia is one of the few countries where English
is an elective rather than a compulsory subject at primary level. However,
parents are strongly in favour of early language learning, putting pressure
on schools to introduce English in their curriculum (Sulistiyo et al., 2020). As
Kirkpatrick (2012, p. 337) put it, "a primary school that did not offer English
would be unlikely to attract many learners".' (Copland et al., 2024, p. 12–13)

D 'In our survey, [teachers of English] are generally qualified and experienced. In
addition, case study data from rural and urban areas and from classrooms in
both high and low income countries, shows that teachers use what resources
and skills they have to create lively and caring classrooms. Many do not use
what we might consider modern pedagogies, and this may explain why
teachers ranked "training in the new teaching methodologies" highly in terms
of what would improve their teaching. However, as Zein (2022) suggests,
rather than criticizing teachers for not attaining an ideal, researchers could
instead be identifying how "traditional" activities are done well and how
teachers can effectively adapt their pedagogy to local contexts. Our data
on the activities used in class confirms that most teachers take an eclectic
approach and adapt their pedagogy to the context, whatever the curriculum
guidelines say. And we suggest that this indicates that they are effective
rather than ineffective teachers.' (Copland et al., 2024, p. 34)

Activity 2.12

What CPD opportunities are there for teachers of English in your context? Make a list.
Would you consider any of them? Are there any challenges that might demotivate
TESOL teachers in your context from joining those opportunities?

Activity 2.13

Think about CPD for teachers of English beyond your immediate context and complete the table below with potential sources of CPD:

Professional journals/ magazines	Websites	Podcasts	Social media (e.g. popular trainers/teachers, social media groups)

Activity 2.14

This activity consists of three parts:

Part 1. Without looking at anything, make a mind map of what you have learnt in this chapter.

Part 2. Go over your notes and the different sections of this chapter. Turn the mind map into a concept map that can help you establish relationships among the concepts addressed in the chapter.

Part 3. Feel free to discuss your concept map with a peer.

Activity 2.15

AI-assisted English language learning and/or the learning of English through digital platforms and apps illustrates that language learning does not only happen in schools, universities or a classroom. In such a context, do you think there is a TESOL curriculum? How are the teaching and learning processes organized? Who enacts it? To answer these questions, you may wish to search for quality information online.

2.8 Further Reading

If you would like to read more about the seminal and influential works of John Dewey, you can explore these resources:

- Dewey, J. (2023). *The child and the curriculum*. Legare Street Press.
- Diaz Maggioli, G. (2023). *Initial language teacher education*. Routledge.
- Pring, R. (2014). *John Dewey*. Bloomsbury.
- Villacañas de Castro, L. S. (2020). Deweyan democracy, neoliberalism, and action research. *Studies in Philosophy and Education, 39*, 19–36. https://doi.org/10.1007/s11217-019-09664-1

For those interested in problem-based learning, inquiry-based learning and project-based learning, these titles could be helpful:

- Greenier, V. T. (2020). The 10Cs of project-based learning TESOL curriculum. *Innovation in Language Learning and Teaching, 14*(1), 27–36. https://doi.org/10.10 80/17501229.2018.1473405

- Murdoch, K. (2022). *Getting personal with inquiry learning: Guiding learners' explorations of personal passions, interests and questions.* Elevate.

- Savin-Baden, M., & Fraser, H. (2024). *Rethinking problem-based learning for the digital age: A practical guide for online settings.* Routledge.

If you are interested in the teaching of English with very young learners, these references could show you general as well as specific discussions:

- Bland, J. (2022). *Compelling stories for English language learners: Creativity, interculturality, critical literacy.* Bloomsbury.

- Otto, A., & Cortina-Pérez, B. (Eds.). (2023). *Handbook of CLIL in pre-primary education.* Springer.

- Rixon, S. (2019). Developing language curricula for young language learners. In X. Gao (Ed.), *Second handbook of English language teaching* (pp. 277–95). Springer.

- Valente, D., & Xerri, D. (Eds.). (2023). *Innovative practices in early English language education.* Palgrave.

Chapter 3
What Does the TESOL Curriculum Include?

Summary

The aim of this chapter is to describe the core elements of curriculum design: goals (this includes aims and learning outcomes), principles, content, materials (published and teacher/student-made), activities and assessment. It is worth clarifying that the section on principles makes reference to educational theories, theories of language and language teaching approaches. The section on assessment also refers to testing. In this chapter, activities foster the analysis of these core elements in a range of curricula, syllabi and coursebooks from around the world.

3.1 Warm-Up

In Chapters 1 and 2, we set out the basis of TESOL curriculum development by discussing what a TESOL curriculum is and the roles that learners and teachers play in its enactment. In this chapter, we will be gravitating towards the mesosystem in the ecological framework of the TESOL curriculum. Why? Because what gets included in a TESOL curriculum reflects not only the institutional context but also wider dynamics (e.g. Ministry of Education) and policies. Also, through those dynamics and policies, we will make connections to the macrosystem as policies and other decision-making processes may be informed/influenced by social values, expectations and beliefs around language, teaching and learning.

As we discussed in Chapters 1 and 2, the process of designing a TESOL curriculum could be understood as a roadmap. Curriculum developers and other relevant stakeholders may have a strategy and a concomitant plan in place to engage in exploration, environment analysis, needs analysis and a preliminary evaluation. These stages provide evidence of stakeholders' views and practices; therefore, the curriculum to be developed will be evidence-based as well as informed by research/theory. However, I am aware that this may not always be the case, as we saw in Chapter 2, Section 2.3, about learners' age and learning English. I am also aware that even when a TESOL curriculum may have been based on evidence coming from needs and environment analysis, as well as relevant theories and research, these aspects may not be explicitly acknowledged in the official curriculum. So, do not assume that a curriculum did not draw from contextual evidence or research just

Activity 3.1 What's Kept Internally in TESOL Curriculum Development?

Look at the following possible reasons for not making some TESOL curriculum development stages public. Could you think of why? Could you think of other reasons?

A The environment analysis may reveal that there are many tensions among stakeholders (e.g. conflicting views about what the curriculum should do, the type of English that should be taught).

B The needs analysis reveals that the employer (e.g. university, Ministry of Education) may need to increase the budget to make curriculum implementation sustainable.

C The institution (or a publisher) designing the TESOL curriculum (or a coursebook) does not want potential competitors to profit from the data they have gathered.

because it does not have references to academic articles or data from needs analysis. This simply shows that some stages in the roadmap of TESOL curriculum development may be internal, while others may be external, i.e. publicly available.

What a TESOL curriculum may include responds to the notion of the formal/official/expected curriculum. In other words, I am taking a surface view since by *what is included* I mean what appears on the actual curriculum in writing. For example, Table 3.1 summarizes the published 2023 TESOL curriculum for primary education in Uruguay (Administración Nacional de Educación Pública, 2023a).

Table 3.1 is just one example. Thus, it should not be seen as a model to follow. However, it does include some elements which are often recurrent in educational curricula around the world. Macalister and Nation (2020) suggest that a language curriculum should consider the following elements: goals, content and sequencing (i.e. how contents will be organized), format and presentation (i.e. how activities, materials, etc., respond to the goals as well as principles, and how the support content and sequencing), monitoring and assessment (formative and summative assessment of learners' progress), principles (key notions informing the overall curriculum) and evaluation (i.e. collecting information about relevant stakeholders' views and experiences with the curriculum implemented). Some of these proposed elements are found in the sections summarized in Table 3.1, such as goals (Sections 1, 2, 9 and 11), content and sequencing (Sections 3 and 10), monitoring and assessment (Sections 5 and 13), and principles (Sections 8 and 12).

In my experience as a curriculum developer, teacher educator and researcher, I have found that curricula in the area of (language) education usually have the following interconnected elements:

- Goals: these provide a sense of direction in terms of what is that it is to be achieved by implementing the curriculum.

Section Title (my translation from Spanish)	What the Section is About (my summary)
1 Justification	The section briefly states what the general goal of including English in primary education is.
2 Specific competences	A list of competences (e.g. to develop oracy) aligned with the national (Uruguay) curriculum framework.
3 Structuring contents	A list of key contents (e.g. writing, metalinguistic reflection) that act as axes around which the specific competences can be developed.
4 Methodological orientations	A list of suggested approaches and ways of learning (e.g. inquiry-based learning, project-based learning, flipped classroom). Please note that these refer to learning in general.
5 Assessment orientations	It states that assessment should be process-oriented and formative, together with summative assessment at certain points in time.
6 Orientations on curricular autonomy	This section specifically states that teachers have the autonomy (and agency) to contextualize the proposed curriculum to meet the needs of their learners in context. In other words, the official curriculum allows teachers to enact a learner-centred curriculum.
7 Justification of the subject	The section argues why learning/using English is important in our globalized world.
8 Pedagogical and didactic guidelines	The section states that the overall TESOL curriculum is based on a sociocultural view of learning. Different authors are mentioned (e.g. Vygotsky, Bruner, Hattie).
9 Specific competences according to year	List of competences such as introducing oneself, understanding simple texts.
10 Contents	These are organized into six thematic units, which include goals, macro skills (listening, speaking, reading, writing), alignment with specific competences and suggested language components (e.g. grammar, vocabulary, language functions).
11 Learning outcomes for end of year assessment	A list of three core outcomes against which learners need to be assessed.
12 Specific methodological orientations	Suggestions for teaching English, with an emphasis on communicative approaches. Contents should be approached in a recursive manner.
13 Assessment	Suggestions around testing and assessment. It provides details on the orientations included earlier.

Table 3.1 TESOL Curriculum from Primary in Uruguay

Section Title (my translation from Spanish)	What the Section is About (my summary)
14 Bibliography	A list of references to policies and volumes on language teaching for teachers.
15 Web resources	A list of links to resources which can support teachers when planning their practice.
15 References	Full references of the authors cited in the curriculum.

Activity 3.2 What Does a Curriculum in Your Context Include?

- Browse a general education curriculum or a curriculum for TESOL from your context. This could be from any level of education (kindergarten, primary, secondary, university, etc.). What sections does it include? Are there any sections which seem to be similar to the curriculum summarized in Table 3.1 or those proposed by Macalister and Nation (2020)?
- Based on your browsing, you may want to create a table similar to Table 3.1 so that you can then expand it as we navigate the chapter.

- Principles: these provide a conceptual background or understanding of the theoretical underpinnings supporting the curriculum; they may also include guidelines around language education pedagogy.
- Content: this refers to what learners will learn; it may be arranged in different ways.
- Materials and activities: these include the resources to be used in the implementation of the curriculum.
- Assessment: this includes guidance on which information about learners' progress will be collected and how (e.g. an oral test at the end of a unit/term).

As I said above, goals play a pivotal role because they are the element on which the other elements revolve. This is not a capricious design. It is one way of guaranteeing that the curriculum is internally coherent. Drawing on what we have discussed so far, I would like you to complete Activity 3.2.

3.2 Goals

Goals may provide an answer to the question 'Why do people learn languages?' Broadly speaking, goals could be defined as descriptions of purposes. For example, I would say that the goal of a TESOL curriculum is to provide relevant stakeholders (e.g. teachers, parents, school principals, superintendents, learners) with a map that organizes how English might be taught. That is the goal of the curriculum as an official document.

According to Cook and Singleton (2014), reasons may vary, but in the context of formal education, learners primarily need to pass the subject. Cook (2013) once distinguished between two types of goals:

1 external (what L2 users want to do with the language outside the classroom), and

2 internal (what L2 users wish to achieve through the language apart from social interactions).

Sometimes, these goals work in contexts where students choose to study English in a language school or as an option course within a programme. However, in other settings, English is just another subject alongside Mathematics or History. In those cases, the first goal that learners may have is to pass the subject. Instrumental, you may say, but pragmatic. Perhaps the question we should be asking is more specific: Why should English (or any other additional language) be included in the school curriculum? I will not address this question here, but you can take a look at policies and documents in your context to see whether policymakers have justified the inclusion of English in the school curriculum.

There will be goals associated with what is being sought by teaching English to, for example, children in kindergarten or university undergraduates. In relation to learning, in our case English, goals could be operationalized as aims, objectives or outcomes depending on where the focus resides. Table 3.2 provides a summary of these operationalizations and some examples. At this point, I would like to include a word of caution: Terminology around goals varies across languages and settings; therefore, do not feel confused when examples you find in/beyond this textbook contradict the terms I have used so far. What is important for you to remember is that they all provide a sense of purpose and/or direction from the perspective of learners, teachers or an educational system as a whole. You may also notice that goals are usually written as to-statements (e.g. To describe places) or affirmative sentences, sometimes featuring future forms (e.g. By the end of this course, pupils will be able to express likes/dislikes).

Table 3.2 Goals

Type	Definition	Examples
Learning aims	A broad purpose or general teaching intention of the programme/course/session. It can also serve as a statement of introduction to a course and help potential participants decide if the course is right for them. It might also give an indication of prior experience necessary to participate for the requirement of a professional or academic qualification. An aim could be a paragraph in length. It does not need to be written in one sentence. Learning aims are usually articulated from learners' perspective.	'To allow students to develop their academic writing skills to be able to operate successfully at postgraduate level.'

Type	Definition	Examples
Learning objectives	Brief descriptions of how the learning aims are going to be fulfilled. They explain the operational aspects of the teaching and learning in more detail than the learning aims, and they are written from the perspective of the educator.	'Students will read sample essays and published articles to identify features of academic writing such as cohesion.' 'Students will write drafts that will receive peer as well as tutor feedback'
Learning outcomes	They describe what learners will be expected to be able to do if they have been successful, and they indicate the appropriate level of learner achievement. These outcomes are expected to have been attained by the end of a course/school year. They describe observable, measurable (assessable) demonstrations of knowledge, skills and understanding.	'By the end of this course, students will be able to use general academic language to write a range of writing tasks at postgraduate level.'

Based on the input provided so far, I would like you to read Vignette 3.1 and then complete Activities 3.3 and 3.4.

<table>
<tr><td>Vignette
3.1</td><td><h2>Goals in an English for Business Masters (EBM) Six-Week Course</h2></td></tr>
</table>

In 2023, English Language Edinburgh offered a pre-sessional English course for international master's students. The course included two learning aims and five learning outcomes.

Learning aims:

'EBM aims to develop and improve your confidence and academic language & literacy skills to a sufficient level to bridge the gap between your entry language level and that required to participate successfully in a range of Business School Masters Programmes. It further aims to raise your awareness of what you should expect on their programme and of what is expected of you by the Business School.'

You may notice that both aims are general and student-oriented. They are about what the course will 'do to' students.

Learning outcomes:

'Intended Learning Outcomes On successful completion of this course, you will be able to: Read academic texts in business fields such as Management and Finance, making critical use of genre knowledge and strategies appropriate to their purpose. Write clearly and appropriately in genres common in their discipline. If required by the genre, synthesizing and critically evaluating content from sources to create their argument. Understand and respond critically to academic lectures in their discipline. Use clear and appropriate English to respond critically and contribute meaningfully to group discussions and deliver academic presentations in their business fields. Reflect on and make autonomous decisions regarding their learning.'

You may notice that all the learning outcomes are measurable and observable because they are specific and clear about students demonstrating their knowledge through a range of language-mediated practices, such as reading academic texts or participating in group discussions.

Activity 3.3 A Bit of Backward Engineering

In Vignette 3.1, you found a set of learning outcomes from a business English course. What kind of activities could lead to them? For example, in the first learning outcome, students are expected to be reading and making critical use of genre knowledge. So, for example, as a teacher, I would give them brief academic texts and I would ask them to tell me what the purpose(s) of those texts is/are, and what linguistic items (vocabulary, phrases, grammatical structures) are evidence of those purposes. Use the spaces provided to jot down some ideas:

(a) ____

____

>> Read academic texts in business fields such as Management and Finance, making critical use of genre knowledge and strategies appropriate to their purpose.

(b) ____

____

>> Write clearly and appropriately in genres common in their discipline. If required by the genre, synthesizing and critically evaluating content from sources to create their argument.

(c) ____

____

>> Understand and respond critically to academic lectures in their discipline.

(d) ____

____

>> Use clear and appropriate English to respond critically and contribute meaningfully to group discussions and deliver academic presentations in their business fields.

(e) ____

____

>> Reflect on and make autonomous decisions regarding their learning.

Activity 3.4 Goals

In Activity 3.2, you were asked to browse a general curriculum with a section on TESOL, or a TESOL curriculum from your context. If you can, go back to that curriculum you browsed. This time, I would like you to see if you can identify any goals. The following questions can help:

- *Are there any general goals?*
- *Are there any specific goals?*
- *What types of goals can you identify? (Refer to Table 3.2)*
- *If there are goals, are they written from the perspective of the teacher, the learners or somebody else?*
- *Are there any learning outcomes?*
- *In your experience, are such goals realistic?*
- *If you could rewrite them, what changes would you make to them? Why?*

3.3 Principles

As I have discussed before, the TESOL curriculum is an organizer of language teaching and learning in a given context. It provides an organization of what is/can/should be taught and when, as well as why and how English will be taught. In Table 3.1, Sections 4, 8 and 12 attest to the inclusion of principles in TESOL curriculum design.

I understand principles as a set of key concepts that form the basis of and provide directionality to the TESOL curriculum. These concepts are mainly pedagogical and are based on theory as well as research-informed practice and practice-based research. Regarding 'pedagogical', principles comprise general pedagogy as well as specific language teaching, what others may call specific didactics (or sociodidactics), a term not usually found in Anglo-centric research and practice, but very much in use in, for example, francophone (e.g. Châteaureynaud, 2022) or Spanish-speaking academia (e.g. Ballester Almagro, 2024; Terán Ñacato et al., 2024). As Macalister and Nation (2020) rightly note, the principles that curriculum developers use to frame the TESOL curriculum need to be flexible, varied, inclusive and coherent to ensure their implementation and/possible context-responsive adaptation. Such a decision may contribute to aligning the official curriculum and the enacted curriculum.

In terms of general pedagogical principles, educational/learning theories such as constructivism, sociocultural theory, inquiry-based learning, cognitivism, interactionism, spiralling learning, connectivism, experiential learning or critical pedagogy, among others, may provide the basis for developing the TESOL curriculum. For example, the Uruguayan curriculum to teach English refers to general theories such as sociocultural theory or inquiry-based learning. While discussing educational theories exceeds the scope of this textbook, Section 3.8 provides some reading suggestions. Usually, a curriculum will draw from different theories in a coherent manner. Therefore, you may find a curriculum that refers to sociocultural theory, taxonomies and critical approaches to education. Such practices illustrate that the complex ecology of education may necessitate the contributions of a handful of educational theories to create a coherent and logical framework that is inclusive of beliefs, people and directions.

When we focus on the TESOL curriculum, we then need to consider specific theories and research-based findings of language learning and second language acquisition. It is important to note that these theories need to be 'handled with care' since some of them describe language learning in naturalistic settings or in settings in which users are immersed in the additional language, which is quite different from a classroom setting or macro-context in which the additional language, in our case English, is not the dominant language of communication, or in monolingual settings (i.e. all the learners share the same L1 such as Mandarin or Arabic).

For example, in terms of language-specific principles/findings, we can think of:

- Implementing the i+1 principle or input hypothesis put forward by Krashen (1981) (e.g. in the classroom, a teacher adjusts their English to that of the students and adds just one level of difficulty to make the input comprehensible and the linguistic challenge manageable).

- Integrating language skills (e.g. for a speaking activity focused on discussion, students are first asked to read an article).

- Finding and using a new word/phrase/expression several times and in different contexts to make it memorable (e.g. teaching phrasal verbs used in different situations).

- Deliberate focus on forms (grammatical structures) and focus on meanings (semantic and sociopragmatic functions).

- Organizing content in a sequence which recognizes students' sequential development of linguistic items (a.k.a. developmental sequence or learnability hypothesis) (Long, 2009).

Therefore, a TESOL curriculum may contain references to general educational theories as well as theories/approaches/pedagogies which concentrate on additional language education. This is when approaches such as communicative language teaching, task-based language learning, CLIL, technology-enhanced language learning, total-physical response, the lexical approach, grammar-based language teaching, inclusive language education, translanguaging pedagogy, etc., come into play. Once again, a TESOL curriculum may combine these and other approaches in different ways depending on contextual circumstances. For example, when I designed the TESOL curriculum for secondary schools in the province of Chubut (Argentina), teachers were suggested to use communicative and task-based language teaching approaches. However, for those teachers working in technical secondary schools or schools with specific orientations (e.g. business and finance), CLIL was suggested so as to harness connections between language learning/use and specific subject knowledge.

At this stage, it is vital to remind ourselves that developing a TESOL curriculum is a complex enterprise which needs to be guided by coherence and agreements. It must be seen as a whole, where all the pieces fit together harmoniously. Thus, the first logical connection we need to find is that between goals and principles. For example, if the learning outcomes of a TESOL curriculum suggest that learners should be able to use English to communicate in different informal situations, then it seems that (language) learning theories with a focus on collaboration, interaction and communication need to have a pivotal role. Or if the learning aims of a programme are about enabling learners to expand their vocabulary, then the lexical approach should become the theoretical backbone of the TESOL curriculum behind that programme.

Activity 3.5 Identifying Principles of Language Teaching

1. Do an online search with the aim of identifying key principles for language teaching. Make sure you use quality sources.
2. If you can, get together with a peer and discuss your search and agree on five key principles for a context of your choice (e.g. higher education students doing English for Academic Purposes in your city).
3. If you are happy, share your five key principles on TESOLand. Use Figure 3.1 to access our digital space and find the Chapter 3 section.

Figure 3.1 QR code access to TESOLand

Activity 3.6 Principles in a TESOL Curriculum

1. If you can, go back to that curriculum you browsed in Activity 3.2. This time, I would like you to see if you can identify any principles. The following questions can help:
   1. *Are there any principles related to teaching and/or learning in general?*
   2. *Are there any language learning principles?*
   3. *What types of goals can you identify? (Refer to Table 3.2)*
   4. *In your experience, are such principles context-responsive?*
2. From the list of five principles you put together in Activity 3.5, are there any commonalities? Would you include any of them in the curriculum you're analysing?

3.4 Content

It is vital that there is a logical connection between goals, principles and content. Why? Because the TESOL curriculum needs to offer an organized and coherent roadmap. For example, if the goal of a TESOL curriculum is to provide primary school students with the opportunity to learn English through content coming from other subjects in the school curriculum so that they develop academic literacies, then principles of CLIL will need to be called in so that pedagogy and aims are in sync. Similarly, the content and its sequencing will also need to respond to those goals and principles.

What do we mean by content? This refers to what is taught. Content often combines declarative/descriptive knowledge (e.g. knowledge of grammatical rules, knowledge of the situations in which it's OK to say 'Hey' instead of 'Hello') and procedural knowledge (e.g. knowledge of how to write an effective message, knowledge about how to solve a task). I would like you to complete Activity 3.7.

Activity 3.7 What Did You Learn?

Think about the last time you took lessons to learn English. Look at the list below and cross out those items you were NOT taught (Note: Perhaps the teacher did teach them, but you don't think you learnt them!).

1. Differences between two sounds.
2. Strategies to record and remember vocabulary.
3. Grammatical structures.
4. Formal and informal ways of expressing your personal likes.
5. Knowledge about cultural practices in different contexts.
6. How to give a presentation.
7. How to use artificial intelligence to proofread your writing.
8. Topic-specific vocabulary.
9. Reading skills.
10. Studying skills.

The items included in Activity 3.7 show that teaching English is not just about knowledge of discrete linguistic items. According to Macalister and Nation (2020), the content in a TESOL curriculum may be organized around several categories, as shown in Figure 3.2, within a course/year or across several courses and years. You can also take a look at the content pages of a coursebook used in your context and see the sections

Figure 3.2
Possible types of content found in a curriculum

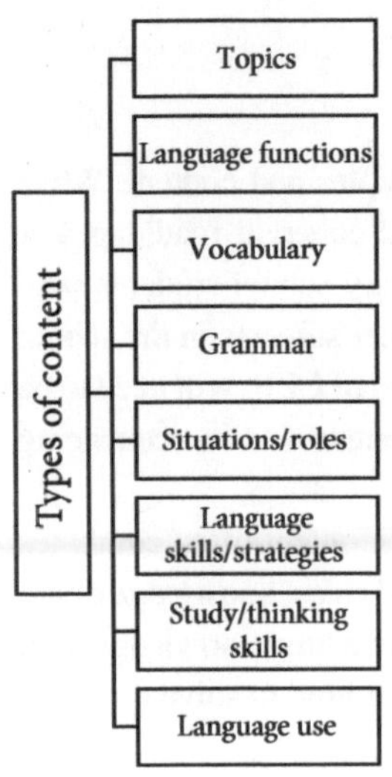

into which units are broken down. If a coursebook claims to be communicative, I would expect that the first column in its contents page refers to a situation or topic so as to show coherence between communicative approaches as a principle and the type of content that seems to be the organizing element of other types of contents, such as grammar or vocabulary.

In Table 3.3, I provide further guidance on what the types of content included in Figure 3.2 may mean. Please, this does not mean that a TESOL curriculum or a unit within a curriculum/syllabus/coursebook must contain all of these types. What to include is worth discussing with those involved in curriculum design, implementation and evaluation.

Let's imagine that as part of a TESOL curriculum driven by CLIL principles, we wish to design a unit of work around the

Table 3.3

Examples of Content Types

Type of Content	Examples
Topics	Friends and families, the solar system, higher education in the UK, healthy eating habits
Language functions	Describing, narrating, arguing, explaining, suggesting, asking, reporting, thanking
Vocabulary	Parts of the body, phrasal verbs, adjectives, prepositions
Grammar	Tenses, reported speech, conditional forms, complex clauses, coherence and cohesion
Situation/roles	Checking in at the airport, making a complaint, interviewing for a job, opening a bank account
Language skills/ strategies	Speaking, pronunciation, listening, reading and writing, language awareness
Study/thinking skills	Making lists, using graphic organizers effectively, developing critical thinking skills, finding and curating information online, ethical use of AI
Language use	Expressing concerns in formal and informal situations, sociopragmatics (denotation and connotation), language appropriacy according to context and interlocutors

topic of volcanoes, as this is a topic that our students are also addressing in their Science lesson. As a teacher, I would have the following content:

- Topic: volcanoes and volcanic eruptions in our continent.
- Functions: describing a volcano, describing volcanic eruptions, explaining the benefits and challenges of volcanic eruptions.
- Vocabulary: parts of a volcano, types of volcanoes, words (adjectives, nouns, verbs) needed to describe volcano formation and eruption.
- Grammar: simple present, when/if clauses to describe processes, passive voice in the present.
- Language skills: reading a text to find specific information (scanning), watching a video to identify stages in volcanic eruption, oral discussion of environmental/ social/economic issues related to volcanoes, writing a summary of the benefits and challenges of volcanic eruptions.
- Study/thinking skills: note-taking (while watching a video), using graphic organizers to record benefits and challenges, interpreting information.

The following example comes from the 2023 TESOL curriculum for secondary education in Uruguay (Administración Nacional de Educación Pública, 2023b). As part of that curriculum, the contents for Grade 9 are divided into six units: (1) Fun and entertainment in Uruguay, (2) Human rights, (3) My social life, (4) My social responsibilities, (5) Making my decisions about the future and (6) Teen media. Such topics appear to indicate that the curriculum is topic-driven and connected to teenagers' experiences. Now, let me zoom in on Unit 2 so that we can take a look at the content in more detail (Table 3.4).

As can be seen in Table 3.4, the curriculum designers sought to construct alignment between learning outcomes and content. It is worth noting that the integrated and balanced development of language skills appears to take centre stage, and that target grammar and vocabulary items are expected to be used recursively throughout the unit. Last, it is also worth highlighting the agency that teachers are given when it comes to the competencies they would like to foster in the unit, as the curriculum recognizes the particularities of each context and the uniqueness of each classroom and students.

In Vignette 3.2, you will find another real-life example of relations between aims and content, and how the latter is arranged into types of content that somehow illustrate those included in Figure 3.2.

Based on your knowledge developed so far, you can complete Activity 3.8 (see p.65).

Let me now share with you Vignette 3.3, written by a former master's student of mine. In the vignette, the student looked at the elements of goals and content in the TESOL curriculum in China. You can then complete Activity 3.9 (see p.66).

So far, we have discussed what content refers to in the TESOL curriculum and the importance of seeking alignment between goals, principles and content. It is also relevant to discuss how such content could be arranged so that stakeholders in the meso and microsystems can maximize their investment in it. Hence, it is time to talk about sequencing.

Table 3.4 Unit 2 of the TESOL Curriculum for Grade 9 (translated and adapted from Administración Nacional de Educación Pública, 2023b, p. 13)

UNIT 2: HUMAN RIGHTS

Learning outcomes

By the end of this unit, students will

- know more about their rights and the rights of others.
- understand the struggles of minority groups and their rights.
- describe actions related to promoting human rights.
- become aware of the role of elderly people and immigrants in society.
- understand why migration occurs and present arguments on how migrants are regarded in our country.
- compare some rights taken for granted in Uruguay and how they are expressed in other countries

Macro skills		Competencies	Suggested language components
Speaking	Students • describe their rights and compare them with those of Uruguay's nineteenth-century reality. • present ideas about topics related to human rights and weakened populations. • share ideas about ways of promoting the protection of human rights.	[Note: In the original document, this column includes a list of competencies from a larger set. These competencies refer to knowledge of the language, procedural and attitudinal knowledge. This column also states: 'Choices made by the teacher in charge based on needs, context and proficiency levels may well determine to foster others.']	• Simple present • Simple past • Comparatives and superlatives, … as well as … • Modal verbs: should, must, have to, ought to • Will • Going to • Present perfect • enjoy + verb(ing) love + verb(ing) • Expressing agreement and disagreement • Expressing partial agreement • Expressing opinions and justifying them • If I were you …
Reading	Students • read articles and studies related to the protection of human rights. • read NGOs' websites as well as laws that protect human and animal rights. • read accounts of people who advocated for their rights. • compare legal texts that speak of human rights in different times and places.		
Listening	Students • listen to people who suffered human rights' abuse. • listen to immigrants with different accents and levels of proficiency in English and understand what they say. • watch and listen to speeches of famous people (e.g. Martin Luther King, Mandela, Gandhi, Malala Yousafzai) advocating for freedom and respect.		**Vocabulary** Related vocabulary is expected to be presented gradually, in a contextualized and motivating way. Recycling vocabulary is also beneficialfor students in the process of acquisition.
Writing	Students • create different types of written communications to promote human rights. • write a speech advocating for one of their rights. • write about their own rights and the actions they can put forth to protect others. • write short opinion essays about topics related to human rights.		

Vignette 3.2	**TESOL Curriculum for Secondary Education in Indonesia, by Alif Winarno**

As of 2024, there are two types of curricula employed in secondary education in Indonesia, comprising the Merdeka curriculum for grade seven and the Kurtilas curriculum for grades eight and nine, respectively.

In the Merdeka curriculum for teaching English in the seventh grade, the content or elements that teachers are expected to cover are listening, speaking, reading, viewing, writing and presenting, such as introducing oneself and others. The learning objectives included in the curriculum become the topic of the lessons themselves, and it includes objectives such as 'Learners being able to greet others', as well as 'Learners being able to introduce themselves and others'. In the example of the topic of greeting others, the learning materials consist of common expressions used for greetings. In addition, the materials and worksheets in the Merdeka curriculum are generally based on the textbook Bright and English Course for SMP/MTs Grade VII.

In the 2013 Curriculum, commonly known as Kurtilas, the teachers are expected to cover content that aims to foster knowledge development and skill competencies. In Kurtilas, the content is made up of three main parts, which are the social function, language elements and the lesson topic. For teaching English in the eighth grade, the social functions taught in the lessons are in regard to maintaining personal relationships. An example of the social functions included is 'Identifying, introducing, praising, criticizing, and admiring'. As a whole, the language elements in Kurtilas largely focus on speaking skills, covering elements such as speech, word stress and intonation. The grammatical aspects that are included are the elements of spelling, punctuation and handwriting. It is generally mentioned in Kurtilas that any interactions or events that is reflective of the core competencies (CC) is encouraged to become the topic of the lesson. The suggested activities include listening and imitating the teacher, asking and answering questions, creating texts, describing and reflecting.

The social functions taught for grade nine learners are also related to maintaining personal relationships, with the specific addition of competency in a particular social situation. An example of a specific social situation would be 'Choosing healthy and safe medicine/food/ drinks, avoiding negative effects, and getting the best results'. The language elements in grade nine lessons remain the same speaking and writing elements of speech, word stress, intonation, spelling and punctuation. The lesson topic for grade nine must also be reflective of the CC, and the suggested activities, too, include listening and imitating the teacher, asking and answering questions, creating texts, describing and reflecting.

Activity 3.8 Content in a TESOL Curriculum

Go back to that curriculum you browsed in Activities 3.2–3.6. This time, I would like you to see if you can identify the content of the curriculum. The following questions can help:

1. *What content does the curriculum include?*
2. *Is it organized/arranged in any way? If so, how?*
3. *Is there alignment between the goals, principles and content of the TESOL curriculum?*
4. *Do you think that the content is suitable for the context and target students of the curriculum?*
5. *Does the curriculum say anything about teachers having the freedom to change the content according to their students' needs?*
6. *If you could make changes to the content of the curriculum, what changes would you make? What would be the rationale for such changes?*

According to Macalister and Nation (2020), we can find curricula, syllabi, or coursebooks with two types of sequencing: linear or modular. What does each mean? In a linear curriculum, content is organized with a clear sense of progression, and what is to be taught in, for example, Year 2 builds upon what has been taught in Year 1. This linear approach explains why, in some institutions, students have to undertake an entrance exam or diagnostic/placement test to determine in which 'level' (e.g. elementary,

<table>
<tr><td>

Vignette 3.3

</td><td>

Goals and Content in TESOL in Secondary Schools in China, by Yilin Liu

</td></tr>
</table>

Secondary education in China comprises two stages: secondary school (3 years, ages 13–15) and high school (3 years, ages 16–18). The curriculum goals focus on developing students' key competencies in language skills, cultural awareness, quality of thinking and learning skills. The high school English curriculum, revised in 2020, is structured around thematic modules that align learning content with overall educational goals.

In the Chinese high school context, the TESOL curriculum's primary goal in developing **language skills** is to instill a robust linguistic awareness in students, empowering them to effectively communicate within various contexts. This entails a thorough comprehension of both spoken and written texts, coupled with the capability to engage successfully in oral and written interpersonal communication (job interviews, report of sports events). In parallel, the aim for **cultural awareness** is to provide students with cultural knowledge (traditional festivals, customs, sports, tourism) and deepen their understanding of its implications. Through learning to compare and appreciate cultural differences (reaction to compliment, political and economic situations), students are expected to cultivate character traits such as self-respect and self-confidence. Fostering **quality of thinking** is another cornerstone of the curriculum. Students are expected to critically analyse and evaluate phenomena in language (idioms, slang) and culture (value orientation of mass media, drama, poems) and proficiently organize and summarize information. They should be adept at evaluating diverse viewpoints critically and embracing multiple perspectives to thinking. The curriculum's **learning skills** goals encourage students to embrace a positive and proactive attitude towards English learning. It guides them to effectively access various English learning resources (library, Internet, newspaper, magazine, broadcast) and thoughtfully plan their study schedules. By continually monitoring, evaluating, reflecting on and adjusting their learning trajectory, they enhance their capacity to use English across different academic disciplines.

Central to the curriculum are six foundational contents that run across the goals above. **Thematic contexts** serve as the broad umbrella under which the curriculum is designed, encompassing themes on 'Individual and Self' (civil rights, social responsibility, occupation development), 'Society' (public welfare, international organization, legal knowledge, technology innovation) and 'Nature' (environment protection, disaster prevention, universe exploration). **Discourse types** are diverse, spanning both oral and written forms. The curriculum includes a wide range of genres, from narratives and expositions to arguments, as well as interviews and dialogues. Additionally, students interact with non-linear texts like charts, diagrams, web pages, advertisements and comics, which all serve as authentic linguistic learning materials. Underpinning these types are the core **linguistic knowledge** components: phonetics, vocabulary, grammar, discourse and pragmatics. **Language skills** are split into two main categories: receptive skills (listening, reading and viewing: multimodal discourse) and productive skills (speaking and writing). The curriculum also places a strong emphasis on **cultural knowledge**. By including both Chinese and international content, it aims to foster a global perspective, encouraging students to appreciate the diversity of human thought and spread Chinese culture to the world. Lastly, **learning strategies** introduce students to metacognitive (identification, implementation, research, reflection), cognitive (word formation, cohesion and coherence), communicative (gesture, eye contact) and affective (collaboration, emotion-regulation) strategies.

Activity 3.9 On Vignette 3.3

1. Re-read Vignette 3.3 and think/discuss with peers whether there is alignment between the goals mentioned in the second paragraph and the content outlined in the last paragraph.
2. Think about what changes you would introduce to make the curriculum more coherent and context-responsive.

pre-intermediate, advanced or CEFR bands A1, A2, B1, etc.) they should be placed to continue progressing with their English language development. This linear approach is usually found in coursebooks. Therefore, a student needs to pass Year 1 to be promoted to Year 2. In this linear curriculum, students may have plenty of opportunities for spiralling learning as there is repetition and recycling of content with different topics and with increasing level of difficulty. For example, conditional form type 0 (present simple+ present simple in a complex sentence) necessitates students who are familiar with the rules and uses of the present simple in, for example, simple sentences.

On the other hand, a curriculum in which the content is organized in a modular fashion understands that each course/unit of work is self-contained and that no previous knowledge of other courses or units is required. This type of organization is sometimes found in courses which are online and self-paced and usually targeted at adult students or students who have already developed a satisfactory, whatever that means, command of the language. In the case of coursebooks, for example, this could be found in the book *Academic vocabulary in use* by McCarthy and O'Dell (2008). The book consists of more than fifty units organized in different sections, such as working with academic vocabulary or opinions and ideas. In the preliminary pages, the authors tell users how the book should be used:

> We recommend that you work through the nine introductory units first so that you become familiar with key aspects of academic vocabulary and how best to study it. After that you may work on the units in any order that suits you"
>
> (McCarthy & O'Dell, 2008, p. 7)

The quote shows that the coursebook appears to feature both types of sequencing. While the first nine units are meant to be completed in a linear fashion, the rest of the book could be used in any direction, and this depends on the user's needs.

Based on your knowledge of linear and modular sequencing in a curriculum, I would like you to complete Activities 3.10 and 3.11.

Activity 3.10 On Sequencing in a TESOL Curriculum

3. Go back to the curriculum you have been analysing so far and try to identify whether there are instances of linear and/or modular sequencing of the content.

Activity 3.11 A Coursebook for Children

1. Use Figure 3.3 to watch a short clip in which author Carol Read talks about her coursebook *Mimi's Wheel*, published by Macmillan. Just watch up to minute 1:04.

Figure 3.3 QR code access to video by Carol Read

2. Based on what Read says about her coursebook, is content organized in a linear or modular way? Why did she choose that type of content organization? Justify your answer.

3. If you can, find a sample unit of the coursebook to see what it looks like.

3.5 Materials, Activities and AI

Materials are usually ubiquitous in the ecology of curriculum development. When selected and used critically, they can be extremely helpful resources for those in the microsystem (teachers and students) and represent/reinforce/challenge the discourses emanating from the meso and macrosystems. At this point, I should also recognize that in some contexts, for different circumstances, materials such as coursebooks or screens are nowhere to be seen. In those cases, the students' experiences and the overall context can be the optimal tools and conduits for learning. Meddings and Thornbury (2009) put forward the idea of Dogme ELT to underscore the possibility of teaching and learning based on whatever students and teachers bring to the classroom, i.e. themselves, and whatever happens to be in the classroom. Dogme ELT is not only a move to resist coursebooks, but also an approach to mitigate the overreliance and overabundance of materials in language teaching.

For the purposes of this section, it will suffice to define materials as anything created/modified/used by teachers and students to facilitate language learning (Tomlinson, 2011; Tomlinson & Masuhara, 2018). In other words, these materials could become pedagogical tools to support teaching and learning in TESOL. These include published pedagogical materials (e.g. a coursebook to teach English; an app), teacher-made materials (e.g. worksheets, a webpage, a game, pictures), student-made materials (e.g. a game), as well as any materials which are not originally intended to be used to teach/learn English in a formal sense, but are then given a pedagogical orientation by their users (e.g. a social media reel, a novel, a song, a Telegram message, a picture book, a podcast, a painting, a recipe, a recorded talk).

In connection with materials, we can briefly mention the use of tools which are used to present materials and the use of generative artificial intelligence (GenAI). In relation to the former, Lu and Xie (2022) conducted a systematic review of the use of digital tools in TESOL and found that such tools are usually used to expose students to speaking and listening materials as well as embed activities that promote interaction, such as online forums. As for the latter, I am not saying anything new, as in one way or another, we have all been surrounded by conversations around and content produced through GenAI. As Lee and Low (2024) suggest, critical thinking for learners and also for teachers who use GenAI to create materials and activities needs to be prioritized. For example, if as part of the TESOL curriculum, learners are asked to interact with/use AI chatbots to design or complete a task, what are the educational goals behind their use? What purpose do they serve to make learning meaningful and a powerful cognitive experience? These questions are important because we do not want our learners to pay the consequences of cognitive offloading (i.e. learners asking AI to do the thinking for them).

According to Mishan and Timmis (2015), materials encapsulate five purposes:

1 Offer psychological support: materials can enhance motivation and autonomy, provide a sense of direction and progression, and scaffold learning.

2 Provide language exposure: materials often include written (reading) and aural (listening) exposure to language calibrated to be just above students' level of understanding.

3 Become a source of information: materials do not only provide linguistic input (e.g. grammar rules) but also content input (e.g. traditional celebrations in a country). This purpose is a core feature of any materials for CLIL or any type of curriculum-language integration (e.g. de Oliveira et al., 2024).

4 Provoke students' response: materials include activities, but they can also generate students' spontaneous reaction to a topic or text.

5 Act as teacher education: materials which come with a companion book for teachers (a.k.a. teacher's book) can help teachers understand the rationale behind a coursebook and make the most of its features.

While the purposes listed above are certainly worth keeping in mind with all materials, and regardless of whether we use GenAI or not, for the TESOL curriculum, it is vital that there is coherence between goals, principles, content and materials. In some contexts, the same group of people who design the TESOL curriculum are also responsible for designing the materials that will help teachers deliver the curriculum as intended. In other contexts, the Ministry of Education may commission a publisher to design a curriculum-compliant coursebook series that will be implemented across schools. And in other contexts, teachers have the freedom to choose any materials as long as these respond to the goals, principles and content of the curriculum as well as their specific circumstances and students. In this regard, a TESOL curriculum could prescribe what materials to use (e.g. a specific coursebook series), suggest what materials could be used (not just a coursebook), suggest possible materials and resources, or refrain from offering any guidance. In any case, I would say that what matters is that the choice of materials and activities to be part of the enacted curriculum emanates from informed decisions and, if possible, agreements among teachers so that the overall enacted curriculum across classes is coherent. That said, we need to be aware that in some settings, deciding on materials is a top-down activity where

Activity 3.12 Coursebooks and the TESOL Curriculum

Read the following extract from an encyclopedia entry, and think about the sentences in italics. Can you make a list of the relationships that you, as a teacher, would expect to find between a coursebook and the TESOL curriculum?

Course books, usually referred to as language teaching materials, consist of a range of language teaching and learning tools. They generally serve an important function in the ELT world and are an integrative part of many language programs. Similarly, curricula serve an important function in the ELT world and are an indispensable element of effective language programs because they set the specifications of language instruction. *The relationship between a course book and a curriculum takes on various forms and depends on many teaching and context-driven variables. The most direct one is that of the correlation between the contents and quality of the course book and the contents and quality of the curriculum.* (Kleckova & Dalle, 2018, p. 1)

Activity 3.13 On Materials in a TESOL Curriculum

1. Go back to the curriculum you have been analysing so far and try to identify whether the curriculum says anything about the materials that should/could be used to guarantee its successful implementation.

2. In connection with your answer to the first part of this activity, what are your views on teaching/learning materials and the TESOL curriculum in your context? What suggestions would you make as (a) a curriculum developer, (b) a teacher or (c) a student?

3. If possible and applicable, find a coursebook (or similar) that is used in the context of the curriculum you are analysing. Choose any unit of the coursebook. Does it respond to the goals, principles and content the curriculum includes?

teachers have no say. I personally find this unfortunate because it does not allow teachers to exercise their agency. However, this does not mean that they will be critical implementers of materials. Even when they have no say in what is used in their own classrooms, there is often some leeway for them to engage in materials adaptation.

Based on the brief discussion in this section, I would like you to complete Activities 3.12 and 3.13.

3.6 Assessment

How do we know that a TESOL curriculum is working? How do we know that the aims, goals and learning outcomes included in a TESOL curriculum are achieved? To these questions, my answer is that evaluation is paramount. Evaluation, which we will flesh out in Chapter 4, includes gathering information about learners' progress. This is when assessment and testing come into the TESOL curriculum picture. In this section, I am only touching the very surface of this topic. If you would like to gain a broader and deeper understanding, please take a look at the titles I have included in Section 3.8.

I understand assessment as a set of procedures to collect information about/monitor what learners know and can do, with the aim of offering support when it is needed. In many contexts, the intention is to measure students' progress against expected learning outcomes. Assessment is often conceived as a process that is an ingrained element of learning. Therefore, there needs to be coherence between the goals, principles, content, materials, activities and assessment. For example, if a TESOL curriculum has a clear focus on aural skills, and learners are systematically asked to engage in group activities such as role-play or presentations, then learners passing a course cannot depend on an individual written exam.

Assessment can take many forms. For example, teachers can ask learners to complete tests with open-ended (e.g. give their opinion about an issue) and/or closed-ended (e.g. multiple choice questions where only one option is correct) activities, submit an essay or deliver a group or individual presentation. Usually, assessment can be formative or summative. Formative assessment refers to activities which allow learners to check their progress and work towards improvement. For example, this may include the use of portfolios, or process writing by which learners submit drafts, and the teacher provides feedback that will enable them enhance their writing until they are ready to submit a final version. It could also entail a teacher keeping observation notes while learners are working in class to understand how they are achieving the learning goals.

On the other hand, summative assessment refers to measuring learners' progress and may have more definitive consequences, such as passing or failing a course, or being accepted or not into a course (think about entry exams). Summative assessment is often associated with testing, which occurs at specific points in time (e.g. start of a course, end of a unit of work, end of a course, end of a programme). However, essays and oral presentations could also be part of summative assessment. Summative assessment is characterized by providing learners with a grade/mark or a pass/fail. Many education systems take summative assessment as the main source of information to evaluate the merits of any curriculum, and institutional budgets may be allocated according to learners' performance in tests. This is why, sometimes, some tests could be high-stakes.

Vignette 3.4 illustrates formative and summative assessment in the context of TESOL with primary school learners in Brazil. Vignette 3.4 shows that in the Brazilian curriculum, there are no prescribed approaches to assessment, as it empowers schools to do what is best for their learners depending on institutional goals and contextual features. This decision illustrates how an official curriculum could provide agentic spaces for educators. The vignette also illustrates forms of assessment in practice. It is interesting to note that formative assessment seems to be connected to speaking, while summative assessment is associated with writing development skills. However, formative and summative assessment could be adopted with any language skill or type of content found in the TESOL curriculum. Last, the vignette mentions rubrics to provide feedback to learners. As you may have experienced yourself as a language learner, feedback can take many forms. For example, teachers can:

A Ask students to monitor their own progress through self-assessment exercises, such as learners agreeing or disagreeing with can-do statements (e.g. I can express likes and dislikes).

B Construct rubrics to assess learners or ask them to use the rubrics to assess their peers (peer feedback) and themselves.

C Provide aural or written comments indicating what learners did well and suggesting areas which need improvement.

D Marking errors and providing the right answer.

Although feedback provides information on something that learners did, teachers can also provide comments as feedforward so as to support learners in the future. The combination of feedback and feedforward constitutes a powerful pedagogical tool to support learning. In TESOL, as well as in other areas of the curriculum, there has been

<table>
<tr><td>Vignette
3.4</td><td>

Meaningful Assessment with Young Learners in Brazil, by Julia Landau

</td></tr>
</table>

As the coordinator of an extended day English language enrichment programme, and now as the leader of the elementary division of a Brazilian bilingual school, I work first-hand with assessment in practice – in all its challenges and possibilities. The teaching of English as a foreign language in Brazil, particularly with young learners, has migrated more and more towards the internal work of schools, though private language courses still play a role in the language education landscape. Different models exist, for example, English Language as a discrete curricular component (in which subject-area teachers enter the homeroom class to teach), extended day enrichment programmes (in which extra time at the end of the day is dedicated to English Language learning, usually through content), fully integrated bilingual schools and international schools, to name some prominent formats. As the Brazilian National Common Core (BNCC) (our curricular guidelines) addresses English Language Learning only beginning in sixth grade, and our National Curricular Guidelines for the Offer of Plurilingual Education (as of this writing, not officially ratified into law) do not prescribe specific assessment practices, those schools working with young learners must design curriculum and assessment according to their learning community's needs and vision.

In my experience in Brazil, focussing on abilities-based assessment rather than deficit-based frameworks will best favour our learners. This has meant assessing based on what a student *can do* rather than what they *have not consolidated* yet. An assessment is, in this perspective, an opportunity for a student to use their linguistic resources. An existing tool that I have worked with in diverse contexts, using them institutionally in assessment building, are the World-class Instructional Design and Assessment (WIDA) standards. This framework does not offer ready-made evaluative activities, but rather tools with which we can create our assessments, descriptors with which we can identify our students' abilities, and more. It is geared towards language learners (from Kindergarten to High School), in a content-driven context.

And how has assessment been carried out in my experience? An effective assessment asks the right questions, and so an abilities-based approach is differentiated, and relevant to a student's (in this case, children's) reality. Formative assessment can be formal or informal, and can be considered even within routine classroom moments, as long as there is documentation regarding this. Summative language assessment will refer to a longer period of time and will represent more or less a culmination of a certain unit of study.

Examples of assessments I have carried out with teams in the past include, while working in contexts driven by Content and Language Integrated Learning (CLIL):

Formative Assessment, Interpretive Listening, Grade 1: students execute steps in a science experiment according to oral commands, integrating instructional language with key academic vocabulary (*'Now make a mixture with the blue and yellow liquid in the bowl'*)

Formative Assessment, Oral Language, Grade 4: learners record a video for the class about their family's origins, their immigration story and how it shapes their family traditions (*'My grandfather came from Nigeria and taught us some words in Yorubá, and how to make asaro'; 'My aunt has emigrated to Portugal and now we talk on video every Sunday'*).

Summative assessment, Writing, Grade 2: Learners write a 'thank you' letter to a guest interviewed during their project or lesson, with the support of some sentence stems. They use a rubric to self-check if they have included the expected textual elements and discursive aspects. (*'Thank you for your visit to our class. My favorite part was using the stethoscope' / 'I enjoyed learning about how compost helps a garden.'*)

With Wide tools, for example, rubrics can be designed to evaluate individual assessments. The institution can decide, within its grading system, where WIDA levels map onto specific grades. Learners have access to rubrics and routinely engage in self-evaluation to bring metacognition and ownership to their learning and assessment processes.

Without a doubt, as educators, assessment is our friend. When leveraged well and often, it tells us what has worked and what hasn't, how to adjust our differentiation, when to go back and when to accelerate. In my experience working with young learners in the Brazilian additional language context, this means we seek out assessment that is relevant, adaptive and meaningful.

a shift towards assessment *for* learning. In other words, assessment should not only be used to measure what learners know or can do at one specific point in time; it should be primarily used to enable them to reflect on their learning and improve. If you wish to read about assessment for learning in general education, Wiliam (2011) is a very good start. In TESOL, Liu and Xu (2017) provide a compelling discussion in the context of China. What does assessment for learning mean in practice? You can read Vignettes 3.5 and 3.6.

Although Vignettes 3.5 and 3.6 describe practices on assessment for learning with different learners and in different contexts, they both demonstrate that it can be beneficial. It is interesting to note that in both cases, learners could work both individually and collaboratively and that there was a degree of agency involved as they could choose which tests to take home (Vignette 3.5) or which activities to solve as part of their classroom test (Vignette 3.6). In this regard, the assessment component of the curriculum is directed

<table>
<tr><td>Vignette
3.5</td><td>

Assessment for Learning with Very Young Learners (Hobbs & Mourão, 2025)

</td></tr>
</table>

The first author, Hobbs, decided to improve their young Thai learners' motivation test engagement by introducing regular, short take-home tests couples with motivational strategies over 25 weeks. The intervention combined formative and summative assessment and embraced both as opportunities for learning. In other words, even summative assessment (short tests) was used for formative purposes.

In terms of formative assessment, the teacher introduced a visual aid that they called 'The Learning Wall' which consisted of simple can-do statements so that the learners could monitor their own progress (self-assessment).

The teacher also designed short pencil-and-paper tests, with varying degrees of difficulty, that allowed the learners to go over the content covered in their textbook every two weeks. First, the learners collaboratively discussed the tests to understand what was required. Second, each learner chose a test and took it home to complete. Fourth, the learners brought the test back to class and edit them before receiving peer feedback on strengths and weaknesses. The teacher also provided written and oral feedback in relation to the assessment criteria displayed on The Learning Wall.

The experience, according to the authors' data collected during the intervention, resulted in an increase in learners' motivation and systematic engagement with take-home tests.

<table>
<tr><td>Vignette
3.6</td><td>

Assessment for Learning with Teenagers

</td></tr>
</table>

Back in the day, when I used to teach English to secondary school students in Esquel, Argentina, I used to do the following once a twice a year with my class:

At the end of a term, I would design a summative assessment-oriented written test aimed at integrating all the content included in the term. The test consisted of two parts. Part 1 included a reading passage followed by comprehension questions and an open question connected to the topic of passage. For Part 2, I designed several activities (multiple choice, gap filling, matching, correcting mistakes, finding the extra word, rearranging a sentence, etc.) connected to functions, grammar and vocabulary in context, all of them with similar levels of challenge. I would make several copies of each activity and place them on desks at the back of the classroom. I would ask my students to choose any three activities, stick them below their answers to Part 1 and complete them. As they were completing the test, I would take note of the activities most chosen and the ones that had been disregarded. The students would hand in the test, and I would take them home to grade with a numerical mark, and I would simply underline their mistakes. I would also make a note of common mistakes made by most of the students.

In the following lesson, I would go over those mistakes, explain a linguistic point, and encourage students to engage in self- and/or peer-correction. Their homework was to take the test back home and hand in a revised version of it. This would not receive a grade but I would provide formative feedback. Then, I would randomly distribute all the activities that had been left out and ask them to work on them in pairs in class. At the end of the class, we would check them and I would ask what made them choose some over others.

By doing so, the test became an opportunity for the students to learn from their mistakes, and the discarded activities allowed us all to reflect on what areas or procedures seemed to be more challenging.

towards learner-centredness, and aspects of assessment are negotiated between teachers and learners so that the latter can meaningfully engage with tests. In Vignette 3.6, there is recognition that, although the test initially was an example of summative assessment since the learners did receive a mark, that was not the end of the test as an instrument. It was transformed into a set of follow-up activities to engage learners in assessment for learning. These examples come to show that even though the official curriculum may provide some indications about summative and/or formative assessment, teachers and learners can engage in different forms of checking progress in order to achieve a curriculum's learning outcomes.

3.7 Bringing It All Together

This section contains a set of activities aimed at recapping as well as extending some of the concepts discussed in the chapter.

Activity 3.14

Read the following quote and reflect on/discuss whether you (dis)agree with it, and whether this is currently the case in your own context/country:

> Educators have disagreed on the issue of whether or not young learners should be assessed and tested for many years. Traditionally, the primary purpose of paper-and-pencil summative tests has been to rank students and divide them into 'winners and losers' (Stiggins 2007: 22). The prevalent culture of competitiveness in Thailand places tremendous pressure on young language learners and can lead to anxiety and demotivation. Although there has been a recent shift towards assessment for learning rather than summative assessment in primary education (Britton 2021), there is still an over-reliance on summative testing in Thailand (OECD/UNESCO 2016: 174).
>
> (Hobbs & Mourão, 2025, p. 22)

Activity 3.15

Go back to the curriculum you have been analysing so far and try to identify whether the curriculum says anything about assessment, testing and/or feedback.

- Take note of any types or examples prescribed or suggested.
- If information about assessment is provided, check whether this coheres with other elements of the curriculum such as goals, learning outcomes, content and materials.

Activity 3.16

Read Vignette 3.7. The author mentions different instruments for assessment. When does she seem to be referring to formative assessment? When does she seem to be referring to summative assessment?

<table>
<tr><td>Vignette
3.7</td><td>

Assessment of English for Specific Purposes (ESP) Students: An Example from the Context of Higher Education in Uzbekistan, by Komila Tangirova

</td></tr>
</table>

Decisions regarding assessment practices in most ESP courses at state higher educational institutions (HEIs) in Uzbekistan are made at the level of institutions. These practices differ from institution to institution.

In one of such HEIs, the ESP course is taught in first- and/or second year of a four-year undergraduate programme. Whether the course is run in the first or the second year or both depends on each individual programme based on the credit value of the ESP course within it. Regardless of the duration of the ESP course, students are assessed through the same framework every semester (18-week period). This includes ongoing assessment, two assessment points during the semester, assessment of independent work (all these constitute 50 per cent of the total mark) and the final assessment (another 50 per cent). The results from these are then added and constitute the overall score (100 per cent) for that semester. Students can see all their marks by logging in the system called 'Hemis' (used by all state HEIs in the country) where all marks for all subjects are displayed.

Students participate in classes, do homework, and get marked for their class work. All these are parts of ongoing assessment, which contribute to students' overall mark. Teachers mark students' performance at each lesson. Homework is compulsory too, and it is checked at each lesson. Both participation in classes and homework allow ESP instructors to monitor each student's progress and gather evidence for making decision about their mark at each of the two assessment points during a semester. The total mark is the average of ongoing assessment together with the result at the assessment point.

The first of the two assessment points take place in the middle of the semester and the other closer to the end. Teachers are given freedom of choice as to how to assess their students. While some teachers take a test that includes all four skills, others may only do a spoken assessment since the assessment of other skills is reflected in the marks of continuous assessment at classes.

Self-study tasks are a part of assessment too. Students are given options of tasks for them to complete outside the classroom hours and in addition to regular homework. Self-study tasks differ depending on students' majors, students have options of tasks they can complete (e.g. portfolio, presentations). The common ratio of contact hours and self-study is 70/30 respectively, which means that completing self-study tasks is important for students to achieve a good score at the end of each semester.

The final assessment is usually a computer test that includes reading, lexis and grammar items based on topics covered during the semester. A pool of test items is prepared by a group of teachers assigned by the head of the department and submitted to the Hemis system support team for them to make a random selection of items for each student. Students are given test tasks (without answers) beforehand so that they can prepare for the test. An assigned teacher accompanies students to the computer rooms and invigilates the test. Students can see their results as soon as they complete their test. The overall score for the semester is revealed by Hemis.

Activity 3.17

Read Vignette 3.8. Based on the topics discussed in this chapter, what elements are included in the Chilean TESOL curriculum? Do you think that the curriculum tries to feature congruence between its elements? How different/similar is the Chilean curriculum to one from your context?

<table>
<tr><td>**Vignette 3.8**</td><td>**Compulsory Education English in Chile (2024), by Maria-Jesus Inostroza**</td></tr>
</table>

In Chilean public education, English is part of the compulsory curriculum from Grade 5 to Grade 8 in primary school (4 years, 10+ to 13+), and continues in secondary school (4 years, 14+ to 18+). However, many schools start earlier, in Grade 1, following a suggested, non-compulsory curriculum provided by the Ministry of Education.

According to the National Curriculum, the general goal of English language learning is for students to become proficient in the language and use it as a tool that will enable them to navigate communicative situations in everyday life, as well as access new knowledge and learning. To achieve this, it is intended that students develop the four language skills (listening, reading, speaking and writing) in English through authentic and meaningful communicative tasks. Additionally, the curriculum explicitly mentions its alignment with the guidelines of Communicative Language Teaching, together with contributions from other approaches that emphasize communication, such as The Natural Approach, Cooperative Language Learning, Content-Based Instruction and Task-Based Language Teaching.

The Common European Framework is used to define the target attainment goals. Thus, by the end of primary education (Grade 8), students are expected to achieve A2, and B2 by the end of secondary education. There is progression only in terms of language skills; attitudes and cross-curricular aims are the same for all the grades.

The syllabus for each grade is organized into four units, two for each semester. The English textbook is different for each grade, and is provided by the Ministry of Education, but sadly, they do not always match the curriculum structure. There are several references to aspects related to teaching, emphasizing the importance of communication and interaction as well as critical thinking; unfortunately, these are less addressed in the classrooms, as the textbook's activities are beyond students' actual proficiency. Thus, it provides examples of teaching and suggestions for tasks and resources to be used for each unit in accordance with each unit's learning objectives.

The curriculum is topic-oriented and includes themes such as family, animals, places in the city, festivals, transport, foods, countries and cultures around the world, technology, outstanding people, environmental issues, sustainability and globalization. Each unit covers reading, listening, speaking, grammar and vocabulary.

Another aspect mentioned in the curriculum is that assessment is part of the learning process. As a result, there is an emphasis on the implementation of formative assessment focusing on measuring progress in achieving learning outcomes, which serves as a tool for student self-regulation and provides information for understanding students' strengths and weaknesses. This information should be the basis for feedback on teaching and enhancing expected achievements, and should be used for guiding planning. It includes assessment indicators for each of the learning objectives, providing suggestions for learners' assessment, including samples of assessment activities which are consistent with the focus on interaction and communication, such as coursework, oral presentations, graphic organizers, posters, etc. Additionally, it contains suggestions for measurement instruments such as rubrics or checklists, when appropriate.

Useful links (in Spanish):https://www.curriculumnacional.cl/portal/Documentos-Curriculares/Fundamentos/https://www.curriculumnacional.cl/portal/Documentos-Curriculares/Bases-curriculares/https://www.curriculumnacional.cl/portal/Documentos-Curriculares/Programas/

3.8 Further Reading

Below, I list a few titles on educational theories, with some of them connected to language education. I have particularly included titles on sociocultural theory since it tends to inform TESOL curricula across settings. I have also included an extremely helpful title on approaches, methods and materials development in language teaching.

- Aubrey, K., & Riley, A. (2022). *Understanding and using educational theories*. Sage.

- Bates, B. (2023). *Learning theories simplified … and how to apply them to teaching* (3rd ed.). Sage.

- Griffee, D., & Gorsuch, G. (2024). *Using theories for second language teaching and learning*. Bloomsbury.

- Poehner, M. E., & Lantolf, J. P. (2024). *Sociocultural theory and second language developmental education*. Cambridge University Press.

- Richards, J. C., & Rodgers, T. S. (2014). *Approaches and methods in language teaching* (3rd ed.). Cambridge University Press.

- Tomlinson, B., & Masuhara, H. (2018). *The complete guide to the theory and practice of materials development for language learning*. Wiley.

On the topic of assessment and testing, the following volumes are highly recommended:

- Barnawi, O. Z., Alharbi, M. S., & Alzahrani, A. A. (Eds.). (2024). *Transnational English language assessment practices in the age of metrics.* Routledge.

- Cheng, L. (2023). *Language classroom assessment* (2nd ed.). TESOL International Association.

- Green, A. (2020). *Exploring language assessment and testing: Language in action.* Routledge.

- Phakiti, A. (2024). *Language testing and assessment: From theory to practice.* Bloomsbury.

Chapter 4
How Can the TESOL Curriculum Be Evaluated?

Summary

The aim of this chapter is to understand that a curriculum is a dynamic entity that is subject to change. It stresses the necessity of practising curriculum evaluation as a necessary exercise in curriculum development. The chapter provides tools to carry out curriculum analysis of the expected/official curriculum through examples. It then promotes engaging in curriculum evaluation by taking an ecological approach to TESOL education. The chapter discusses ethical considerations around curriculum evaluation, such as transparency, participation, representation, confidentiality, anonymity and the wellbeing of all those involved in curriculum evaluation.

4.1 Warm-Up

In Chapter 3, we discussed some of the key elements that are usually found in the official TESOL curriculum. You may remember that Chapter 1 (Figure 1.7) shows that once an official curriculum is published, it is then put into practice, which we call curriculum enactment. As the TESOL curriculum is enacted, and students are assessed, it is also worth involving stakeholders in curriculum evaluation.

As a warm-up, you can complete Activity 4.1 (see p.80) to take a moment to reflect on your experience as a student of English, maybe when you were a kid, or when you were a teenager, or even as an adult if that is your case.

What you did in Activity 4.1 could be regarded as an exercise of curriculum evaluation because you took some time to reflect on your English language learning experience, even when this may have taken place quite some time ago. If you wish, you can take a look at TESOLand and see what other students around the world have shared in terms of their 'looking back' at their experiences. Perhaps, you can find some commonalities, or even differences rooted in some of the elements of the TESOL curriculum or the ecology of the TESOL curriculum.

Now that I have just used the word 'ecology', I shall say that curriculum evaluation is a process that may include different stakeholders. Primarily, it will involve TESOL teachers and learners (microsystem), but as we know, a curriculum is enacted as part of an institution

Activity 4.1 Looking Back on Your Learning English Experience

Try to visualize yourself at a particular point in time when you were learning English. As you think about that specific stage, think about: *How old were you? Who were your classmates? Who was your teacher? Did you have a textbook to learn English? What did you like about that class? Why? What didn't you enjoy about that class? Why? What puzzled you at the time? What did you find surprising about that class?*

You can use a piece of paper or a digital device to take notes on those questions. With those notes, write a brief reflective text. If you are happy, you can share it with other folks by posting it on TESOLand (Figure 4.1).

Figure 4.1 QR code access to TESOLand

Activity 4.2 Mapping SDG 4

The United Nations has set out a series of targets to achieve SDG 4. Below, you will find some of these. Alone or with a peer, discuss the ways in which your government may be (not) contributing to these targets. You may also want to focus on the teaching and learning of English in particular.

SDG 4 Targets

1. By 2030, ensure that all girls and boys complete free, equitable and quality primary and secondary education leading to relevant and effective learning outcomes.

2. By 2030, ensure that all girls and boys have access to quality early childhood development, care and pre-primary education so that they are ready for primary education.

3. By 2030, ensure equal access for all women and men to affordable and quality technical, vocational and tertiary education, including university.

4. By 2030, substantially increase the supply of qualified teachers, including through international cooperation for teacher training in developing countries, especially least developed countries and small island developing States.

(e.g. a school, a language institute, a company, an online provider). Therefore, evaluation also involves the mesosystem as policies, guidelines and institutional dynamics and resources play a fundamental part in the practice of TESOL. Curriculum evaluation also involves the macrosystem since evaluation may be in response to socio-political expectations, language in use in society, and demands from different sectors and key players. At this level, we can think of United Nations Sustainable Development Goal (SDG) 4, which seeks to guarantee inclusive and equitable quality education for all. You can find more information about this goal if you just type 'United Nations Sustainable Development Goal 4' in your preferred search engine. Last, we can also think of the chronosystem to capture what factors may impinge on curriculum development over time and how curriculum evaluation may change as different elements in the environment vary.

4.2 Defining Evaluation

What do we mean by curriculum evaluation in TESOL and beyond? I often see it as a systematic attempt to collect information about the TESOL curriculum (intended, enacted, taught, learnt, assessed, hidden) to make a series of decisions. In other words, if someone wishes to change the TESOL curriculum in a school, region, country, what information do they have about the current curriculum? What has or hasn't worked in practice? In a similar vein, Richards (2016) understands curriculum evaluation in language education as a set of

> procedures used to determine the overall effectiveness of a language course, and may involve many different procedures such as interviews with teachers and students as well as classroom observation. Students' performance on texts may also be used as one component of evaluation.

> (no page)

The definition refers to *procedures*. While these may vary from context to context, I suggest the following based on personal experience and the literature. I organize procedures around stages as Table 4.1 shows. Sections 4.3 and 4.4 provide details about these two stages.

Stage	Procedures
1. Analysis of the official/ intended curriculum	1. Review of policies that may have impacted on the curriculum design. 2. Review of the (im)material conditions and resources operating in the context of the curriculum (e.g. What's the budget for education? Is there a budget for the training of teachers of English? Is English offered as a subject in all schools?) 3. Review of the curriculum as a text. 4. If possible, meetings with the curriculum developers to understand their aims, principles, wants and constraints. 5. Mapping a set of implications for the context of the curriculum based on Procedures 1-4.
2. Analysis of the curriculum in practice (this encapsulates the taught/ learnt/assessed/enacted/ hidden curriculum)	1. Meetings/interviews/focus groups with teachers, programme coordinators, school heads. 2. Meetings/focus groups with students. 3. Classroom observations. 4. Review of students' evidence of learning and grades.

Table 4.1 Stages of Curriculum Evaluation

4.3 Curriculum Analysis

As mentioned in Table 4.1, comprehensive curriculum evaluation first necessitates the presence of a curriculum analysis stage. In other words, we need to understand what the official TESOL curriculum states. Posner (2004) understands curriculum analysis as

> an attempt to tease a curriculum apart into its component parts, to examine those parts and the way they fit together to make a whole, to identify the beliefs and ideas to which the developers were committed and which either explicitly or implicitly shaped the curriculum, and to examine the implications of these commitments and beliefs for the quality of the educational experience.
>
> (p. 14)

This definition seems to align with the first stage proposed in Table 4.1. Thus, to carry out a robust analysis of the TESOL curriculum, we may need to (1) examine the parts of the curriculum (i.e. goals, content, materials, assessment, etc.), (2) understand curriculum developers' beliefs, and (3) examine implications. To this effect, in Figure 4.2, I put forward a set of questions that can aid with the analysis of a TESOL curriculum. The questions are organized into four steps. Step 1 represents the contextual conditions that look at the first elements that may trigger curriculum design. Step 2 refers to the ideological (see Chapter 6) forces operating behind the design of a curriculum. Step 3 helps understand

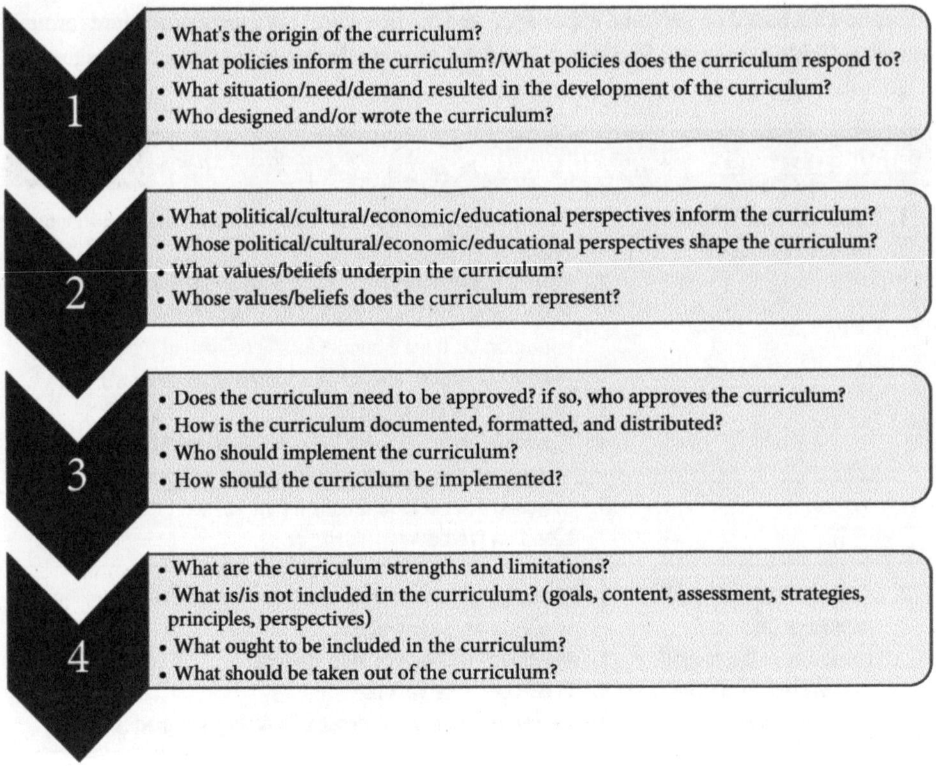

Figure 4.2
Questions for
curriculum analysis

1
- What's the origin of the curriculum?
- What policies inform the curriculum?/What policies does the curriculum respond to?
- What situation/need/demand resulted in the development of the curriculum?
- Who designed and/or wrote the curriculum?

2
- What political/cultural/economic/educational perspectives inform the curriculum?
- Whose political/cultural/economic/educational perspectives shape the curriculum?
- What values/beliefs underpin the curriculum?
- Whose values/beliefs does the curriculum represent?

3
- Does the curriculum need to be approved? if so, who approves the curriculum?
- How is the curriculum documented, formatted, and distributed?
- Who should implement the curriculum?
- How should the curriculum be implemented?

4
- What are the curriculum strengths and limitations?
- What is/is not included in the curriculum? (goals, content, assessment, strategies, principles, perspectives)
- What ought to be included in the curriculum?
- What should be taken out of the curriculum?

the expectations around a curriculum once it is published/approved. Last, Step 4 involves the analysis of the curriculum as text as well as discourse, which may involve engaging in content and/or discourse analysis.

Above, I have mentioned that curriculum analysis involves examining a TESOL curriculum as published text (Spolsky, 2004). What does this mean? This refers to analysing what is said, portrayed and stated. For this level of analysis, we may need to engage in content analysis. According to Krippendorff (2019, 24), 'content analysis is a research technique for making replicable and valid inferences from texts (or other meaningful matter) to the contexts of their use' (p. 24). This may involve counting, coding, comparing, contrasting, and categorizing the elements of a text (words, illustrations) forming a corpus of textual data. Curriculum analysis may need to account for the beliefs and ideologies that seem to inform the decisions made in the curriculum. In this case, we are going beyond words, and this is when (critical) discourse analysis (Jørgensen & Phillips, 2002) becomes helpful. In Chapter 9, you can find details about content analysis.

Shall we do a bit of curriculum analysis? Vignette 4.1 is based on my experience as a consultant for a university in Colombia. The vignette partially illustrates Steps 1–3 from

---

Vignette 4.1

A Curriculum to Combine English Language Learning and International Relations

In 2018, I was invited to deliver a series of workshops for a group of TESOL teachers at a university in Barranquilla, Colombia. The aim of the workshops was to enhance their knowledge and use of content and language integrated learning (CLIL) in English language courses at university level. The workshops made particular emphasis on teaching strategies, materials adaption and design, and assessment (see Banegas et al., 2020).

The workshops were part of a strategic move towards the redesign of a programme that combined the fields of international relations and English language learning. The origin of the curriculum was the university's need to provide students with an outstanding learning experience based on what they called at the time 'the latest' developments in educational and language teaching approaches, which drove them to select CLIL as a conducive approach for learning. They were also interested in a communicative approach to language learning with a focus on meaningful and authentic opportunities for language in use. This interest in the 'outstanding experience' was based on the university's vision and mission of being at the forefront of higher education pedagogies and an example of internationalizing the curriculum, in this case, by introducing courses framed within the umbrella of English medium instruction (EMI).

Before and after the workshops, I had meetings with the head of department and programme coordinators, who were in charge of writing the curriculum. In the meetings, I provided some insights about what a future curriculum could look like. I then provided feedback on a draft of the curriculum. The draft was also shared with the staff who would be teaching in the programme. Feedback from them and me led to some curriculum modifications before it was formally reviewed and approved by a programme committee at the University.

The published curriculum for the programme states:

English for International Relations at the Universidad del Norte aims to develop progressively and cumulatively the four basic communication skills (listening, speaking, reading, and writing) and the skills necessary for success as a professional in international relations. The complete program consists of 8 levels/courses. Each level is 64 hours. The courses are divided into two cycles, the basic (International Relations English I to IV) and professional (International Relations English V to VIII). The basic cycle aims to develop communicative competence in English, critical-analytical skills, and intercultural thinking. The professional cycle, which is mandatory for all students of International Relations, aims to continue the development of students' language skills together with the professional competencies of international relations (i.e. negotiation, diplomacy, critical analysis, etc.).

In terms of English language proficiency, the entry requirement is an A2 level in the Common European Framework of Reference, and the exit level is somewhere between B2 and C1.

These are the learning outcomes of the programme:

Students will be able to: (1) Understand the main ideas of complex text on both concrete and abstract topics, including technical discussions in his/her field of specialization. (2) Understand and follow complex lines of argument. (3) Read a variety of texts concerned with contemporary problems and related to their field of specialization. (4) Interact with fluency and spontaneity, taking active part in discussions accounting for and sustaining their views. (5) Produce clear, detailed texts on a wide range of subjects, including text types related to International Relations. (6) Explain a viewpoint on a topic giving the advantages and disadvantages of various options.

Activity 4.3 On Vignette 4.1

Go over the questions in Steps 1–3 (Figure 4.2) and Vignette 4.1. Which questions are answered, even if minimally in the vignette?

Step 1:

What's the origin of the curriculum?

What policies inform the curriculum?/What policies does the curriculum respond to?

What situation/need/demand resulted in the development of the curriculum?

Who designed and/or wrote the curriculum?

Step 2:

What political/cultural/economic/educational perspectives inform the curriculum?

Whose political/cultural/economic/educational perspectives shape the curriculum?

What values/beliefs underpin the curriculum?

Whose values/beliefs does the curriculum represent?

Step 3:

Does the curriculum need to be approved? Who approves the curriculum?

How is the curriculum documented, formatted and distributed?

Who should implement the curriculum?

How should the curriculum be implemented?

Figure 4.1. I say 'partially' because I could not collect enough information from relevant stakeholders to answer all the questions about ideologies and perspectives included in Step 2. We will also use this vignette for Activities 4.3–4.5.

Below, you will find a summary of Courses 1 and 8 of the International Relations English (IRE) programme. As you read the main goal ('students will develop … ') and the learning outcomes ('At the end of this course, students will be able to … '), think about the programme's overall learning outcomes included at the end of Vignette 4.1:

International Relations English I: In this course, students will develop the four basic language skills. Students will learn to understand and produce short simple texts about daily situations requiring a simple, direct exchange of information. This course focuses on using language to communicate and interact with others about topics of immediate relevance. Students will have the opportunity to recognize and give opinions with support. At the end of this course, students will be able to: (1) Identify main ideas and details in level appropriate texts, conversations and talks. (2) Identify the purpose of a written text. (3) Identify opinions and distinguish them from facts. (4) Produce a well-organized opinion paragraph using simple, compound and complex sentences. (5) Ask and answer questions in a series of linked phrases and respond to simple statements. (6) Give a presentation expressing opinions with basic support. (7) Accurately use Level 2 grammar. (8) Accurately produce Level 10 pronunciation concepts.

(Note: Level 2 and Level 10 refer to an in-house sequencing of grammar and pronunciation instruction and development).

International Relations English VIII: This course, the last of the professional cycle, gives students the opportunity to further develop language, grammar, and vocabulary. Through a thorough analysis of academic articles, international literature, films/ documentaries, and research, students achieve both learning of content as well as how to communicate issues of high importance to the field. Students also develop their professional skills in this level related to job interviews and CV construction. At the end of the course, students will be able to: (1) Identify main ideas and specific details, make inferences, and draw conclusions from academic texts, films, and literature. (2) Discuss themes, supporting ideas with observations and specific examples. (3) Respond to questions as part of a job interview. (4) Participate in class discussions. (5) Write a research report, citing sources. (6) Write formal emails and complete CV and portfolio related to the professional field. (7) Synthesize information from various academic texts, films, and literature and write a response. (8) Identify themes in literature and film and relate them to relevant issues in International Relations. (9) Identify and analyse the interrelatedness of historical, cultural, economic, environmental, technical and/or current events on local, national, and international issues through research. (10) Disseminate research through a digital product highlighting the potential local, national, and global impact of findings.

As you may have noticed, there is alignment between the programme's learning outcomes and the learning outcomes of Courses 1 and 8. For example, at programme level the learning outcome 'Understand the main ideas of complex text on both concrete and abstract topics, including technical discussions in his/her field of specialization' is matched by 'Identify main ideas and details in level appropriate texts, conversations and talks' (Course 1) and 'Identify main ideas and specific details, make inferences, and draw conclusions from academic texts, films, and literature' (Course 8). It seems that the level of complexity of texts that the programme aspires students to understand is supported throughout the programme since they start with 'level appropriate' texts (at the level of A2) in Course 1 until they work with 'academic texts, films, and literature' (beyond B2) in Course 8. Now, you can move on to complete Activities 4.4 and 4.5.

Activity 4.4 On Goals and Learning Outcomes

Above, you have only been provided with the main goal and the learning outcomes of Course 1. Try to answer these questions related to Step 4 in Figure 4.1:

What are the curriculum strengths and limitations regarding learning outcomes?
What is/is not in the curriculum in relation to goals and learning outcomes?
What ought to be included in the learning outcomes?
What should be taken out of the learning outcomes?

Activity 4.5 On Learning Outcomes and Content

Choose the learning outcomes either from Course 1 or Course 8 and think about what content you would need to teach in order to achieve them.

First, you may want to brainstorm all the contents that spring to mind. Once you have a list, you can organize it in a table with areas/categories (e.g. vocabulary, language skills, grammar, topic).

If possible, swap tables with another student to discuss.

Now that you have explored some aspects of a curriculum in the area of TESOL, I would like you to analyse a TESOL curriculum from your context.

Activity 4.6 Analysing a Curriculum from Your Context

Choose one curriculum for TESOL in your context (this could be the same curriculum you used to complete the activities included in Chapter 3) and complete the following prompts, thinking about the elements of the curriculum (e.g. goals, content, assessment, teaching principles and strategies):

Strengths:

Limitations:

What should be reconsidered:

What should be included:

What should be taken out:

4.4 Curriculum Evaluation

As noted in Section 4.2, curriculum evaluation may be organized around two stages: (1) analysis of the official curriculum, i.e. what the curriculum says as a text, and (2) analysis of the curriculum as practice, i.e. what teachers and students do with and think about the curriculum. Hence, practices and beliefs play an important role in curriculum evaluation, and both are interconnected. Although teachers may say one thing, but then they do the opposite, their behaviours may be guided by their beliefs.

Let us begin by unpacking *practice* in relation to the curriculum. As we said above, the official curriculum could be understood as policy, and its examination may be taken following a policy-as-text approach. However, as we know, that is only the tip of the *pedagogical iceberg* since we are interested in what teachers and students do in response to and beyond the official curriculum. What is below the surface is what Bonacina-Pugh (2024) calls *policy as practice*. In the context of the TESOL curriculum development, this includes getting to comprehend different behaviours:

- Understanding how the official curriculum is implemented (i.e. the curriculum *in* practice).

- Understanding how teachers and students enact a curriculum which may (not) respond to the official curriculum.

- Understanding what teachers teach (the taught curriculum), what students learn (the learnt curriculum), and what is actually assessed and how (the assessed curriculum).

As you read above, evaluating the curriculum also entails finding out what teachers, students, and other stakeholders (e.g. school heads, parents) think about the TESOL curriculum. Their beliefs very much depend on different circumstances and roles. For example, a teacher may know what the official curriculum states, but this is not something that students or parents may be aware of. Parents' beliefs about the TESOL curriculum may be based on their children's grades and what they may tell them about their English lessons. Thus, beliefs need to be approached in context, i.e. within the ecology of the TESOL curriculum.

In the case of teachers, their beliefs could be understood through the notion of *cognition*. Simon Borg, an influential scholar in the area of teacher cognition, states:

Teaching can be described with reference to what teachers say and do – these are observable behaviors. But teaching is not a purely behavioral enterprise; in the same way that icebergs have an exposed surface beneath which lies a significant hidden mass, teachers' behaviors are also powerfully shaped by a complex range of unseen influences. Some of these are obviously external – explicit school policies which prescribe the way learning is organized or assessed, for example – but many are internal to the teacher, such as their beliefs, knowledge, feelings, perceptions, attitudes, and thoughts. Teacher cognition is the established term for describing these personal, unseen aspects of teachers' work.

(Borg, 2019, p. 1149)

As the quote says, teachers' practice will be informed by a whole array of beliefs, knowledge, feelings, perceptions, attitudes, as well as previous experiences. Therefore, it is important to explore them, as, for example, what teachers think about the official curriculum and their rationale for the enacted curriculum may be informed by their own internal theories and principles about what *good* language teaching or education in general should be about. In order to capture behaviours and beliefs, curriculum evaluation needs to include different instruments (meetings, interviews, focus groups, classroom observations, evidence of learning, etc.). In Section 4.5, you will find an example of how curriculum evaluation may be conducted.

4.5 Conducting an Evaluation Exercise

A few years ago, I was contracted as a consultant to conduct a curriculum evaluation of the International Relations English programme described in Section 4.3. To this effect, I carried out an analysis of the curriculum as well as an analysis of the curriculum in practice, together with teachers' and students' views. Therefore, my evaluation included: (1) interviews with two teaching staff, (2) focus groups with 10 students, (3) analysis of each course syllabus, (4) analysis of assessment samples, (5) analysis of course materials, and (6) analysis of the programme website. Unfortunately, classroom observations could not be conducted as I could not stay in Colombia for long. Table 4.2 summarizes how I gathered information.

In Vignette 4.2, I have included snapshots of the report I submitted to the programme's coordinator.

In Vignette 4.3, I have included a part of my recommendations to the director of the programme under evaluation.

Table 4.2 Curriculum Evaluation Exercise

Information Gathered	Details
Individual interviews with staff teaching in the programme	The programme director provided me with a list of teachers and their contact emails. I sent out an email to all of them (n = 6) and two accepted to be interviewed. These took place in person, and I used my mobile phone to record them. I sent them my initial questions in advance: 1. How long have you taught in the programme? 2. If you were to tell another teacher about what the programme is like, what would you tell them? 3. What do you like about the programme or course(s) you teach? Why? 4. What would you like to change in the programme/course(s)? Why? 5. Are there any aspects/areas of the course(s) in which you feel more confident than others? 6. In what aspects of the delivery of the course would you like to be more supported with?
Focus groups with students from different levels of the programme	The programme director provided me with a list of students and their contact emails. I sent out an email to all of them (n = 117), and from those who accepted to be interviewed (n = 28), I randomly selected 10, making sure that all the courses were represented. I carried out two in-person focus groups (5 in each focus group). I used my mobile phone to record them. I sent them my initial questions in advance: 1. What is your course about? 2. If you were to name three things you like about your course, what would they be? Why? 3. If you were to name three things you think may need to be revisited in the course, what would they be? Why? 4. Does the course make you want to learn English? 5. Do you feel that your English and knowledge about international relations is improving?

Information Gathered	Details
Analysis of each course syllabus	After analysing the aims and rationale behind the programme as a whole, I analysed each course syllabus. The following questions guided my analysis: 1. What is the course about? 2. Do the course aims and learning outcomes cohere with those of the programme? 3. Is there coherence between the aims, content and teaching principles? 4. How is content organized? 5. Is there constructive alignment between the aims/learning outcomes and assessment? 6. Is content organized and sequenced in a logical manner within each course and from one course to the next? 7. In what ways does the course align with CLIL principles, which is the main approach underlying the programme? (This question informed Questions 2–6) 8. What principles are also implicitly/explicitly present in the syllabus?
Analysis of assessment samples	The programme director provided me with samples of tests, assignment briefs, assessment criteria, and evidence of learning (e.g. tests submitted by some students). The following questions guided my analysis: 1. What content is being assessed? 2. How? 3. Is there constructive alignment between the aims/learning outcomes of the course and the assessment? 4. Are instructions clear? 5. Is it clear what the assessment criteria are? 6. What do the students' answers show in terms of their achieving learning outcomes? What does the evidence of learning show?
Analysis of course materials	The programme director provided me with access to an online space in which the teachers have all their teaching materials (coursebooks from international publishers, worksheets, teacher-made handbooks, slides, videos, etc.). I analysed the materials in tandem with the syllabus of each course. These questions guided my analysis: 1. Do the course materials cohere with the syllabus? 2. Are there opportunities for differentiation, personalization and contextualization? 3. How is language support embedded? 4. Are there opportunities for the balanced development of content *and* language in an integrated manner? 5. How are materials organized, sequenced and formatted? 6. Is there enough variety?
Analysis of the programme website	The programme director asked me whether I could also analyse the programme website to understand their outward-facing message. For this task, I came up with these questions: 1. If I were a student, would I feel motivated to sign up to this programme? 2. Is it clear what the entry requirements are, what the aims are, how I will be learning? 3. If I have questions, is it easy to contact someone? 4. Can I see the same information in both Spanish and English to check my own understanding? 5. Is the page appealing and easy to navigate? 6. Does the course have a profile on social media?

<table>
<tr><td>Vignette
4.2</td><td># Snapshots of Curriculum Evaluation</td></tr>
</table>

The snapshots summarize the main information gathered from teachers, the syllabi, assessments, materials, and students. This is organized into strengths and areas for improvement.

Strengths
Interviews with teaching staff
- Strong cohesion between learning goals and assessment.
- Assessment proves to be meaningful given its formative nature and the employment of different formats (e.g. videos) to measure students' development.
- As tasks have become more language-orientated, students exhibit stronger linguistic awareness and an increase in transforming language learning into language using.
- Content (i.e. international relations) continues to be a source of student and teacher motivation.

Focus groups with students
- Relevant and motivating content of the International Relations programme and its integration with the English Language.
- Importance of integrated language and coverage of all the skills, especially the interconnectedness between writing and speaking.

Syllabi
- There is horizontal and vertical coherence in terms of intended learning outcomes connected to academic discourse and critical thinking skills.

Assessment samples
- There is a consistent wide range of tasks, formats, and modes of engagement for students to exhibit the new knowledge developed in the modules.

Course materials
- There is explicit reference to links between learning outcomes and discrete curriculum areas such as content and grammar.
- The materials feature language-exclusive sections ('spotlight on … ') on grammar and vocabulary learning.

Areas for improvement
Interviews with teaching staff
- There needs to be more room for explicit content-driven language learning across the levels.
- Students may benefit from systematic CALP (cognitive academic language proficiency) development for both written and oral skills.

Focus groups with students
- There was a sense that the language course needed to be about much more than key vocabulary.
- There was some discussion around the language foundations for the programme at Levels 1–4. Here was a focus on the grammatical structures of English. The students felt that whilst it could be argued that this is an essential part of the language learning process, the lack of application of the language to discussing real-world issues and the paucity of authentic speaking opportunities meant that the 'leap' at Level 4 did not provide adequate opportunities for developing confidence in speaking.

Syllabi
- The themes which structure Level 2 seem to be a bit disconnected. I understand that this may be due to the use of a global coursebook. Is it time, perhaps, for the programme to develop its own materials for the lower levels, too?
- Level 5–8 may need to include more explicit linguistic goals/objectives, with stronger vertical coherence to guarantee recycling and scaffolded complexity. Perhaps, the team can agree on having at least an X number of linguistic goals which are then recycled, for example, every (other) unit and at every level.

Assessment samples
- I wonder whether a detailed rubric could be included for the written component of the exams.

Course materials
- There needs to be systematic inclusion of language work across Levels 5–8. Having a clearly delineated scope and sequence for each level can help with recycling and advancing students' CALP (grammar, vocabulary, pronunciation, presentation skills, and academic writing within and beyond sentence level).

Activity 4.7 Proposal for Change

Go back to Vignette 4.2 and select one of the areas for improvement listed. What suggestions would you make to address the area selected? What's your rationale for those suggestions?

| Vignette 4.3 | **Recommendation Snapshots** |

Language learning across the levels
I encourage the programme leader and tutors to engage in the development of an IRE-based language learning syllabus that considers areas such as academic vocabulary and grammar, pronunciation and spoken academic discourse, functions (e.g. describing, defining), pragmatics (helpful for verbal interaction and presentations), and textual grammar (coherence and cohesive devices) for a selected range of genres, which are sequenced and recycled over the levels. This will help achieve consistency and systematicity in relation to language learning. Also, it will help strengthen constructive alignment between learning outcomes, exam instructions, and assessment rubrics.

In relation to constructive alignment, module syllabi could include a table which sets clear content and language learning objectives and how these are materialized in the different assessments (coursework, projects, videos, presentations, mid-term exams, assignments, reports, etc.) that the students need to complete to pass a module. These objectives need to be sequenced and recycled across the levels so that the students can engage in deeper learning and therefore transfer academic (cognitive and linguistic) skills from one situation to another with different degrees of complexity and support (e.g. from collaborative to individual writing, from shorter to longer texts, from basic interpersonal communication skills (BICS) to cognitive academic language proficiency (CALP), or from general academic language to subject-specific language).

In line with CLIL frameworks, language learning could align more closely to the language triptych, which provides room for (1) the language of learning, (2) the language through learning, and (3) the language for learning. The triptych guarantees that students are provided with the necessary tools to engage in a number of linguistic functions and genres as well as concepts and discourses for knowledge building. I recommend the most recent book on CLIL authored by D. Coyle and O. Meyer, *'Beyond CLIL: Pluriliteracies Teaching for Deeper Learning'* (Cambridge University Press, 2021).

A systemic functional approach for disciplinary literacies
'How does IR speak and write?' Closer alignment between how language learning is approached in IRE and how it is used in the field itself, particularly when coded in English, is of paramount importance, since the aim of the IRE programme, as far as language development is concerned, is to help students develop IR literacies, i.e. the specific ways in which IR professionals speak and write. I understand that the IR is a vast field that contains several professions and profiles, but perhaps the team may wish to choose those which might prove more relevant (and maybe more challenging) for students to receive support. I also recognize that the linguistic points of departure between IR and IRE differ since the students are already developing their CALP in Spanish, though they may experience similar issues with text organization and sentence construction regardless of the language used.

Systemic functional linguistics (SFL) takes the text as its main unit of analysis. This perspective can help move beyond sentence level (which is still important) and support students in the construction of coherent and cohesive pieces of work. This approach is intimately associated with a genre pedagogy and the notion of the different genres that coexist within a text. For example, a (research) report includes genres and functions such as describing, defining, explaining, comparing, illustrating, summarizing, highlighting, and recommending, among others. Therefore, approaching tasks such as deconstructing a news item, an essay, or a report, may take several lessons to support students in the writing process, which includes awareness raising at word, sentence, paragraph, and section levels. In connection to a genre pedagogy, I suggest the adoption/adaptation of the teaching learning cycle to provide students with a model/sample text that they can 'dissect' before they write their own piece.

In addition, I suggest the inclusion of longer texts as sources of input so that students can exploit them at the levels of content, coherence, and cohesion. A progression from shorter to longer text, more lexically dense, can provide the programme with a stronger sense of contributing to content learning while offering L2 support.

At this point, I should acknowledge two facts: (1) SFL and a genre pedagogy are far from new or innovative, and (2) the course materials do feature work on textual grammar and textual support with writing. However, the latter needs to be systemically informing each module so that students are provided with operational tools they can utilize to build new knowledge and skills as they navigate the IRE component of the overall programme.

Activity 4.8 On Recommendations for Change

Go back to Vignette 4.3. What do you think of the recommendations suggested? Are they similar to the suggestions you made in Activity 4.7?

4.6 From Evaluation to Informed Decisions

As discussed above, curriculum evaluation may leave stakeholders with a set of recommendations for them to consider and act upon, or ignore. In either case, a decision is made since doing or not doing are both agentic moves informed by a set of reasons.

The literature in language curriculum offers a few examples of initiatives which, even when badged as exploratory, led to changes in the curriculum. For example, in 2020, Crites and Rye (2020) published an article in which they describe how the analysis of a TESOL curriculum in paper and in practice led to the exploration of the notion of design thinking in education (e.g. Melles et al., 2012) to enhance the very development of language curriculum design. In other words, the evaluation exercise they conducted led to the implementation of changes that were scrutinized in order to collect evidence of their pertinence.

If we remind ourselves of the ecological framework of the TESOL curriculum, it is important to understand that the journey from evaluation to informed decisions could be crystallized in different directions, as Figures 4.3 and 4.4 illustrate.

Figure 4.3 The micro impacting on the meso

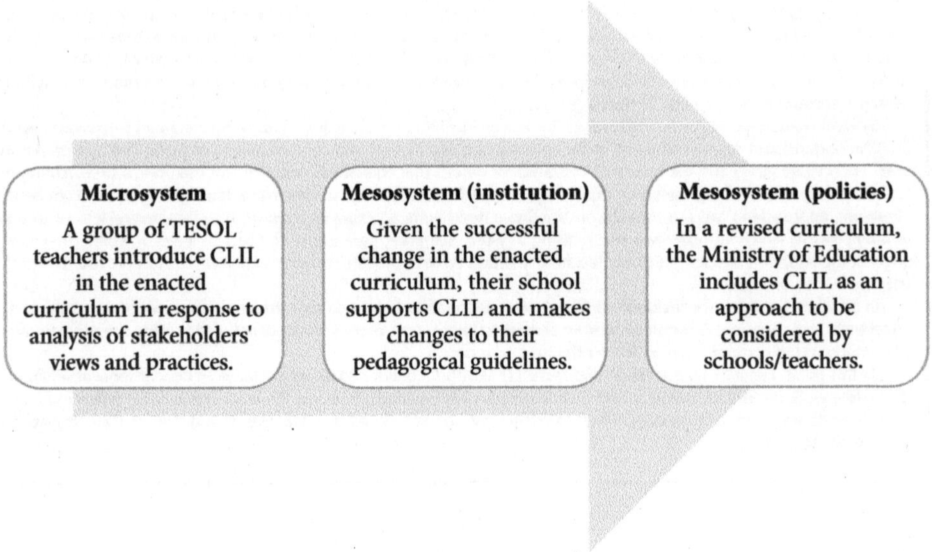

Microsystem	**Mesosystem (institution)**	**Mesosystem (policies)**
A group of TESOL teachers introduce CLIL in the enacted curriculum in response to analysis of stakeholders' views and practices.	Given the successful change in the enacted curriculum, their school supports CLIL and makes changes to their pedagogical guidelines.	In a revised curriculum, the Ministry of Education includes CLIL as an approach to be considered by schools/teachers.

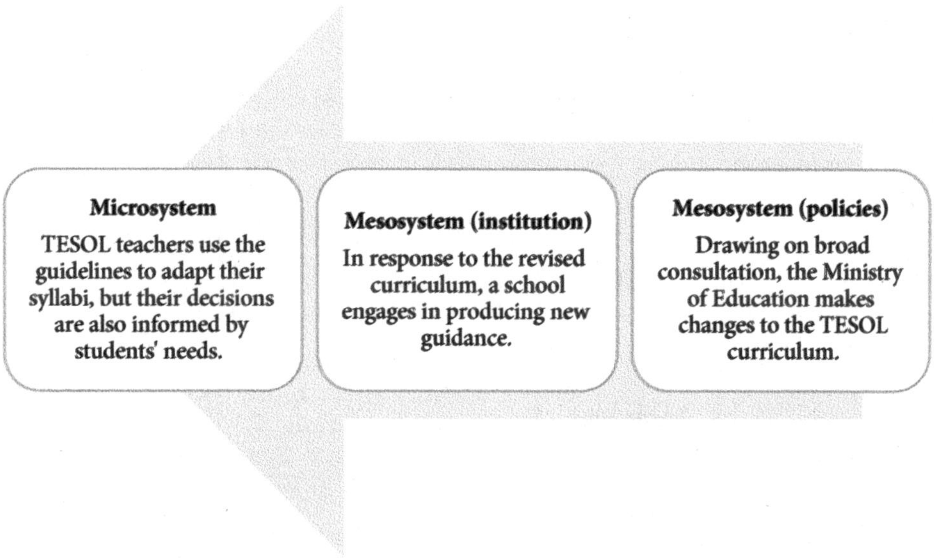

Figure 4.4 The meso impacting on the micro

Figures 4.3 and 4.4 show the impact of teachers on policies and vice versa. In addition, the process that starts with evaluation and culminates (or also starts) with informed decisions can be initiated at the institutional level, and therefore, when a school engages in curriculum evaluation, the outcomes can impact teachers and policies. Regardless of the direction of travel, translating recommendations into decisions for (in)action is a complex journey, for it involves a number of stakeholders as well as (im)material resources such as time, planning, personnel, budgets, policies, guidelines, support from key players (e.g. teachers' union), etc.

In response to Activity 4.9, I would say that if I were the programme director, I would consult the recommendations and potential changes to introduce to the teachers who are part of the programme. I would also involve a head of department and colleagues teaching in similar programmes elsewhere. I would also inform my decision on recent empirical studies that show evidence of the benefits and challenges of introducing the recommended changes. Last, I would also consider what resources I need to (re)deploy in order for the changes to come to fruition. For example, do I need to recruit more TESOL teachers? Do we need to increase the number of teaching periods? Do we need to include more workload for the teachers to redesign their materials? Do I need to organize training to support the teachers in understanding and implementing the changes in a critical and sensitive manner? How long will it take us to implement the changes? Do we make all the changes in all the courses/levels of the programme at once, or do we introduce them progressively? Who will be in charge of writing up all the changes so as to produce a revised curriculum? Do we need to communicate the changes to students?

Activity 4.9 Informing Decisions

Imagine that you are the programme director who received the recommendations included in Vignette 4.3. What/Who will inform your decisions to act on those recommendations? Use the figure below to help you organize your ideas.

Who?
:
:
:

What?
:
:
:

As you may have noticed, evaluating the TESOL curriculum is a complex, but necessary exercise that teachers and institutions need to carry out. While most of the examples included in the chapter start with the official curriculum, it is also fair to say that curriculum evaluation could happen at the level of teachers, as in Figure 4.3. For example, a teacher engaged in reflective practice (e.g. Farr & Farrell, 2023; Mann & Walsh, 2017) may begin to examine their own enacted/taught curriculum by keeping a journal, talking to colleagues and students, watching presentations, reading papers, and so on, until they make some decisions based on the voices and evidence gathered. We will return to this issue in Chapter 9.

4.7 Bringing It All Together

This section contains a set of activities aimed at recapping as well as extending some of the concepts discussed in the chapter.

Activity 4.10

In Activity 4.1, I asked you to write a reflective text about your memories of learning English. Go back to the TESOLand using Figure 4.1 and read what other people have posted. Can you identify any common themes?

Activity 4.11

Go to Google Scholar and type in the phrase 'TESOL curriculum evaluation' in English or the equivalent in another language. Browse the first few pages of the hits returned to find five examples of how evaluation of the TESOL curriculum has been done in different contexts. You can use a table like the one suggested (Table 4.3) to organize your findings.

Table 4.3 Examples of TESOL Curriculum Evaluation

Title & Authors	Context	How Evaluation Was Conducted	Evaluation Findings	Any Decisions Made

Activity 4.12

The following paragraph is an abstract from Carol Chapelle's *Encyclopedia of Applied Linguistics*. The entry is entitled 'Language programme evaluation'. Some words are missing. Can you fill in the blanks by using some of the words in the box included below the abstract? Two words are not needed. Once you complete the quote, check out the answer key in Chapter 10.

Language program evaluation entails systematic collection of (a) __________ that is useful for making (b) __________ about the value of a program. The specific types of information gathered and the value judgments depend on the intended (c) __________ of the evaluation. In applied linguistics and social science more broadly, evaluation generally treats the whole program as the unit of analysis even though the definition of a program can vary widely. Contemporary language program evaluation practices have been motivated by both external accountability-driven forces as well as the need for improvement and (d) __________ recognized internally within some language programs.

The diverse needs of audiences for program evaluations have prompted the adoption of utilization-based evaluation, which requires examining the intended uses of evaluation outcomes early in the process of evaluation. Language program evaluation holds the potential for guiding positive change to meet the (e) __________ of an evolving society, but professional development of prospective evaluators in applied linguistics is needed to realize the potential. (Chapelle, 2021, p. 1)

CHANGE, AGENCY, INFORMATION, NEEDS, USES, ECOLOGICAL, JUDGEMENTS

Activity 4.13

Read Vignette 4.4 written by Eric Ekembe. The author refers to his experience as being involved in different forms of curriculum evaluation. What are your thoughts on the sentences in italics? How could you link them to what we have discussed in this chapter?

Vignette 4.4	**Experiences with Becoming Involved in Language Curriculum Development in Cameroon, by Eric Ekembe**

In 2018, I was reached by the Inspectorate General of the Cameroon Ministry of Basic Education on a consultancy basis to review the primary school curriculum in use in Cameroon. I was assigned to test the practicability and responsiveness of certain English language learning activities in Grade 3 in one of the most renowned primary schools in the Yaounde 6 Municipality, from which permission and consent had been sought. I was also asked to review the use of English in the curriculum and not to focus any content. In this brief narrative, I share my experience in completing these two tasks.

For my first consultancy task, I met the classroom teacher in Grade 3 and presented the purpose of my visit to him and he acknowledged having been informed about my visit. I went to his class and introduced myself to the pupils and told them I was going to be their new teacher only for a day and checked with them if they'd be happy to have me as their teacher. They all agreed and expressed their willingness to collaborate. I moved further to inquire if they'd be happy to do an activity and they all expressed their willingness. I got the activity that had been designed from the syllabus and asked them to complete it. It took me over seven minutes to no avail to cause them to understand the activity demands. I noticed time was fast running and I had not got them to sit on the activity. I reminded myself of the need to break down my language for them to understand what I wanted them to do. I did so, but it still didn't work. I sought help from the classroom teacher, who, in less than 50 seconds, got the pupils working on the activity. I observed the way he got the pupils to sit on the desks and noticed that they had co-constructed a culture of communication that was based not only on the kind of instructor-pupil language, but had codes that needed to be applied for effective communication and response. While the activities were being done, I noticed that the classroom atmosphere was serene and a little tense – far more than the kind of episode I had initiated when I entered the class. I asked the class teacher to leave the room so I could continue to run the activity. My intention was to find out if I had learnt his classroom language and could use it. Immediately he stepped out, three pupils came running to me requesting permission to go use the toilet. Indeed, they really needed to use the restroom, as they came back to class running after that. Two others came to pose personal challenges they were experiencing while doing the activities. The consultancy task was completed and I graded it and wrote my observation for the Ministry. *It was their singular responsibility to do whatever they wanted to do with my report and I never was consulted for that subsequently.*

In the second assignment, I revised the English of over ¾ of the curriculum sent to me and, although I noticed issues with the curriculum targets and contents, I was asked never to make any comment on these. My job at this level was to revise basic sentence-levels, punctuation, shifts in tense and person, faulty parallelisms, faulty predication, dangling modifiers, concord etc that could interfere with comprehension. *In other words, I was being consulted as an editor/proof-reader almost. The assumption of the Inspectorate General at the Ministry of basic Education, by the time I was assigned the task, I suppose, was that the curriculum had been developed by experts in primary education of which I was considered not to be one, even when I am qualified to teach English in different levels of education.*

4.8 Further Reading

Below, I list a few titles on curriculum evaluation in education in general:

- Hewitt, T. W. (2006). *Understanding and shaping curriculum: What we teach and why*. Sage.

- McCormick, R., & James, M. ([1988] 2018). *Curriculum evaluation in schools*. Routledge.

- Okumura, Y. (2023). *Educational evaluation and improvement in Japan: Linking lesson study, curriculum management and school evaluation*. Springer.

In connection to evaluation, there are also a few titles connected to the field of language education, though not always necessarily connected to the TESOL curriculum, but to key stakeholders or elements:

- Howard, A., & Donaghue, H. (2015). *Teacher evaluation in second language education*. Bloomsbury.

- Martínez Agudo, J. (Ed.). (2020). *Quality in TESOL and teacher education: From a results culture towards a quality culture*. Routledge.

- Rea-Dickins, P., & Germaine, K. (1992). *Evaluation*. Oxford University Press.

Chapter 5
How Can We Change the TESOL Curriculum?

Summary

The aim of this chapter is to understand curriculum change by discussing the notions of agency and sustainability to contribute to innovation in the TESOL curriculum. Agency is discussed in relation to both teachers and learners as central actors in planning, enacting and evaluating curriculum change. The main premise of this chapter is that curriculum change can be actioned by positioning teachers and learners/teachers and learners positioning themselves as agents of change. Agentive curriculum change is discussed in relation to ethics as well as sustainability. In line with recent developments in the field, the latter is associated to two aspects: (1) strategic sustainability (capacity building, resources, time), and (2) socio-environmental sustainability (topics around climate change, forced migration, etc.). The chapter emphasizes that curriculum change can contribute to learner motivation and engagement as well as teacher motivation and continuing professional development.

5.1 Warm-Up

We closed Chapter 4 by reflecting on what to do with the recommendations emanating from and/or outcomes of curriculum evaluation. If, for example, those involved in teaching English, or any other language, at a state school or university department, or private language school decide to engage in curriculum change, they need to stop to think and discuss what they are (not) willing to do to become fully immersed in adaptation since change can 'throw' them into uncertainty and chaos … for a while, until the new curriculum begins to take shape. Change is an opportunity to leave our comfort zone and push ourselves to live different experiences. As Eagleman (2015) explains, new experiences can change our brain, and these 'accumulate to make you who you are, and to constrain who you can become' (p. 20). With these ideas in mind, I would like you to complete the activities that follow.

Indeed, change can be a complex or complicated process, and people can navigate it differently. I am sure that, if you are on social media, you may have come across inspirational quotes about change. Some of these could be meaningful, while others can make our eyebrows rise.

Activity 5.1 Change: Benefits and Challenges

Imagine yourself, in turn, as (1) a novice teacher of English, (2) an experienced teacher of English, (3) a TESOL programme director, and (4) a TESOL curriculum developer working for the Ministry of Education in your country. What benefits and challenges would you associate with curriculum change? Use a graphic organizer (e.g. a table), photos from the internet, memes or anything visual to represent those benefits and challenges.

Activity 5.2 Online Quotes About Change

Use a search engine to look for quotes. You can type 'inspirational quotes on change' or 'inspirational quotes on curriculum change'. Make a list of your top five quotes and think why they resonate with you. If possible, share your top five quotes with a peer and discuss the one that each has placed at the top of the list.

5.2 On Change

Change is a complex phenomenon. What makes it complex? According to Markee (2013), change is complex because it shapes and is shaped by a set of interrelated contexts, which could be hierarchically placed. The preceding sentence should make you think of the ecological view adopted in this book. Regardless of where it starts (if it is really possible to determine where and when change begins), change can operate at the classroom level (microsystem), institutional-educational-administrative level (mesosystem), social-political-cultural level (macrosystem) and over time (chronosystem). Therefore, change is inherently contextual. Change is bound to time, place, practices and people. Change can be personal (e.g. a teacher wanting to change the way they provide oral feedback), collective (e.g. teachers from the same school agreeing to change the learning outcomes of their classes), or institutional (e.g. English as a subject will be reorganized not according to class/age but according to students' level of English proficiency).

Change needs to be constructive, realistic and planned as it may lead to renewal and innovation. The literature in TESOL boasts quite a few titles that have described innovation in different settings as a result of change (e.g. Chong & Reinders, 2024; Mideros et al., 2023; Phung et al., 2024). To introduce change in a manner that helps to guarantee success, Macalister and Nation (2020) suggest a series of steps (Figure 5.1).

While the steps in Figure 5.1 can help rationalize and organize change, curriculum change practices around the world show that approaches to change could be grouped around three types (Figure 5.2). A power-coercive approach takes place when 'change is

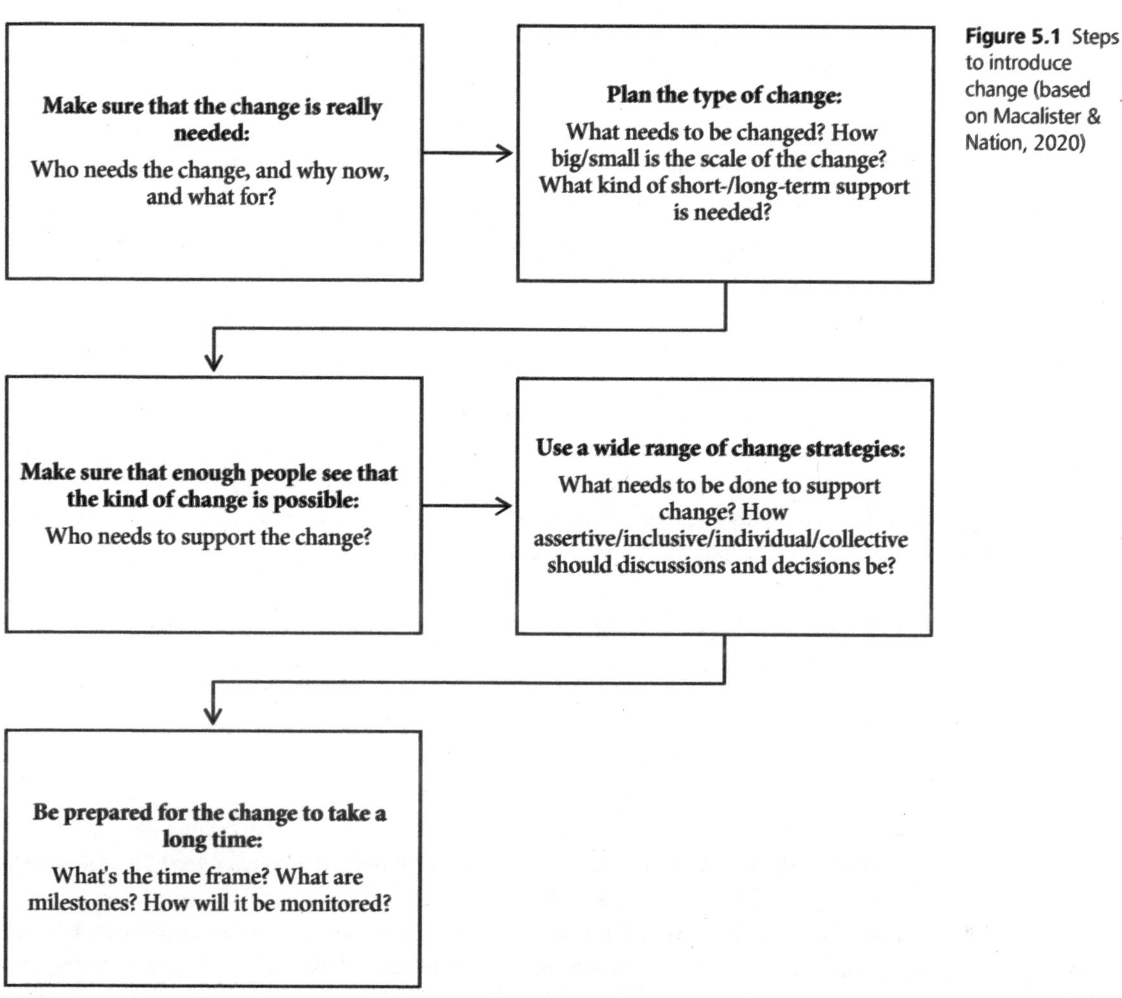

Figure 5.1 Steps to introduce change (based on Macalister & Nation, 2020)

Figure 5.2 Approaches to change (based on Macalister & Nation, 2020)

achieved through authority' (Macalister & Nation, 2020, p. 202), and it is usually used when there might be reluctance to change for a variety of reasons (e.g. arbitrariness, lack of consultation, different types of leadership styles, lack of rationale). A rational-empirical approach emanates from research in the field of (language) education, and it may be reinforced by organizing conferences, talks and seminars for teachers and other stakeholders to explain what the changes proposed are and the justification for them. This is often triggered by experts and/or researchers. Last, a practical-situational approach occurs when teachers (or just a single teacher) wish to enact change in response to an issue they find in their practice. This need may lead to teachers carrying out action research or becoming involved in continuing professional development initiatives, such as *ateneos* (Banegas & Glatigny, 2021) in which they negotiate change with other colleagues. These types of approaches to change should not be understood as completely removed from each other, but as complementary and interconnected.

Let me illustrate each approach with examples from my own experience.

Power-coercive strategy: When I was working as a teacher of English for a private language school, I used to prepare students for the Cambridge First Certificate of English, which is known at the time of writing as B2 First (Cambridge English Qualifications). At that time, there were changes in the assessment: one type of activity (students identifying extra words in a paragraph) was removed, and the writing component became shorter. These changes triggered changes in the coursebooks used for preparation, as well as goals, etc. In this case, the change was completely top-down. Cambridge English made the change, and all providers preparing students for the qualification had to adapt. The change was decided (and I want to believe it was informed) in Cambridge English (the centre), and from there it spread to language centres around the world. In this case, curriculum change was introduced by the owners of the qualification (authority). That said, Cambridge English may have decided to introduce the change based on in-house evaluation/consultation/research. In formal education, teachers usually understand curriculum change (e.g. the imposition of a new coursebook, a shift from grammar-based teaching to task-based language teaching, a change from summative to formative feedback) as top-down and exercised through power and rules (the curriculum itself as policy).

Rational-empirical: When I was working at the Ministry of Education in Chubut (Argentina), I was also doing research on CLIL in secondary schools. I showed my results to my line manager to explain/justify why I thought that introducing CLIL as another educational approach in the TESOL curriculum was good and necessary. A couple of years later, I was invited to lead the renewal of the TESOL curriculum. With a team of teacher educators and researchers and in consultation with practitioners, the new TESOL curriculum suggested CLIL as another approach that language teachers could consider. While the change started as rational-empirical, there was consultation/negotiation to some extent, which is more akin to practical-situational. The change then became policy. In other words, a rational-empirical strategy supported a power-coercive approach to change. In my experience, this type of approach usually precedes top-down curriculum change, and it can also support a practical-situational approach when teachers are working collaboratively with other teachers, teacher educators and researchers as part of a project. While it is academic-driven, it often includes opportunities for teachers to understand what the change is about and ask questions.

Practical-situational: When I was teaching English to pre-service teachers of Geography using an English for Specific Purposes (ESP) approach, I was concerned with their demotivation and their feeling that they lacked subject-specific knowledge. In response to this issue, I carried out action research through which I combined CLIL with ESP (Banegas, 2018b). This change was negotiated with the students and discussed with my line manager. In this case, the change responded to a very practical problem, which led to changes in the syllabus of the course, but not the overall curriculum of the programme. With this type of approach, I had a great degree of agency and autonomy to shape the change, which was mainly informed by my students' feedback and my own professional knowledge of CLIL.

In relation to curriculum change, Wedell and Grassick (2018) have edited a volume of cases from around the world in which they highlight how teachers navigate curriculum change in English language teaching. In the volume, the editors refer to barriers to curriculum change, which may be connected to many of the issues and concepts already discussed in this chapter. In their view, the main barriers are: (1) lack of consultation, (2) coercive strategies, (3) tight timescales (i.e. the change has to be implemented in a very short period of time), and (4) lack of (im)material resources (e.g. teachers have not been trained to implement a new teaching approach; long-term support has not been planned).

Based on the issues discussed so far, you can now complete Activities 5.3 and 5.4 which follow in this section.

Below, you will find two vignettes with activities to help you bring together some of the issues discussed and extend your reflective thinking about curriculum change in practice. Vignette 5.1 comes from Japan and takes a look at changes to the teaching of English in high school.

As you read these pages, you know that generative artificial intelligence (GenAI) continues to shape and reshape our experience with the world and ourselves. Thus, two questions are worth asking ourselves at this stage: What role may generative artificial intelligence play in curriculum change? How can it help with designing a TESOL curriculum?

Activity 5.3 On Supporting Teachers with Change

Above, you came across the term *ateneo* as a form of continuing professional development. Scan Figure 5.3. Read the article by Banegas and Glatigny (2021) and complete these sentences:
  (a) An ateneo could be defined as …
  (b) In this study, the ateneo helped the teachers to grapple with curriculum
      change by …

Figure 5.3 QR code access to Banegas and Glatigny (2021)

Activity 5.4 Experiencing Change

What are your experiences with change in the TESOL curriculum? Depending on your professional identity and roles, what kind of changes have you lived/implemented/challenged/led/designed? Think about one experience in particular and share it on TESOLand (Figure 5.4). Just make sure that you provide a little bit of context for others to understand your story. How did you feel about? In what ways does your experience illustrate or challenge some of the concepts and ideas included in this chapter?

Figure 5.4 QR code access to TESOLand

Vignette 5.1	**Japanese National Curriculum for High School English, by Kota Kawakami**

In 2017, the Japanese national curriculum for high school English underwent a major reform, spearheaded by the Ministry of Education, Culture, Sports, Science and Technology (MEXT). The revision involved modifications to the educational objectives, curriculum structure, and learning content. This reform was initiated in response to the growing demand to cultivate global citizens, as well as the mounting criticism towards traditional grammar-based instruction, which has long been the dominant approach.

The new curriculum presents the goal of English learning as developing communicative competence to exchange ideas accurately and appropriately. It also aims to equip students with intercultural perspectives to communicate effectively with people from various backgrounds. One of the most salient aspects of the revision was to place greater emphasis on the interactive use of English, which has been considered a particular challenge for Japanese learners. This emphasis led to the promotion of interactive learning tasks such as role-play or poster sessions. Furthermore, it is recommended that English lessons should be conducted primarily in English, with the intention of providing students with extensive language exposure. These suggestions are informed by the Communicative Language Teaching approach, which promotes creating opportunities for language use in authentic contexts, based on the functional view of language.

The educational reform has received mixed reactions from teachers in the field. While some acknowledge the importance of developing practical English skills, others are perplexed by the gap between the lofty goals advocated by the new curriculum and the reality of their teaching context. For instance, the new curriculum suggests incorporating performance tests (e.g. presentations) into the assessment process. However, teachers who are accustomed to the traditional accuracy-based assessment often encounter difficulties in evaluating students' performance based on its appropriateness or effectiveness. Furthermore, the policy of teaching only in English poses challenges for some teachers who lack confidence in their oral skills. Perhaps the greatest source of confusion arises from the fact that many prestigious universities continue to employ translation-based entrance exams, which is at odds with the prevailing educational trend towards communicative competence. Teachers are faced with the challenging task of reconciling the need to adapt to the new communicative-oriented curriculum with the necessity of dealing with the traditional entrance exams.

Although MEXT has implemented measures to improve the situation, such as sharing teaching resources and holding training seminars, further action is required to bridge the discrepancy between the desired outcome and the status quo.

Activity 5.5 Reactions to Curriculum Change

Read Vignette 5.1 again. There were some 'mixed reactions' among teachers. In what ways could these mixed reactions be explained through the lens of curriculum change as discussed in Chapter 5 this far?

According to a large-scale study carried out in global higher education institutions, Abassi et al. (2025) found that

> frequent use of AI, the extent of the faculty knowledge, institution support to faculty, and the future expectation about AI are promoting curriculum development. Furthermore, the effectiveness of AI-driven tools in personalizing learning experiences, enhancing student engagement, identifying and addressing individual needs, providing real-time feedback, improving the quality of teaching and learning materials, and promoting critical thinking and problem-solving skills is driving curriculum development. Moreover, the challenges limiting AI integration in curriculum development include its ability to personalize learning, adapt content based on student needs, ethical concerns, and hesitations in recommending AI use to other educational institutions. Besides, with respect to cultural and educational contexts in AI-powered tools, the integration of AI in global higher education curriculum development is hindered by its inability to align with and navigate the complexities of these contexts. In addition, educators' and leaders' perceptions and attitudes also influence AI's role in curriculum development. Factors such as AI's ability to create personalized learning experiences, familiarity with current AI tools, its effectiveness in identifying student learning gaps, willingness to undergo training and professional development, and its capacity to address biases in curriculum content stimulate development yet also present limitations. Importantly, our findings indicate that, while AI has enormous potential to revolutionize curriculum development, strategic approaches and policies are required to overcome the identified issues and improve AI integration in varied educational settings.
>
> (p. 547)

While the quote above portrays an exciting and attractive use of GenAI in higher education curricula, we may need to discuss how GenAI can support stakeholders in planning (e.g. needs analysis), designing, implementation and evaluation change in the TESOL curriculum. These ways need to be ethical, ecologically situated and robust, as we cannot entirely rely on GenAI or assume that whatever it provides will be accurate or trustworthy. In other words, let's handle GenAI with care. It is a powerful tool, but *we* are in control of it.

Activity 5.6 Curriculum Change and GenAI

Revisit the quote from Abassi et al. (2025, p. 457). Make a list of things you can do with GenAI to support TESOL curriculum change considering an ecological perspective. For every item, think of benefits and challenges. The final product of this activity should be a table.

5.3 Teacher Agency

Picture the following situation: You are a university student, and you know that in three weeks you have a 3,000-word essay to submit for one core module. The essay is 100 per cent of your overall grade for the module, which means that you have to give it all so that you can pass the essay. You know that you want to pass the essay with a very good grade because you would then like to apply for a scholarship to continue your studies. Thus, you have devised a plan, which you know you are capable of achieving. You have decided that, in preparation for the essay, for every article you read, you will write a brief summary or take notes (you don't want to just highlight bits here and there). You have decided to read between ten and twelve articles. You have also planned that at least you will write 200 words a day so that you can see small wins every day. You have also decided that you will begin to revise and tidy up once you have a full draft. This is your plan based on your previous experiences. And you know you've got this!

The fictional (or probable) scenario I have just described shows that you have the ability to think of a course of action to achieve an aim and that you know what you need to do and how. You also know what you do not need to do (e.g. 'just highlight bits here and there'). Now, let us transfer this knowledge and/or ability to TESOL teachers. Now, imagine that you are a teacher of English working at a university language centre. The centre has decided to upgrade its English for Academic Purposes courses, which are organized in four levels. You are in charge of one of the levels. The centre has asked you and your fellow teachers to submit a revised syllabus of your course so that each shows what changes you would like to implement. After considering your teaching of the course, you have decided that you do not want to change the goals, the content or the materials. However, you want to introduce changes to the assessment and how students will receive feedback so that there is more constructive alignment. In other words, you have designed a course of action based on your aims and you have planned what to do and not do.

In both scenarios, you have shown your capacity to act, which is a very minimalist way of conceptualizing *agency*. According to Lipponen and Kumpulainen (2011), agency can be defined as 'the capacity to initiate purposeful action that implies will, autonomy, freedom, and choice' (p. 813). It is worth noting that the authors connect agency to autonomy, since the latter refers to someone's capacity to make decisions on their own. However, autonomy and agency differ in the sense that while the former is about one's capacity to make decisions, the latter is about being able to act and acting on those decisions.

What about teacher agency? According to Banegas and Gerlach (2021), teacher agency may be defined as 'teachers' dialogical and relational sense of progression towards their professional goals, and it includes teachers' capacity to plan and direct change through regulated actions' (p. 3). This is just one definition of teacher agency. If you review the literature, you will find others. What is worth remembering is that there are different conceptualizations and perspectives. In their review of language teacher agency, Tao and Gao (2021) arrange such perspectives into four:

1 Agency as individuals' intentional acts: This conceptualization is rooted in social-cognitive theory, and from this perspective, agency is directly connected to intentionality, reactiveness and reflectiveness. In other words, teachers engage in agentic moves in reaction/response to different events in their environment. As Kayi-Aydar (2019) suggests, this perspective emphasizes agency as a result of internal cognitive processes that influence a person's ability to act intentionally.

2 Agency as a socioculturally mediated capacity: From a sociocultural perspective, teacher agency occurs at a social/interpersonal plane (teachers in interaction with others) as well as at an intrapersonal plane (a teacher reflecting on their own self), and it is mediated by tools such as a TESOL curriculum, technology, etc., and interaction with stakeholders (e.g. students, parents, school heads, policy makers).

3 Agency as a temporally situated achievement: This conceptualization is based on an ecological perspective and it pays attention to teachers' context as well as their own lived history and experiences over time. This perspective considers teachers' past, present and future. Thus, agency is a phenomenon transactionally negotiated between individual capacities and contextual, material, as well as historical conditions. As we have discussed since Chapter 1, there are micro, meso, macro and chronosystems, all interconnected, through which teacher agency operates.

4 Agency as a discursive practice: From a post-structuralist perspective, teachers engage in agentic moves when they are positioned/position themselves to 'speak up' and take on responsibility and roles which are legitimated by their collective. Differently put, the collective empowers some individuals to step up and assume leadership in one way or another to, for example, embrace or resist (and everything in between these two extremes) curriculum change.

What I have just given you is an extremely brief and crude summary, and if you would like to understand the differences and similarities between these perspectives, I recommend that you read Tao and Gao (2021) as they provide examples taken from published studies. However, not all their examples are connected to the TESOL curriculum per se. What is worth understanding is that when English language teachers engage with bottom-up curriculum change, or are the subjects of top-down curriculum change, their agency (or lack of) could be approached from different theoretical lenses to understand what pushes teachers to plan and execute (or refrain from doing) a series of actions to bring about curriculum change, and how teachers use their agency to continuously learn to teach and develop professionally. Now, I would like you to complete Activities 5.7 and 5.8.

Regardless of the lens used to understand teacher agency, it is important to bear in mind that the core of teacher agency is the course of action teachers of English decide to take when there has been a curriculum change in their context. Vignette 5.2 provides one example.

Activity 5.7 Perspectives in Empirical Study About Language Teacher Agency

Read the two abstracts below. Which teacher agency perspectives do they illustrate? You can then check your answers by going to Chapter 10.

ABSTRACT 1

This study explores how teachers enact agency to facilitate their professional development during curricular reform at a Chinese university. An analysis of data derived from life history interviews with eight language teachers complemented with field notes reveals differential agentic choices and actions. The teachers' learning, teaching and research endeavours in relation to the new curriculum are directed by various identity commitments and enacted in highly individualised ways, as mediated by their prior experiences. By situating teachers' agency in their individual professional trajectories, this study conceptualises interaction of teacher agency and identity commitment to professional development during curricular reform. (Gao & Tao, 2017)

ABSTRACT 2

Scholarship on language teacher autonomy and agency has demonstrated that both constructs are central components of teacher identity and, hence, teacher performance. However, few studies have examined the role of these constructs in language teacher identity, particularly how power mediates their co-constitutive implications for identity construction. This study reports on how institutional power was a key factor in shaping Iranian English language teachers' autonomy, agency, and identity construction. Drawing on data from narrative frames and semi-structured interviews, we show how institutional power discursively shaped the teachers' professional performance in three major areas: (1) power as a normative impetus; (2) policies as hierarchical forces; and (3) power as weakening the nexus between autonomy and agency. Our findings reveal that in the space between power and practice, the teachers viewed institutional power as discursively constraining their own personalized understandings and performances. However, the teachers considered the overarching discourse that power bore as positive in helping establish systemic organization. The article closes with implications for teachers, teacher educators and policymakers in establishing context-specific discourses that positively contribute to institutional and teacher growth. (Nazari et al., 2023)

Vignette 5.2 shows the interactions between the meso, the micro and the chronosystems. How? It appears that curriculum change was not completely top-down. There was an element of consultation, which, as in the case of Kathy, may have acted as a drive to become involved in supporting the implementation of the new curriculum

Activity 5.8 On an Ecological View of Language Teacher Agency

Read the following open-access article (Wang, 2022) at https://doi.org/10.3389/
fpsyg.2022.935038 or just by typing 'English Language Teacher Agency in Response to
Curriculum Reform in China: An Ecological Approach' on your browser. As you read it,
have these questions in mind to guide your reading. Please note that you may not need
to read the whole paper, so it's OK to skip some paragraphs or sections altogether.

Question 1: How does the author understand teacher agency? What are its main
features?

Question 2: Based on the findings and discussions, what are the main practical
takeaways for language teachers interested in enhancing their agency?

Question 3: Is there anything suggested by the author to which you are in
disagreement? What makes you say so?

Vignette 5.2

On Vilches (2018)

In her book chapter, Vilches (2018) describes the case of Kathy (pseudonym) and her account of implementing curricular change in Philippine
basic education. Kathy had 18 years of experience as a teacher of English and was a teacher as well as a mentor to novice teachers in her
school. In 2013, the K-12 curriculum reform entailed that a grammar-based approach would be replaced by a communicative approach to
help students develop their English language proficiency for international communication and professional opportunities.

Given her experience and school role, Kathy was invited to be part of a consultation process, which contributed to her awareness of
the rationale behind the curriculum change. With a group of experienced teachers, she was also tasked with writing a textbook series that
would accompany the new curriculum. The author highlights that Kathy saw the textbook as a tool among others. As part of the change,
she decided not to rely only on the textbook she had co-authored. She also designed other activities and made some changes to the course
syllabus since she firmly believed that teachers can make changes because they know what needs and opportunities their students bring with
them. In the chapter, Kathy remarks that the curriculum change and the textbooks are a stimulating opportunity for teachers to revisit their
practices, assume new roles and take a more leading position in their schools. Given her involvement with the consultation process and the
new textbooks, she also participated in the curriculum change by facilitating professional development courses that would enable fellow
teachers understand the rationale behind the new curriculum and the textbook series.

In the chapter, the author includes a paragraph which summarizes the ups and downs of Kathy's case:

Kathy's story portrays a teacher who believes in the new curriculum and who wants to make it work in her classroom and for other
teachers in the system. While Kathy seems to be coping well in implementing the new curriculum, she is aware of the challenges
faced by other teachers in terms of what the new curriculum is asking them to do in the classroom and the kind of support they have
had (or not had) to be able to understand and make these changes. These challenges can be identified as the changing role of the
teacher, the mismatch between the new curriculum goals and the reality of state school teaching and learning contexts, and the flow
of communication between different people and levels of the education system. (Vilches, 2018, p. 30)

---

to teach English. These are powerful acts of agency since Kathy could have disregarded
the invitations. Not only did she mentor fellow teachers and co-authored a new textbook
series, but she also introduced agentic changes in her own practice driven by a sense of
contextualization and learner-centredness, which she seemed to have developed over
time. Although this is one single case, it shows that when ministries activate curriculum
change, involving teachers from the very start pays off because there is the potential of

<table>
<tr><td>

Vignette 5.3

</td><td>

Balancing Teacher Agency and Curricular Demands in Austrian EFL Teaching, by Tatjana Bacovsky-Novak

</td></tr>
</table>

While Austrian schools and EFL teachers tend to enjoy greater measures of autonomy than their counterparts in many other countries, the introduction of a standardized leaving exam in 2016 has led to more defined curricular demands being placed on EFL teachers and students. However, the Austrian education systems remains highly differentiated especially at secondary level, which is reflected in English as a foreign language (EFL) curricula for different school types prescribing different degrees of standardization. For Hannah, a second-year teacher at an upper-secondary vocational college specializing in business, this means closely following a list of content topics dictated by her school type's curriculum. Alina, a teacher with 9 years of experience teaching at an academic secondary school, has more agency in that regard, as her school type's curriculum formulates learning goals in term of competences without specifying any particular content topics. While Alina is thus free to 'follow a fairly individual approach', Hannah feels that her curriculum mandating the topics she covers restricts her agency and limits her creativity. She notes that 'topics tend to repeat themselves', which can lead to English lessons becoming 'quite boring and superficial' unless teachers expend a great deal of additional effort on sourcing alternative materials.

What both teachers have in common is that they almost completely rely on their respective coursebooks to meet curricular goals in their short-term planning. Alina uses approved coursebooks extensively, trusting that 'they follow the curriculum anyways', but frequently substitutes a class's primary coursebook with additional materials. Hannah cannot make use of this option to the same extent, as her school strongly encourages EFL teachers to closely follow the coursebooks: this ensures that teachers are able to cover for each other in case of illness and allows them to model their assessment measures after a school-internal standard. While Hannah considers the coursebook 'a very helpful tool', she feels that the strict 'by the book' approach adopted at her school forces her into a more passive teaching role than she would like. It also limits her options when it comes to mitigating some of the problems associated with a coursebook becoming the unofficial curriculum: although EFL coursebooks for the Austrian market generally follow the respective curricula, long production times mean that they can be out of date regarding curricular changes and current topics of interest. While both teachers address the first part of this issue by referring to their curricula in their long-term planning, only Alina is afforded the agency to pursue different topics of interest and can thus make up for a coursebook being out of date on a topical level. She considers this agency 'crucial to enrich the classroom and adapt to the needs and interests of one's students'. Ultimately, while both Hannah and Alina navigate the challenges of standardization and curricular constraints, Hannah's adherence to a more rigid curriculum restricts her ability to innovate and engage creatively in the classroom, whereas Alina's greater flexibility allows her to meet her students' interests and needs more fully.

raising awareness among practitioners. In this case, it was not an 'expert' or someone removed from teaching who was co-authoring the textbooks and providing training to in-service teachers; it was 'one of them', which may add legitimacy and criticality to curriculum change. On the one hand, Kathy was cognizant of the benefits that the curriculum change would bring in terms of adding meaning and authenticity to English language learning. On the other hand, she was aware of the limited resources available to make implementation successful and equitable.

Now, allow me to introduce Vignette 5.3, which integrates teacher agency, curriculum change and the use of coursebooks in an Austrian context.

As you may have noted, Vignette 5.3 illustrates how teacher agency can support or hamper changing a coursebook-based enacted curriculum. As the author notes, while both teachers rely on coursebooks, what they do with them differs due to how the institution, i.e. the mesosystem of curriculum development, seems to promote or limit their agency. I would now like you to complete Activities 5.9 and 5.10.

Let me bring this subsection to a close with Vignette 5.4, which is not about curriculum change but more about how a curriculum includes spaces for teacher agency. The vignette is situated in the context of Hong Kong, known for its understanding of the curriculum as a school-based organizer/policy even when there is a central curriculum. According to Yuen et al. (2018), the aim of a school-based curriculum is to cater for the needs and interests of individual schools' students, provided their initiatives comply with the requirements outlined in the central curriculum.

<table>
<tr><td>Vignette
5.4</td><td>

Teacher Agency in a TESOL Curriculum from Hong Kong, by Ivy Chau

</td></tr>
</table>

In Hong Kong, children start learning English from kindergarten. English is one of the core subjects in both primary and secondary schools. English is classified as a key learning area where subject knowledge and skills are presented in the form of learning targets under three strands: interpersonal, knowledge, and experience. The curriculum aims to support not only students' English language proficiency for study, work, and leisure but also how they connect themselves to the world as global citizens while preparing to meet the socio-economic demands in a fast-changing society. To achieve the overall aim of the English language curriculum, teachers are expected to connect the subject knowledge with components including transferable skills (e.g. literacy), positive values, and attitudes.

The English language curriculum is organized around four Key Stages (KS). KS1 is classified as lower primary, KS2 as upper primary, KS3 as junior secondary, and KS4 as senior secondary. Although language items and communicative functions are outlined in each key stage, schools and teachers are granted great flexibility in implementing this central curriculum. The range of flexibility varies from a single lesson plan to the entire school's English language education curriculum. This practice is also known as school-based curriculum, which allows schools and teachers to adapt the central curriculum and create new materials that suit the ability of students and teachers in a school (Curriculum Development Council, 2001). Teacher agency, in this sense, is promoted both explicitly and implicitly. For instance, although the Education Bureau provides a recommended English textbook list for primary and secondary schools, schools have their own choice in deciding what textbook to use. As a result, many high-ranking English Medium of Instruction (EMI) schools in Hong Kong tend to use international English textbooks instead of the recommended textbooks, which are mostly Hong Kong context-based. Although English teachers may not be consulted in the textbook decision-making, they can decide how to utilize the textbook. In other words, teachers can use/create their teaching materials as the major source of input, and the textbook can play a supplementary role, as long as the level of the materials is similar to that of the textbook, and the materials have covered all language items that will be tested in examinations.

Due to the popularity of school-based curriculum, English teachers, especially secondary school teachers, are also encouraged to adopt a cross-curricular approach in teaching, which is similar to the notion of content and language integrated learning (CLIL). As stated in the central curriculum, English teachers can collaborate with teachers of other subjects. Teachers can decide on a range of themes and create specific materials not only to develop students' language skills but also to broaden students' learning experience through language learning activities related to other subjects. As a result, English teachers generally have greater ownership in planning lessons and even a school curriculum.

Activity 5.9 On the School-Based Curriculum

Based on the professional lives of Alina and Hannah included in Vignette 5.3, create a continuum which allows you to imagine how teachers can exercise their agency to use coursebooks in different ways amid certain institutional constraints. You can use Figure 5.5 to create your continuum or create your own. Note: The icons included in the continuum are simply decorative. You can replace them by meaningful ones.

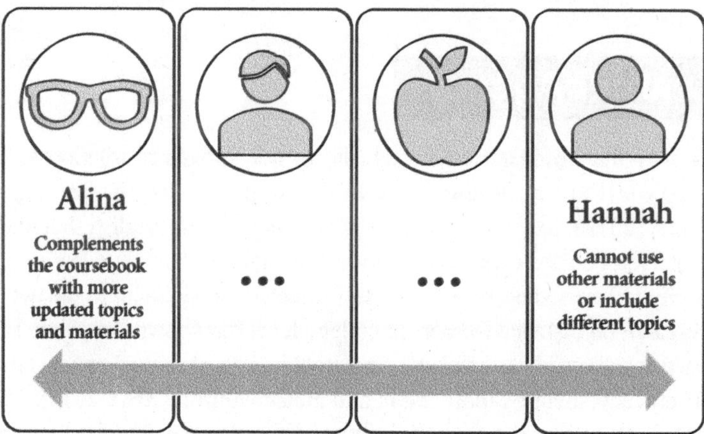

Figure 5.5 A continuum on teacher agency

Activity 5.10 Teachers Mobilizing Their Agency for Curriculum Change

Imagine that you are a teacher of English working with very young learners, and a new TESOL curriculum will be implemented as of the following school year. In response to the new curriculum, you would like to plan and implement a few actions that will enable you to own and shape the curriculum for your own context. Create a timeline that can help you plan your steps and realize that what you are planning is doable. You can use Figure 5.6 to set your points in time using the circles and the bullet points to break down your planned actions. Please, use your agency and autonomy to change the proposed figure in any way you wish. This is just an example.

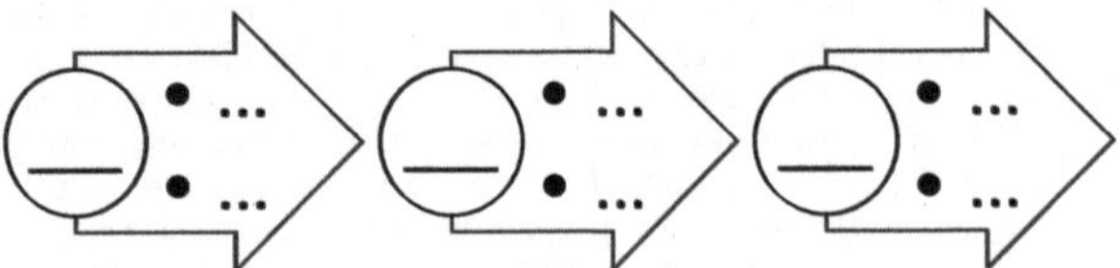

Figure 5.6 A possible timeline to plan a course of action

Activity 5.11 Agency and the School-Based Curriculum

Based on Vignette 5.4, what are the benefits and challenges to teachers as agents of curriculum change in the context of a school-based curriculum? In your view, where and how does a school-based curriculum sit within the ecology of curriculum development?

5.4 Learner Agency

In the same way that teachers can engage in agentic moves in relation to the TESOL curriculum, so can learners. Within research on the psychology of language education, Mercer (2011a, 2012) has noted that *good* or *successful* English language learners attending in-person courses owe their positive and enabling language learning experience to their capacity to orient their beliefs and self-directed engagement to the act of learning. Similarly, research on distance learners at college level has shown that when such learners engage in agentic moves, these can have a positive impact of mutual enhancement on their sense of self-efficacy, identity, motivation, and metacognition (Xiao, 2014). These studies illustrate that learners who exhibit satisfactory performance in English language courses do so because they are intentionally in control of their English language development. Learner agency in the context of language education has been approached from different perspectives. Below, I illustrate two because they broaden the repertoire of perspectives mentioned when we discussed teacher agency.

One perspective is that of complexity theory. Mercer (2011b) has offered a summary of this theory:

> Larsen-Freeman (1997: 157) characterises language learning as a non-linear, complex process and explains that "we will never be able to identify, let alone measure, all of the factors accurately. And even if we could, we would still be unable to predict the outcome of their combination". Thus, rather than trying to extricate and separate the variables involved in a piecemeal fashion, complexity theory recognises the need to explore and acknowledge the dynamic complexity inherent in learning a foreign language. It rejects simplistic cause and effect explanations of language learning and accepts its non-linear, dynamic nature which can vary across individuals and is closely tied to a range of contextual factors.
>
> (p. 429)

From this perspective, we understand that learner agency is part of a multi-faceted landscape and it must be understood as a dynamic whole. Larsen-Freeman (2019) emphasizes that learner agency cannot be seen just as an individual feature. Language learners are inserted in a complexity of interconnected systems and therefore their agency needs to be examined and mobilized as embedded in the contextual, which include social, spatial, material, cultural, temporal, relational and structural dimensions. At this stage, you may be wondering why I did not mention this perspective when I introduced teacher agency. This is because, interestingly enough, it has not fully captured researchers' attention. However, you might as well understand language teacher agency in relation to curriculum development from complexity theory.

Larsen-Freeman (2019) also makes two suggestions about how TESOL teachers and institutions can revisit their curricula to support learner agency. I have used them as prompts to ask some questions, which should be taken as just examples of the many questions you can ask yourself and others to promote agency through the TESOL curriculum.

- Optimize conditions for language learning: Could TESOL courses include a strong digital component to invigorate the language learning experience? Can technology (digital spaces, devices, AI, apps, etc.) be used in a way that enables learners to make decisions?

- Help learners to enhance and enact their agency: Could learners be asked to keep a journal of their language learning strategies and share them with their peers? Could the teacher create a menu of activities/projects and let learners decide what they want to do and how in order to achieve a set of learning outcomes? Could learning outcomes be written together with learners? For writing and speaking activities, could the teacher enable their learners to collectively create an assessment rubric that they can use to provide peer feedback? Could the teacher provide learners with a video and ask them to design an activity for other peers to complete? Could questions and assessment instruments and procedures be negotiated with learners so that they can ask questions in class and decide how they would like to be assessed in relation to the goals/learning outcomes?

Activity 5.12 On Larsen-Freeman (2019)

Larsen-Freeman (2019) postulates that agency has the following characteristics: relational, emergent, spatially and temporally situated, achievable, changeable through iteration and co-adaptation, multidimensional and heterarchical. Copy this link https://doi.org/10.1111/modl.12536 to access the article and find out what each of these characteristics means.

Activity 5.13 Questions to Support Language Learner Agency

On your own or with peers, add questions to the two suggestions put forward by Larsen-Freeman (2019). Feel free to make other macro suggestions and develop questions to illustrate them.

5.5 Sustainability in Curriculum Change

When teachers, learners and other stakeholders invest time, effort, resources and more on curriculum change, they may want to check that the changes they are proposing and actively engaging with are sustainable. This does not mean that the changes will only make sense and be worth acting on if they are to be implemented forever. In their edited volume on TESOL and sustainability, Goulah and Katunich (2020) understand sustainability through a prism of interconnected aspects, which I have tried to represent through a set of quotes from their introductory chapter:

> [H]uman beings now live and work in the Anthropocene era, in which the anthropogenic impacts on the biosphere are so pervasive that they threaten to alter the conditions that sustain human and nonhuman life. [...] For many teachers, researchers, and teacher educators in the field of TESOL, the relationship between the work of teaching English and broader sustainability crises that characterize the so-called Anthropocene era, such as the interconnected predicaments of climate change, habitat loss, food insecurity, and the threat of nuclear conflict. (p. 1)
>
> ... to begin to make more explicit the ways in which the field of TESOL is implicated and, to an important degree, if unwittingly, complicit in the present sustainability crises so that a new ethic of language teaching in the Anthropocene era may emerge. (p. 1)

Once sustainability (including biological, cultural, and linguistic sustainability) is treated as a core consideration in the professional work of teaching English, then an opportunity for a broader professional field of action and theorizing opens. We see this emerging in important if still limited ways, where the interconnectedness of language, culture, education, and sustainability increasingly frames the topic or theme of symposia, conference sessions, and entire conferences in the field. (p. 2)

As you may notice, the authors subsume a wide array of interlinked issues and areas under the concept of sustainability. This is because, in my perspective, they are all part of the nature and conditions of life and how to sustain it. At this point, you may be wondering how these topics are related to changes to the TESOL curriculum. Drawing on Goulah and Katunich's (2020) stance on sustainability, when I think about sustainability in relation to the TESOL curriculum, I think of the key dimensions condensed in Table 5.1. I have spelled out a few connections to TESOL curriculum change. I hope that the questions included help you think about cases and examples.

Table 5.1 Dimensions of Sustainability

	This refers to …
Temporality	… the extent to which any TESOL curriculum change can be maintained and supported over a certain period of time, a period that gives stakeholders enough time to fully implement and evaluate the changes introduced. For example, how long will the new TESOL curriculum be implemented for? At which point in time will there be a review and possible new curriculum change?
Resources	… the extent to which the body (e.g. a school, a Ministry of Education) championing and implementing the TESOL curriculum change has the financial, structural, administrative staff and/or operational means to implement the TESOL curriculum change. For example, if the new curriculum stipulates that students will be provided with a coursebook, is there enough funding to do it year after year? Or, if the TESOL curriculum change states that students will be using a dedicated online platform, will all students have equal/equitable access?
Capacity	… the extent to which there will be enough teachers prepared to implement a new TESOL curriculum. For example, will teachers engage with training/continuing professional development opportunities for them to understand and be supported as the new curriculum is rolled out? Will there be enough teachers to enact the change? Will teachers have time in their workload to, for example, attend training and design new teaching materials?
Ecological	… ways in which a TESOL curriculum can raise awareness of and advocate for environmental issues such as climate change, pollution, green sources of energy, etc. It may also refer to ways in which the curriculum implementation itself will become more environmentally friendly. For example, will the implementers consider a carbon footprint offsetting strategy?

This refers to …	
Cultural	… ways in which changes in a TESOL curriculum can contribute to raise awareness of and advocate for the need to promote, protect, and preserve cultural beliefs, practices and heritage, particularly from minoritized groups. For example, can the TESOL curriculum raise awareness of local practices among students? Can the curriculum promote pluriculturalism and different ways of thinking, doing and being?
Linguistic	… ways in which a TESOL curriculum can contribute to the survival of indigenous and non-dominant languages in a given context by promoting the learning of English in tandem with other languages through multilingual and translingual approaches to English language learning. For example, will the curriculum encourage translanguaging in the classroom?

Activity 5.14 Curriculum Change and Sustainability

Find out if there have been any fairly recent changes to the TESOL curriculum in your context. If there have been, do a search online to see whether newspapers or other outlets have reported any issues with it and whether you can link those issues to any of the aspects included in Table 5.1.

Activity 5.15 On Learners as Co-Creators of Content

Between 2005 and 2016, Zhong et al. (2019) conducted an action research study with the following research questions: (1) What should be done to motivate students to engage in producing and using student content? (2) What routines are to be built to enhance student content quality to make it worthy of language learning? (3) What routines are to be built to facilitate equitable and justifiable assessment of individually created student content? (4) How is student content, together with its use, to be justified to the school management and the public?

You can read the abstract of their publication here:

This paper reports on an action research project designed to develop and integrate a new conceptual learning and teaching approach into four language-related courses in an Australian university. Being named Curriculum 2.0 after Web 2.0, the approach places the production, sharing and learning of student content at the centre. In this paper, we recount the project, focusing on how its aims were methodically pursued through reflective experiments to incorporate student content-based pedagogy into the selected courses. Among others, three major actions will be discussed, namely segmenting content, building a content bank and developing an equitable system for assessing individually created content, which proved effective in implementing the new approach. The course and outcomes of the project, to be presented in this paper, will inform the continuing evolution of the scholarship of language learning and teaching. (Zhong et al., 2019, p. 76)

While the article does not include the term *sustainability* not even once 😊, some students of mine and myself still see it as an example of sustainability connected to the dimension of resources because learners produced content, which could be re-used and recycled by other learners and teachers. What are your thoughts on this connection?

5.6 Sustainable Development Goals

In tandem with the views expressed above on sustainability, there are world initiatives championing sustainability:

The 2030 Agenda for Sustainable Development, adopted by all United Nations Member States in 2015, provides a shared blueprint for peace and prosperity for people and the planet, now and into the future. At its heart are the 17 Sustainable Development Goals (SDGs), which are an urgent call for action by all countries – developed and developing – in a global partnership. They recognize that ending poverty and other deprivations must go hand-in-hand with strategies that improve health and education, reduce inequality, and spur economic growth – all while tackling climate change and working to preserve our oceans and forests.

(United Nations, 2024)

The seventeen SDGs are listed below. You can find details about what each means by using a search engine and typing '17 sustainable development goals'

1 No poverty
2 Zero hunger
3 Good health and wellbeing
4 Quality education
5 Gender equality
6 Clean water and sanitation

7   Affordable and clean energy

8   Decent work and economic growth

9   Industry, innovation and infrastructure

10   Reduced inequalities

11   Sustainable cities and communities

12   Responsible consumption and production

13   Climate action

14   Life below water

15   Life on land

16   Peace, justice and strong institutions

17   Partnerships for the goals

Through change, a TESOL curriculum can contribute to the seventeen SGDS in different ways. First, I would say that SDG 4 is deeply connected to what a TESOL curriculum, or curricula in general, can do. SDG 4 seeks to 'ensure inclusive and equitable quality education and promote lifelong learning opportunities for all'. What does this mean for us? It means that we need to guarantee that goals, principles, content, materials, activities and assessments to teach English are inclusive and equitable and provide a meaningful and enabling learning experience for all students, regardless of their identities, background or beliefs. As you can see, an inclusive TESOL curriculum can therefore contribute to SDGs 4, 5 and 10. My true hope is that by the end of this textbook, you have developed knowledge and skills that can help you design, evaluate, and enact a TESOL curriculum that can support you as well as your students in creating and experiencing quality educational opportunities.

In 2017, Alan Maley and Nik Peachey edited a volume in which English language teaching and the SDGs coalesce. Their publication

> has a twofold aim – to help students learn a language creatively whilst at the same time raising awareness of the SDGs through bringing together a range of innovative ideas for teaching creatively and addressing these key issues.
>
> (Maley & Peachey, 2017, 204)

The volume is freely available online, so, if you go to the full reference included in the reference list of this book, you will find a link to access it. If the link does not work, just type the title into a search engine, and you will easily find it online. The book contains practice-oriented activities, lesson plans and more. While they may be rightly perceived as one-off attempts, they illustrate how teachers can change a TESOL curriculum so that teachers and students become agentic actors for sustainability. You can now complete Activity 5.16.

Activity 5.16 SDGs and the TESOL Curriculum

Find the edited volume by Maley and Peachey online. Take a quick look at the table of contents and choose one chapter in particular. As you read the chapter, think about these questions: (a) In what ways can the practice suggested in the chapter contribute to sustainability? (b) Is there space for teachers and students to exercise their agency? (c) Would teachers in your local context be able to implement this practice or something similar? (d) What changes would you make to it if you were to implement it? (e) How could this example be used to make wider changes to a TESOL curriculum in your context? Provide support for your answers.

Answer the questions by creating a 5-slide, 5-minute presentation you could share with your peers.

5.7 Bringing It All Together

Activity 5.17

Make a concept map which brings together the issues and concepts discussed in this chapter. Share it with a peer and discuss commonalities and differences.

Activity 5.18

Browse a general education curriculum or a curriculum for TESOL from your context. This could be from any level of education (kindergarten, primary, secondary, university, etc.). Are there any indications of (a) curriculum change from a previous curriculum, (b) teacher agency, (c) learner agency, (d) changes based on sustainability? If agency or sustainability are not included, what context-sensitive and doable changes would you introduce? Why? How?

Activity 5.19

Imagine that you have been asked to change the syllabus of an English language course you teach in any way you wish, provided it responds to the United Nations SDGs. Write a syllabus which contains: goals, principles, content, materials, activities and assessment. You may need to revisit Chapter 3 before you embark on this activity. Because this is a syllabus for just one course, it does not need to be more than 2–3 pages long.

5.8 Further Reading

Below, I list a few titles on teacher agency within and beyond the remit of TESOL:

- Durrant, J. (2020). *Teacher agency, professional development and school improvement*. Routledge.

- Priestley, M., Biesta, G., & Robinson, S. (2026). *Teacher agency: An ecological approach* (2nd ed.). Bloomsbury.

- Ríos, R. (2017). *Teacher agency for equity: A framework for conscientious engagement*. Routledge.

- Veliz, L., Slaughter, Y., Bonar, G., & Nguyen, M. H. (Eds.). (2025). *Language teacher agency: Navigating complex and diverse educational contexts*. Bloomsbury.

Chapter 6
What Makes the TESOL Curriculum Political?

Summary

This chapter aims to raise awareness of the TESOL curriculum as an inherently ideological and political tool embedded in the broader and complex ecology of education. It discusses links between politics, ideology and policy. Given the social orientation of curriculum, students are introduced to the notion of social justice as a philosophy of education aimed at disrupting inequity in TESOL. The chapter offers connections to previous chapters as it discusses how decisions about goals, principles, materials, activities and assessment are underpinned by political and ideological forces in the macrosystem of the TESOL curriculum.

6.1 Warm-Up

According to Cantoni et al. (2017), '[b]eliefs, attitudes, and ideology play a fundamental role in human societies: they shape interactions within social networks and in markets, and they underlie political institutions and policy choices' (p. 339). In other words, beliefs, attitudes and ideology drive decisions and practices. For example, in Chapter 5, we discussed how the TESOL curriculum could be changed by adopting sustainability as a powerful perspective. Changing a curriculum by embracing sustainability is part of a decision-making process which involves several individuals and institutions who believe that sustainability should inform educational change. Such notions of what education and the teaching of languages in particular should be like are part of a complex set of ideas, values and beliefs. From the ecological perspective adopted in this book, those ideas are usually placed in the macrosystem of the ecology of the TESOL curriculum. At a personal level, I do believe that language teaching and education in general need to be sustainability-based so that we can protect and value all the (im)material resources, many of which are limited, that we have as human beings on this planet. This belief has driven me to include sustainability as well as other perspectives in this book. This example shows that there is a powerful relationship between ideology and curriculum. I would even say that a curriculum is an ideological tool. In other words, we cannot have an ideology-free curriculum. In the

Activity 6.1 Understanding Key Concepts

First, jot down any words that spring to mind when you think of the terms *politics* and *ideology*.

Now, go online and search for these terms: *politics, political, ideology, ideological*. You can do your search in English and/or in any other language(s). Record two or three definitions that you find. You can choose online dictionaries, encyclopaedias or any other source that you consider trustworthy. We will come back to these definitions in Section 6.2.

context of TESOL, the first questions to ask would be: What does English mean? What does learning English mean? Should people learn English in my context? Why (not)?

Kelly (2009) once said: '[W]e must (…) acknowledge that in making decisions about the content of the curriculum we are dealing with ideologies rather than eternal truths' (p. 33). If you think that a teacher of English does not need to care much about politics and ideologies, I hope that I can help you revisit that belief. If you think that politicians and policy makers and those in power should care about this but not teachers, I hope this chapter shows you that it is more complex than that. If you think that teaching English or education in general should not be instilling any ideologies and political ideas, let me tell you that such beliefs may prove that a dominant ideology has worked so well that it has become normalized/naturalized!

6.2 Ideologies and Politics

Ideologies are collective beliefs resulting from power relations in society. Nozaki and Apple (2002) have defined ideology as 'a system of ideas, beliefs, fundamental commitments, and values about social reality' (p. 381). While it is a complex concept, the authors summarize how it has been understood in two ways:

1 As a system of meanings that justifies the vested interests of existing groups in society.

2 As a set of knowledge and beliefs that provides meaning, that enables people in their everyday lives to make sense of their social reality (Nozaki & Apple, 2002, p. 381).

The authors emphasize that both ways are necessary and complementary. Perhaps, the first way may help you understand why there are ideological systems that have led to hegemonies, cultural and economic reproduction, social control, patriotism, nationalism, economic control (Apple, 2018), and even the *one nation, one language* ideology that has been used by different governments to cement their plans of a so-called harmonious and unified nation-state to develop and implement educational systems, and therefore a curriculum, which is delivered through one dominant, hegemonic language (Hofmann, 2016). For example, in Argentina, Chile or Uruguay, formal education is mostly delivered through the medium of Spanish even when there are other languages in use by different speakers. Spanish represents the hegemonic ideology and social groups in power. At this stage, it is important to become aware that ideology is power.

In her book, Ortaçtepe Hart (2023) conceptualizes ideology as

> the set of unconsciously held beliefs and assumptions by which individuals rationalize and are reconciled to the socio-economic, political, and cultural status quo. These beliefs are not consciously arrived at but are continually being embedded in individuals from a very early age.

> (p. 5)

The second sentence in the quotation may make us think of the context in which children grow and the people they are surrounded by (e.g. family, carers, friends, neighbours). It may make us think of formal education and what beliefs the enacted (and the hidden) curriculum embeds in children. You may wish to (re)read Chapter 2, Section 2.3, in which we discuss governmentality through school systems. As you may know, education has the capacity to transform or reproduce our reality, and therefore, it is a powerful tool and system to construct discourses and practices. This is why it is also said that education is a political act; education is politics (Giroux, 2010; Shor, 1993). In this context, politics refers to the ideological forces and discourses behind the shapes and forms of that transformation (or perpetuation of dominant, usually unequal, discourses).

Ideologies are influential in the thinking and development of politics, which could be minimally defined as a set of activities aimed at shaping the direction of social groups. In other words, politics is about making decisions by people in power among (or against) other groups. It should be noted that politics does not only refer to political parties and government. Politics is about governance, and it relates to institutions, the workplace, opinion and above all, power and what people can do with it and for it.

Activity 6.2 Questions to Raise Awareness

Think about these questions and feel free to add others as you read them:

- In which countries are girls not allowed to be schooled?
- Are all levels of education obligatory in your country?
- Why must some children wear a uniform?
- In your country, can children with special educational needs attend mainstream schooling?
- Is formal education universalized in your country? Are there, for example, schools in rural areas?
- What languages are taught in formal education in your country? Do you know why?

6.3 Ideologies in the TESOL Curriculum

Scholars in the field of language education have discussed some of the ideologies and the politics of TESOL (e.g. Mirhosseini, 2018; Seltzer, 2022; Wicaksono, 2020). The dominant politics in TESOL may be related to neo-colonialism as a powerful ideology which continues to drive what happens in TESOL, particularly when TESOL is understood as an industry. Unlike colonial powers (e.g. England), which used direct force and control to subjugate *developing* nations, those powers, as well as multinational corporations, may use *soft power* (e.g. policies, projects, scholarships, prizes, funding, international networks) and more subtle, non-coercive ways to exercise control. One of those ways is how English is commodified and packaged to be taught and learnt, which has been discussed under the concept of linguistic imperialism (e.g. Altay, 2025; Phillipson, 2010).

Within the umbrella of neo-colonialism, the school curriculum (not just for the teaching of English) may be dominated by Anglo-centric discourse on ways of knowing, cultures, identities and pedagogies, and the notion of English as a lingua franca to facilitate communication or education in a globalized world. You can think of English-medium instruction (EMI) or content and language integrated learning (CLIL) as approaches embraced by educational systems around the world, particularly in higher education and how they seem to reinforce Englishization, i.e. the 'increasing presence, importance and status of English at all levels in the educational domain' (Lanvers & Hultgren, 2018, p. 1), and neoliberalism at the expense of local languages and ways of thinking and constructing knowledge (e.g. Manan et al., 2024; Ohja et al., 2024; Wang & Jiang, 2025). In the specific case of TESOL, not all varieties of English are equal, and therefore, the status of some Englishes is presented as more prestigious. For example, in some educational systems, TESOL curricula or language schools may impose British English as their trademark or type of English adopted. However, it is not any British English. Usually, this is the English spoken by white, upper-class, professional men or what has also been called BBC English. Something similar happens with institutions which appear to have a preference for American English. Again, it is not any variety of American English, but that spoken by the dominant classes. Tied to the hierarchy of some Englishes over others, we can find the pervasive notion of nativespeakerism. This means that the goal of teachers and students is to sound … and probably act and be like a *native speaker*, i.e. someone (almost always someone white, privileged and male) who was born speaking the variety of English presented as the best/purest/most sophisticated/powerful. Nativespeakerism has given rise to the still prevalent, but challenged (e.g. Waddington, 2025), native vs non-native dichotomy particularly among teachers of English (e.g. Aneja, 2016; Llurda & Calvet-Terré, 2024). This ideology may explain racism in TESOL, such as the negative experiences lived by so-called non-native TESOL professionals in leadership roles, as investigated in Raza and Eslami (2024).

Let me briefly refer to two more examples of ideologies in TESOL. One is the (over) use of imported/global coursebooks from UK/US-based publishers to teach English across different contexts. In many settings, teaching and learning English is reduced to following a global coursebook as if it were a script, which has led to the notion of the coursebook as the teacher. Apart from potentially deskilling teachers, these coursebooks ignore contextual particularities and are based on the belief that students should learn English in the same manner regardless of their setting, aims, background, etc. I must stress that I have nothing against such global coursebooks if they are used as tools critically. They can be helpful with novice teachers, unqualified teachers or in contexts where materials are scarce. Another example is the English-only policy in TESOL, which refers to teaching English through English, allowing students to use English only and banning (and even punishing) students using their full linguistic repertoire. In other words, from this view, English is taught through a monolingual lens. Fortunately, the pedagogies behind translanguaging (e.g. Cenoz & Gorter, 2021; Wei, 2024) and own-language use (e.g. Hall & Cook, 2014) are becoming more and more widespread.

Vignette 6.1 provides an example of ideologies and politics in the TESOL curriculum. According to the author, this is reflected in the pedagogical approaches and content included in the curriculum to teach English as a foreign language (EFL). Together with the focus on nationalism and identity, it is worth recognizing that the Algerian curriculum appears to be mindful of diversity in the world, as it includes perspectives closer to inclusion, such as multilingualism and multiculturalism. It is also worth highlighting that English is seen as a vehicle, and therefore, there is a focus, in principle, on developing students' communication skills.

Vignette 6.1

Ideologies in the EFL Curriculum in Algeria, by Sid Ali Selama

In Algeria, English as foreign language (EFL) is taught/learnt as early as the third year of primary school, when students are typically around eight years old. From a contextual perspective, Algeria is a very varied linguistic area, a multilingual territory in which national languages and foreign languages are present. The EFL Algerian curriculum has recently undergone a significant transformation, particularly with the integration of English into primary education. This linguistic policy shift aligns with the nation's goals of modernizing education and preparing learners for global competition. The curriculum aims to enhance students' communicative competence, critical thinking and intercultural awareness, reflecting a broader vision of equipping them with skills for a multilingual and multicultural world.

The curriculum embodies multiple ideologies. First, nationalism is evident through the emphasis on sustaining a unified national identity alongside linguistic diversity. This is reflected in its content, which incorporates Algerian heritage while promoting global English usage. Second, inclusivity and equity are addressed through attempts to standardize access to quality English education, although challenges remain in bridging regional disparities.

These ideological strategies seem to be intertwined with the Algerian socio-political landscape. The curriculum explicitly reflects an educational framework where Algeria's identity politics and globalization interact with the classroom practices in a multicultural context. This dual focus highlights the complexity of integrating global languages into a nationalistic framework without neglecting cultural integrity.

These ideologies significantly shape the teaching and learning process. To illustrate, teachers would find themselves mediating between fostering a national identity among Algerian young learners and, at the same time, preparing them for global challenges. By doing so, the EFL curriculum establishes a case for responding to internal and external challenges. Internal challenges are based on national identity, culture and the freedom of citizens. External challenges are based on globalization: an education in universal values that prepares them for exchanges between peoples. It is for globalization that the curriculum positions EFL education in an intercultural communication context.

About this particular point, it is powerfully stated that the curriculum is designed to help Algerian young learners become citizens capable of integrating into the multicultural world and being able to respect their nation's cultural diversity. To reach these ambitious goals, stronger emphasis should be placed on teacher professional development, equitable resource allocation and addressing practical challenges in multilingual contexts. Reinforcing the integration of intercultural competence and aligning policies with classroom realities can ensure a more effective and inclusive EFL curriculum.

Vignette 6.1 illustrates how broader ideological and political forces can shape key elements of a TESOL curriculum, for example, content, as a way of constructing a certain identity among citizens in a given context. Now, Vignette 6.2 comes from Finland. The author highlights the language education approaches embedded in a curriculum, such as English as a lingua franca (ELF), as a way to depart from nativespeakerism ideologies (Kiczkowiak & Lowe, 2019), and how these inform key curriculum elements such as learning outcomes and principles for language teaching that emphasize communication.

Vignette 6.2

Teaching English at Finnish Universities, by Peter Launonen

Finland is technically a bilingual country, with Swedish being an official language in addition to Finnish. In practice, however, the second-most widely spoken language after Finnish is English. Although proficiency levels can vary considerably, the use of English as a lingua franca (ELF) is firmly established in Finland and other Nordic countries (Peterson & Beers, 2023). Upon graduation from high school, students in Finland are already expected to have attained a high intermediate (B2) level in English, which is why first-year English courses taught at university Language Centres (LCs) are usually pitched at a B2 level. Students at university are generally only required to take 1–2 mandatory English courses during their bachelor's degree, but further English courses may be included in their master's degree programmes, and students can choose to take elective courses as well.

The intended learning outcomes (ILOs) for English courses are written by the LCs or negotiated with the faculties in order to ensure that the skills and knowledge acquired in language courses support and complement students' ongoing academic and professional development. The specifics of course design are generally handled either collaboratively or individually by LC teachers, who aim to ensure constructive alignment between ILOs, teaching methods and assessment practices, as advocated in university pedagogy (Biggs & Tang, 2007). All full-time LC teachers hold, at a minimum, a master's degree, and LC English teams tend to comprise teachers from diverse backgrounds, including both Finnish nationals and non-Finns.

Course design and pedagogical practices are often reflective of an understanding and acceptance of ideas stemming from ELF and World Englishes. Given that these fields emphasize the diversity of English use in a variety of contexts around the world, there has been a shift away from using the *native speaker* as the primary model one should aim to emulate (Vettorel, 2018). Therefore, it logically follows that pronunciation is generally de-emphasized in English courses at Finnish LCs, although it may be addressed (e.g. in feedback) if it leads to miscommunication. Similarly, the attention given to grammar and error correction is often minimal and mostly limited to ensuring successful communication is achieved. Moreover, given that students already have high listening comprehension skills, partly due to the level of extramural exposure to English in Finland (Schurz & Sundqvist, 2022), traditional listening activities tend not to feature in classes either.

Instead, LC English courses in Finland focus considerably on the development of productive skills via practice and communication. Developing such skills is important, particularly for first- and second-year students, as it helps build the confidence required to use English in professional and academic contexts. This emphasis on practice and communication means that courses tend to reflect a variety of principles from communicative language teaching (CLT), task-based learning (TBL) and problem-based learning (PBL). Students are also given opportunities to develop their ability to work autonomously (e.g. asynchronous courses) and collaboratively (e.g. team-based coursework), as well as practice giving and receiving peer feedback. Additionally, allowing students to choose topics or texts that align with their field or major helps make learning more student-centred, which generally has a positive effect on students' engagement. All in all, courses are designed with a view to promoting the development of students' twenty-first-century skills, equipping them for success in their ongoing studies and future careers.

Activity 6.3 Ideologies in a Curriculum from Your Context

Browse a curriculum for TESOL from your context. This could be from any level of education (kindergarten, primary, secondary, university, etc.). Find any indications of the ideologies underpinning the curriculum. Be aware that these may not be explicitly stated, but you can identify them through the choice of words or certain approaches the curriculum stresses. Also, how does it compare to the curricula portrayed in Vignettes 6.1 and 6.2 in relation to the aims of teaching and learning English?

6.4 Policy and the TESOL Curriculum

A TESOL curriculum is policy, for it can guide and/or determine, depending on how prescriptive it is, how English is taught in a certain context. However, as policy, a TESOL curriculum usually aligns, at least in formal education, with broader policies such as a national constitution, education acts and legislation, etc. These policies are also tools used to propagate and instil a set of values, ideologies and political positionings. For example, in Argentina, Article 87 of the 26206 National Law of Education (Congreso de la Nación Argentina, 2006b) states that the teaching of at least one foreign language will be compulsory in all primary and secondary schools in the country, and that the strategies for implementing this article will be agreed through the Federal Council of Education. As such, the article does not determine which language(s) will be taught as *foreign*, but it was the Federal Council that later made more specific decisions that led to the inclusion of English as one of those languages. It is also worth clarifying that in another article of the same law, the government acknowledges the necessity of protecting and revitalizing indigenous languages and their peoples through the creation of bilingual intercultural programmes. In other words, the policy shows that languages play an important role in the construction of a nation.

If we zoom out, the literature shows that policy can be understood as:

- Text, such as a constitutional clause, a law, or the official/intended TESOL curriculum from a specific context (Ball, 1993; Spolsky, 2004).

- Discourse, i.e. a set of beliefs and ideologies, which, for example, could form the (un)intended or the hidden curriculum (Ball, 1993).

- Practice, which refers to a set of implicit rules/norms of interaction, an implicit understanding of what is appropriate or not (Bonacina-Pugh, 2012, 2020). This could be the enacted and/or the hidden curriculum.

As discussed in Chapter 1, there may be different curriculum types. For example, the official or intended curriculum is that produced by a recognized body/institution such as a Ministry of Education. This could vary in how flexible or prescriptive it is. The enacted curriculum is that which is found in practice. The hidden curriculum, in turn, refers to

> what is implied to students by what (and who) is included or left out of the curriculum experience (Apple, 2004). For example, when immigrant student are taught about housekeeping and warehouse jobs rather than how to prepare for a career, the curriculum implies that they are only capable of the former, not the latter.
>
> (Graves, 2016, p. 80)

With these key notions in mind, you can now move on and complete Activities 6.4 and 6.5.

Activity 6.4 Policies and TESOL in Your Context

After a comprehensive search, make a list of all the policies as text that seem to have an impact on how a TESOL curriculum is designed in your context.

Activity 6.5 The TESOL Curriculum as Text

Browse a curriculum for TESOL from your context. This could be from any level of education (kindergarten, primary, secondary, university, etc.). 1. Does it refer to any other policies? 2. How flexible or prescriptive is it? 3. Does it enable teachers to enact their agency? 4. Is there room for schools to adapt the curriculum to meet contextual particularities and their students' needs and wants?

6.5 Social Justice

The tension emanating from ideologies may lead to inequality and inequity as not everyone may be guaranteed the same learning and social opportunities. The concept of social justice recognizes inequality and the need to dismantle injustice.

Social justice seeks to promote equality, diversity, inclusion and equitable access to resources and social participation (Okan, 2019). Lamb et al. (2019) propose that social justice as social inclusion seeks to guarantee individuals' right to participate effectively in all areas of human experience. Against these notions and following the influential works of Dewey (1916/1966), education is a powerful agent/tool of social change. The authors mentioned above agree that teachers are in a privileged position to engage in socially just practices for the equal co-creation of knowledge and experience, as they have a direct socio-political impact in the classroom. I will return to this aspect in Section 6.6.

Based on the views summarized above, we may understand social justice as a philosophy aimed at bringing about social change to empower civic activism and transform society (Banegas & Sanchez, 2024; Freire, 2000). This transformation-oriented stance aligns with a view that embraces education as a platform to 'dismantle[e] the power relations, social hierarchies and cultural hegemonies that currently underpin the canons, the assumed norms and values of inherited curricula and [set] up processes to reimagine more inclusive ways of participating in curriculum and pedagogic practices' (Luckett & Shay, 2020, p. 52). Hence, social justice in education has the power to address entrenched inequities through from-school-into-community activism via school-led projects (Ortaçtepe Hart, 2023). This philosophy is an invitation to reimagine ways of knowing and being, and therefore, even the concept of curriculum itself and dominant forms of schooling may be challenged.

Social justice in education can disrupt inequities based on what/who counts as knowledge and knower, gender and sexuality, ethnicity, religion, cultural practices, languages and non-conforming identities through the creation of empowering frames of action which have activism at its core (Freire, 2000; Goodwin & Proctor, 2019). To address culturally-constructed categories such social class, ethnicity, or gender and disrupt sites of oppression at their intersection, Tikly and Barrett's (2011) propose a set of three interlinked principles of social justice in education based on Fraser (2009): (1) inclusion (redistribution of resources, access to quality education), (2) relevance (recognition, meaningful learning outcomes for all learners) and (3) democracy (participation in curriculum development, advocacy, activism). These principles have the potential to guarantee equity and equality. What we may call activist social justice in education is key to disrupting spaces of oppression and privilege (Lamb et al. 2019; Rodríguez Mejía et al., 2019).

Scholars agree (e.g. Lamb et al., 2019; Porto, 2023a) that for activist social justice in education to become a transformative endeavour, it necessitates a nuanced understanding of agency (see Chapter 5, Sections 5.3–5.4) so that transformation is built on educational actors' agentic knowledge production. Studies (e.g. Caraballo et al., 2017; Porto, 2023a) have demonstrated the power that students and teachers agentically working on collaborative projects can have in schools and their communities.

With a focus on activism for social change, Ortaçtepe Hart (2023) unpacks social justice by stating that:

> Metaphorically speaking, social justice is a verb as much as a noun. As a noun, it refers to a set of individual, social and cultural values that include but are not limited to agency, advocacy, caring, democracy, fairness, equity, diversity, ethics, respect, dignity, recognition, inclusion and worth. As a verb, social justice is the transformation of these values into political, social, economic, cultural and environmental strategies and tactics that will challenge, chip away at and perhaps even eventually demolish existing heteropatriarchal, racist, and capitalist ideologies and hegemonic power relations (Bell, 2016).
>
> (p. 4)

As you can understand from the quote, social justice could be a powerful action-oriented perspective to be considered for the understanding, design, enactment and evaluation of a TESOL curriculum.

Let's take a quick look at the seams of social justice and TESOL. Authors such as Hall (2016) and Lamb et al. (2019) acknowledge such conceptualizations of social justice and agree that learning English as an additional language is no longer a luxury; it is a right through which speakers access a wider range of intercultural practices. However, authors still have reservations about the perpetuation of linguistic imperialism (Mahboob, 2020). Hall (2016) contends that in the broader field of L2 education, social justice talk is stronger than social justice practice. Differently put, language scholars and educators may talk a lot about social justice, but they may fail to enact social justice in their own teaching and research. Chang (2018) underlines that while social justice in second language learning has been influenced by movements led by Indigenous peoples, women, LGBTQ+ groups, working and immigrant families and other marginalized populations, TESOL is far

<table>
<tr><td>Vignette 6.3</td><td>

Social Justice in the South Korean TESOL Curriculum, by Daye Kim

</td></tr>
</table>

In 2022, a revised national curriculum was announced in South Korea. The curriculum change was initiated by the Ministry of Education (MoE) of South Korea with a group of experts. From a social justice perspective, the strengths and weaknesses of the curriculum as text, especially with regards to the section of English Education (i.e. TESOL), can be analysed in terms of the development process, its goal and content.

In terms of the development process, the curriculum included different stakeholders' voices, fostering *participation and democracy*. Throughout 2022, in which the curriculum was announced, feedback from in-service teachers and educational experts was collected through conferences. Through an online platform called Educhannel (educhannel.edunet.net) feedback from learners, parents and other stakeholders was also collected. However, *the development of the curriculum was mainly top-down, and therefore stakeholders' voices were marginal*.

In relation to goals and content, the curriculum emphasizes its educational purpose of implementing ecological *transformative education*. It refers to education pursuing overall change in individuals' behaviour and thought for sustainable ecology and the coexistence of human beings and nature as a reaction to the climate crisis. This curriculum aim is aligned with the Berlin Declaration on Education for Sustainable Development, which highlights the need to embed ESD (Education for Sustainable Development) as a foundation of education systems. Therefore, in the section of English Education of the revised South Korean curriculum, one of the six sub-goals of English education involves community competence as English is promoted as an important tool for *active contribution to global and social issues*.

As discussed above, one of the goals of English as a school subject is to foster community competence, aspiring to *raise learners' cooperative attitude within their community and awareness of social issues including global issues*. However, the curriculum *lacks general or specific guidance on discrimination and inequality*. The second principle of SDGs (Sustainable Development Goals), Leaving No One Behind, highlights the need to reach out to individuals who are victims of discrimination or inequal opportunities because of their social/financial status, gender, or any other characteristics. Considering 'SDG in the Republic of Korea: Progress Report 2024' in which the need of fine-tuned policy for gender equality in employment and gender wage gap was revealed, it is necessary that, since the official curriculum does not, the enacted curriculum promotes the discussion on social issues of gender equality and discrimination, which may lead learners to perceive English as an important tool to engage in social and global issues.

Activity 6.6 Visualizing Social Justice

Based on the key notions around social justice included in this section, make a collage that represents your understanding and what social justice means to you.

You can use a piece of paper, photos or a device to create your collage. If you are happy, you can share it with other folks by posting it on TESOLland (Figure 6.1).

Figure 6.1 QR code access to TESOLand

---

from being diverse, inclusive and empowering. In this regard, second language learning pedagogies are being interpellated to engage in recognition, collaboration, global citizenship and solidarity with the diverse realities that learners inhabit. Then, it is necessary that educators and learners assume an active role in practising social justice to change unjust circumstances. For example, Mortenson (2021) warns that when White TESOL instructors engage with social justice as content, they cannot remain neutral; they need to take a stance to dismantle inequity, otherwise, they run the risk of perpetuating racism. In a study carried out with Iranian teachers of English, Karimpour et al. (2025) showed that teachers may use their own lived histories to foster criticality and advocacy among their students. These two examples illustrate the power that teachers have. In this regard, Lamb et al. (2019) call for bottom-up initiatives or school-university collaborative projects that address social justice in language education. According to these authors, a language pedagogy for social justice can be based on learners, inquiry and agency, and be best channelled through collaborative action research, as this form of inquiry shares the same goals sought through social justice.

Vignette 6.3 shows how social justice may appear in a TESOL curriculum. I have highlighted key words (in italics) which may remind you of some of the fundamental principles underpinning social practice. I have also highlighted phrases which also show problems at the level of actualizing social justice.

6.6 Curricular Justice

You may be wondering how we can infuse social justice into the TESOL curriculum. This would be possible via the notion of curricular justice, which could be defined as the development of a counter-hegemonic curriculum that recognizes systemic injustices and guarantees equitable access to the oppressed and marginalized. I am sure that this definition will remind you of the United Nations Sustainable Development Goal 4 (inclusive and equitable quality education), which we discussed at the start of Chapter 4.

In their conceptual piece on understanding curricular justice and democratic schooling, Mills et al. (2022) state that through curricular justice, educational systems need to guarantee that the curriculum:

- Facilitates the access of young people from less advantaged backgrounds to diverse and meaningful learning experiences to support further and equitable opportunities in adulthood.

- Offers opportunities for specialized knowledge and differentiated learning while guaranteeing access to all forms of knowledge.

- Recognizes differences (cultural justice) and builds on the many funds of knowledge students bring to the classroom.

- Is concerned with representation so that teachers, students and the community have a say in curriculum development and evaluation.

As you may have noticed already, curricular justice is closely interlinked with the learner-centred curriculum and teacher/learner agency as representation, democracy and inclusion are its vital drives.

Before we move further, let me pause and concentrate on the second bullet point. Mills et al. (2022) remind us that a curriculum could be extremely hierarchical and that subjects such as maths or science are sometimes prioritized over, for example, the arts or languages. With this argument in mind, I would like you to complete Activity 6.7 to help you think about the role of TESOL or additional language learning in general in your own context.

Activity 6.7 The Space/Place of TESOL in a Curriculum

Read the following quote and answer the questions below:

The curriculum is also hierarchically organized with some forms of knowledge valued over others. For example, STEM subjects in high school are often favoured over the humanities and social science ones. As such, there have been multiple attempts to address the underrepresentation of girls in STEM, yet few campaigns to address the underrepresentation of boys in the humanities. There are also vigorous debates about the types of knowledge to which all students should have access. The subsequent understandings created in respect of the focus and purposes of education clearly have social justice implications. (Mills et al., 2022, p. 349)

1. From what you know about formal education in your context, is there a hierarchical organization? 2. Are some subjects more important than others? 3. What place (if any) does learning English or other languages have in the curriculum? 4. What resources are focused on language teaching and learning?

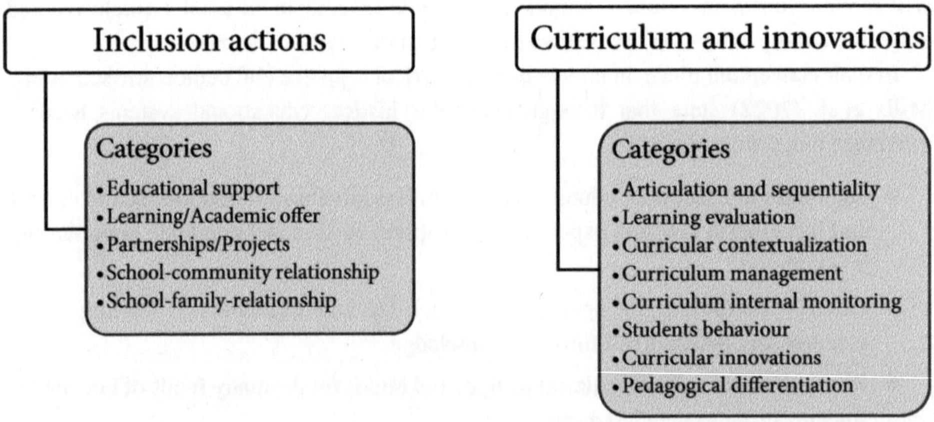

Figure 6.2 Areas of curricular justice

Inclusion actions

Categories
- Educational support
- Learning/Academic offer
- Partnerships/Projects
- School-community relationship
- School-family-relationship

Curriculum and innovations

Categories
- Articulation and sequentiality
- Learning evaluation
- Curricular contextualization
- Curriculum management
- Curriculum internal monitoring
- Students behaviour
- Curricular innovations
- Pedagogical differentiation

According to Sampaio and Leite (2017), for social justice to be a reality, a curriculum needs to be socially just (i.e. curricular justice) by considering equity and inclusion in two connected areas (Figure 6.2).

As Figure 6.2 shows, curricular justice should penetrate all dimensions of the curriculum, not only in its design but primarily in its enactment and evaluation to guarantee that social justice is not just empty rhetoric. In Vignette 6.4, you will find an example of curriculum reform from a social justice perspective. Once you read it, you can complete Activity 6.8 (see p.133).

Now, how can we make the imperative for curricular justice more tangible? Ortaçtepe Hart (2023, p. 53) has put forward four strategies which can help situate social justice at the centre of the TESOL curriculum. Table 6.1 includes such strategies and hints on how to put them into practice.

| Vignette 6.4 | **The New Mexican School: Expectations and Implementation, by Araceli Salas** |

Mexico has a structured educational system since the Ministry of Education (Secretariat of Public Education, SEP) was established in 1921. The system is divided into three stages: (a) basic education, (a) middle high school and (c) higher education. The system considers both, public and private institutions. However, the New Mexican School (NMS) aims to provide free public education to all Mexicans under the age of 23 years at least; as a social right of all Mexican citizens.

In 2019, the Mexican government reformed the previous programmes and established the NMS, with the main purpose and commitment for quality and equity in Mexican education (SEP, 2019). A central element in the NMS is that it integrates all communities prioritizing disadvantaged populations and indigenous communities. For the NMS, the concept of community means to offer the same learning opportunities and excellence in learning for all Mexican citizens. According to the NMS, the learning process should be inclusive, equitable, pluricultural (given the multiculturality of the country) and collaborative. This perspective involves the appreciation and learning of other languages, including English. English is seen as a tool and a facilitator of knowledge that will help students achieve excellence as global learners.

Some of the NMS key principles are: (a) development of a national identity, (b) citizen responsibility and respect for human values, (c) participation in the transformation of society, and (d) respect for human dignity. Following these principles, the NMS views education from humanism considering all aspects of human life: social, economic, scientific, technological and cultural. This perspective may enhance the integral development of students in a fair and free society. Regarding the teaching of English, according to the NMS, the new programme will include topics related to the aspects mentioned, however, teachers are still working with the materials created for the previous program, especially in basic education. Teachers in higher levels can adapt materials to meet the interests and needs of their students. In general, the NMS and the English teachers still have a long way to successfully implement it in terms of materials, training, language certifications and lack of English teachers all over the country.

Finally, the NMS has the objective to contribute to the well-being of teachers and students aligning to the UNESCO SDGs and other intergovernmental organizations. According to the NMS, we all take part in a community of human beings, and we should recognize, respect and coexist with each other across cultures and languages. The implementation of the NMS has become a challenge for all levels of the system to balance the individual and common goals. In my case, for example, the biggest challenge is to prepare teachers who can embody and balance the individual and common goals and objectives of the NMS during the transition and teach English in the different levels of the system. I value the idea of equity and excellence in education; however, the results of the NMS implementation will take time, and we need to engage in its evaluation.

Activity 6.8 Curricular Justice in the Mexican Curriculum

Read Vignette 6.4 and make a list of all the words/terms that seem to show the Mexican government's interest in curricular justice. Are there any key terms discussed so far in the chapter/book you would associate with this vignette?

Table 6.1

Ortaçtepe Hart's Strategies for Social Justice in Language Teaching with Examples

	Strategy	Example
1	Centralizing social justice within lesson planning	A teacher uses discrimination due to social class as a topic to frame a lesson on expressing opinions in English.
2	Cultivating activism for social change	A teacher and their students design a project through which they develop a multilingual campaign to stop bullying at their school and the community.
3	Deconstructing language education materials	A group of teachers and their students create a set of activities aimed at (1) identifying who has been erased from the TESOL coursebooks they use, and (2) collaborating creating materials in which marginalized people and their funds of knowledge are featured. These aims entail having critical discussion of representation and marginalization.
4	Reconstructing materials to develop learners' critical literacy	

To bring this section to a close, let me share with you a project that, in a way, has responded to the strategies condensed in Table 6.1. In 2022-2023, I led a project aimed at mobilizing social justice in the enacted TESOL curriculum. Activities 6.9 and 6.10 will allow you to recap some of the key concepts discussed so far and delve into the teachers' and student-teachers' understanding and practice of social justice English language teaching.

Activity 6.9 Recapping Key Concepts

Use Figure 6.3 to access Banegas et al. (2025). Read the introduction and conceptual background sections. Create a concept map that summarizes the main issues under discussion. You can then enrich the concept map with concepts and references included in this chapter so far.

Figure 6.3 QR code access to Banegas et al. (2025)

Activity 6.10 On Banegas et al. (2025) and Curricular Justice

Continue reading Banegas et al. (2025), but this time read the methodology and findings sections. Make a list of all the very practical things that the teachers did in order to imbue social justice in the enacted TESOL/ELT curriculum. Also, think about how doable these actions would be in your context.

6.7 Bringing It All Together

Activity 6.11

Mambu (2022) describes how a group of TESOL student-teachers learnt about critical pedagogy in an attempt to make the TESOL curriculum more inclusive and socially just. The experience entailed the student-teachers' collaborative work on needs analysis, syllabus design, materials development and lesson planning to raise awareness of inequalities towards English language learners. If you were a teacher educator working at a TESOL teacher education programme, what changes would you introduce so that future teachers are prepared to develop and implement a TESOL curriculum based on curricular justice?

Activity 6.12

In her practice-oriented article, Blume (2021) proposes an inclusive TESOL curriculum through online games which question heteronormativity (i.e. heterosexuality as the norm in society) and include LGBTQ+ characters. In your view, in what ways does this proposal respond to curricular justice?

Activity 6.13

Mortenson (2022) describes a case study in which a teacher integrated social justice-oriented content into English for Academic Purposes (EAP) instruction. The teacher used teaching materials that addressed racial inequities in the US with the aim of dismantling oppression and creating frames of action among the students. In your view, in what ways does this practice respond to curricular justice? Would teachers and students in your context welcome a similar proposal?

Activity 6.14

The following excerpt comes from an article in which López-Gopar and Pérez Nava (2025) describe different TESOL lessons observed at a public primary school in Mexico. As you read the excerpt, think about which of Tikly and Barrett's (2011) principles mentioned in Section 6.5 of this chapter are illustrated.

During oral presentation rehearsals, a lot of the negotiation occurred in Spanish, which shows how the second author acted out her agency (as previously discussed) in promoting decolonizing pedagogies that make room for the students' full linguistic repertoire. Furthermore, the second author accommodated not only the students' first language but also their life realities. Deeply caring about and fully knowing her students, she allowed the students to present 'different' types of families during their oral presentations, as the typical family comprised of 'mom, dad, brother and sister' was the exception in her class.

(p. 562)

Activity 6.15

YouTube hosts a channel called Social Justice in ELT. Use Figure 6.4 to access the list of videos. Give them a quick browse, make a list of your *top 5* and explain why you think they can help embed social justice in TESOL.

Figure 6.4 QR code access to Social Justice in ELT on YouTube

Activity 6.16

Browse a curriculum for TESOL from your context. This could be from any level of education (kindergarten, primary, secondary, university, etc.). Is there anything in it that may indicate that social justice has a place in its theoretical and practice-oriented underpinnings?

Activity 6.17

Vignette 6.5 comes from a master's student's essay in which she analysed the goals found in a curriculum from the perspective of social justice. This was a university TESOL curriculum for four-year English Teaching major students in a Chinese university in Guangdong (China) in 2019. What follows is only the analysis section of the essay. Based on the notions included in this chapter, (a) in what ways does the vignette illustrate them? (b) To what extent do you agree with the analysis included in the vignette? Please, be fair 😊 as you are only reading one part of the whole essay. If you are a user of Chinese, you can check the original curriculum under analysis by following the relevant reference.

<table><tr><td>Vignette
6.5</td><td>

Analysis of Curriculum Goals from a Social Justice Perspective, by Yoyo Jiang

</td></tr></table>

The strengths and weaknesses of the goals in this curriculum will be analysed from the perspective of social justice following the principles of inclusion, relevance, and democracy (Tikly & Barrett, 2011), for it can evaluate the goals better from different levels by connecting the issues which are social class, race and ethnicity in Ortaçtepe's paper (2023). As taken from College of International Studies (2019), the goals of this curriculum are:

Professional aspects: Through four years of specialised study and educational practice, English (normal) majors not only excel at cross-cultural communication and critical thinking, but also have sufficient education and teaching knowledge and skills, qualifying as English teachers in primary and secondary schools, class head teachers and school education management personnel. Both the employment rate and the rate of graduates opting for a teaching career in 2019 reached 96.25 per cent. With the growing demand for teachers, thanks to the rapid development of the education industry in Shenzhen in recent years, more than 88 per cent of English (normal) graduates are employed in Shenzhen, and more than 95 per cent are employed in the broader Pearl River Delta. In addition, a large proportion of graduates have the opportunity to study in world-renowned universities at home and abroad, including Harvard University, University College London and the University of Edinburgh.

First and foremost, to make the analysis more logical and clearer, the goals will first be analysed into learning aims, objectives as well as outcomes. Firstly, the learning aims are 'English (normal) majors not only excel at cross-cultural communication and critical thinking, but also have sufficient education and teaching knowledge and skills, qualifying as English teachers in primary and secondary schools, class head teachers and school education management personnel'. It provides a general teaching intention and gives learners reasons for choosing this programme (Macalister & Nation, 2020). For example, if learners want to be a secondary school teacher, they should choose this programme. Secondly, the learning objectives are 'Through four years of specialized study and educational practice', for it indicates that teachers should provide not only knowledge but practice for students to connect theory with practice to achieve the aims. However, as learning objectives should be in more details (Macalister & Nation, 2020), it would be more appropriate if the objectives have more information. The rest of the paragraph is the learning outcomes, for it illustrates if learners succeed the programme, what they will achieve (Macalister & Nation, 2020).

Strengths of the curriculum

The curriculum has strengths from the perspective of social justice. In the part of the aims, it emphasizes students' cross-cultural communication competence which pays attention to the meaning-making processes in different and diverse cultures and is influenced by students' values and worldviews (Banegas et al., 2021). It's a step to cultivate learners' ability to shift from individual culture perspective to societal/institutional perspective which enables them to challenge the existing cultural hierarchies and break the individual prejudice by language education and language use (Ortaçtepe, 2023). Therefore, focusing on this competence in the curriculum can show that it tries to arise the social justice awareness among learners.

Weaknesses of the curriculum

However, there are several weaknesses of this curriculum which are mainly from learning outcomes. Firstly, the goals fail to satisfy learners from other small cities in Guangdong which is against the principle of inclusion and relevance (Tikly & Barrett, 2011). Guangdong is a province of China which not only includes Pearl River Delta cities such as Shenzhen or Guangzhou but small cities such as Qingyuan or Shantou which doesn't belong to Pearl River Delta. However, the learning outcomes in this curriculum mainly focuses on learner's achievement in Shenzhen. In fact, Shenzhen not only is the city where the university locates and China's first special economic zone but also is a home to learning education hub and has a higher education sector in China which developed rapidly over the last four decades (Fang & Liu, 2023). It demonstrates its position in education industry in China. The goal gives no details about the career situations of other area which marginalizes the group of learners who are not from Shenzhen and makes Shenzhen learners elite (Mills et al., 2022), for it is not relevant to every learner in this context and confirms the superior position of Shenzhen. For example, some students may want to work in small places rather than in Pearl River Delta area or even back to their hometown which is not in Guangdong province. Another example is that, under the influence of this curriculum, teachers mainly provided skills and cases which are suitable for applying for teacher jobs in Shenzhen rather than others which truly marginalized learners who want to be teachers in other cities. In this case, it causes curricular injustice by making marginalized learners' opportunities to learn from curriculum lesser than learners with privileged backgrounds (Mills et al., 2022). In addition, it also treats this language education as a commodity because it provides learners a higher status such as work in Shenzhen to give the feeling of satisfaction from the issue of social class (Ortaçtepe, 2023).

Secondly, the goals reveal the colonization of English countries. At the end of the goals, it includes prestige western universities such as University of Edinburgh and neglects indigenous universities which makes learners feel their local university culture in TESOL area is devalued and marginalizes the local one (Poudel et al., 2022). It indicates that only the western universities own the named language: English and have power to analyse TESOL concept which minoritizes the non-western universities (Macedo, 2019) especially local universities which can also make progress in TESOL area. For instance, teachers will mainly exposed to relevant theory comes from western world which makes the high position of whiteness in TESOL. It is against the principle of democracy because it denies the local participation in the educational outcomes decision and only focuses on institutional participation which owns power (Tikly & Barrett, 2011).

Thirdly, this curriculum fails to confirm other careers in TESOL area. It is true that learners from this programme can be teachers, class head teachers or management personnel in school. However, there are some other jobs related to TESOL area such as business English teachers, teaching materials designers. It erases the different jobs and chances which learners can obtain and remove the 'recognition' in the central part (Mills et al., 2022) of the curriculum which causes curricular injustice.

6.8 Further Reading

If you wish to read about nativespeakerism in TESOL, you can direct yourself to these sources:

Kiczkowiak, M., & Lowe, R. J. (2024). Native-speakerism in English language teaching: 'Native speakers' more likely to be invited as conference plenary speakers. *Journal of Multilingual and Multicultural Development, 45*(5), 1408–1423. https://doi.org/10.1080/01434632.2021.1974464

López-Gopar, M. E., & Nava, D. I. P. (2025). One morning at a public elementary school in Mexico: A decolonial/critical perspective of ELT. *TESOL Quarterly, 59*(1), 552–564. https://doi.org/10.1002/tesq.3264

Mahboob, A. (Ed.). (2010). *The NNEST lens: Non native English speakers in TESOL*. Cambridge Scholars Publishing.

Rose, H., Syrbe, M., Montakantiwong, A., & Funada, N. (2020). *Global TESOL for the 21st century teaching English in a changing world*. Multilingual Matters.

Chapter 7
What Does Decolonizing the TESOL Curriculum Mean?

Summary

The aim of this chapter is to continue the conversation initiated in Chapter 5
(on curriculum change) and Chapter 6 (on social justice), particularly by arguing that
curriculum change may entail decolonizing the curriculum. The chapter problematizes
(de)colonization, and associates it with other key concepts: global citizenship,
culture and interculturality, spatiality and plurilingualism. Through these concepts,
the chapter raises awareness of broader and deeper issues entrenched in TESOL
curriculum development. With this aim, the notion of Epistemologies of the South is
employed as a perspective that reinforces the discussion in previous chapters about
social justice, context and agency.

7.1 Warm-Up

To talk about decolonization, we may need to understand and acknowledge colonialism
in history and neo-colonialism spreading in more subtle ways. In a nutshell, colonialism
is a socio-political system through which one dominant group (an empire) subjugates and
exploits another group of people and their resources. As an Argentinian citizen, I am aware
of the colonial past of my country under Spain, as well as the ways in which other powers,
such as the UK or the United States, have exercised their influence for their benefit, and at
the expense of ours. I am also aware that this very same book, despite having sections on
social justice, decolonization and intersectionality, and my own thinking around curriculum
development, might as well be colonial.

In the realm of education, teaching and learning in some contexts have been monopolized
by certain ideologies, ontologies (study of the nature of being), and epistemologies (i.e.
study of the ways in which we understand and construct knowledge). For example, most
global coursebooks in TESOL are authored by British/American authors and published
by companies with their headquarters in the UK or the United States. The way we teach

TESOL students how to write an essay is often dominated by certain views of what counts as critical thinking and argumentation and how an *effective* essay should be organized. These simple examples illustrate that colonialism has been a powerful and complex system through which hegemonic ideologies and discourses are imposed. With this very crude summary, I would like you to complete Activity 7.1.

As you may suspect, decolonization seeks to interrupt (re)colonization by raising awareness and mobilizing thinking and activity so that those groups of people who have been systemically dominated can reclaim their identity, their rights, their culture, their ways of knowing/being/feeling, their land, their resources, etc. Colonization or colonialism is not historical. It is a practice of control by one people or power over other people or areas. When we talk about recolonization, we may be talking about globalization, which could be viewed as an excuse to advance/perpetuate certain hegemonic ideologies across the globe. In formal education, this may also refer to the concept of one language – one nation, or language-in-education policies which prioritize certain languages (English!) to be taught. At this point, it is worth highlighting that (re)colonization should not just be blamed on external forces. There are almost always internal interests; think about the dominant classes in your own context and how they may quickly accept a foreign master so that they can safeguard their own interests and privileges.

Against this background, why do we hear about decolonizing the curriculum in certain contexts? This is because decolonized education is about creating an inclusive sense of being, belonging and becoming. It is imperative that education is critical, inclusive and empowering by enabling the problematization of power structures and boundaries. For example, UK universities are investing time and resources to decolonize the curriculum. Vignette 7.1 reproduces Keele University's (no date) manifesto for decolonizing the curriculum.

Activity 7.1 Examples of Colonialism in Your Context

1. Make a list of examples of colonialism in the history of your country:

2. Make a list of examples of colonialism in contemporary everyday life:

3. Make a list of examples of colonialism in the teaching and learning of English in your country:

You will return to your answers later in the chapter.

<table>
<tr><td>Vignette
7.1</td><td>

Keele's Manifesto for Decolonizing the Curriculum

</td></tr>
</table>

Decolonization involves identifying colonial systems, structures and relationships, and working to challenge those systems. It is not 'integration' or simply the token inclusion of the intellectual achievements of non-white cultures. Rather, it involves a paradigm shift from a culture of exclusion and denial to the making of space for other political philosophies and knowledge systems. It's a culture shift to think more widely about why common knowledge is what it is, and in so doing, adjusting cultural perceptions and power relations in real and significant ways.

What would it mean to decolonize the University curriculum?

Decolonizing the curriculum means, first of all, acknowledging that knowledge is not owned by anyone. It is a cumulative and shared resource that is available to all. Knowledge (and culture) is collectively produced and human beings of all races, ethnicities, classes, genders, sexual orientations, and disabilities have as much right as elite white men to understand what our roles and contributions have been in shaping intellectual achievements and shifting culture and progress.

Decolonizing the curriculum is to recognize that knowledge is inevitably marked by power relations. Our universities exist in a global economy of knowledge, with a definite hegemonic centre, reflecting hierarchies of race, class and gender. At the top of this hierarchy sit the knowledge institutions of the Global North, databanks and research centres supported by the wealth of European and North American powers. This hegemonic position is not just a matter of the wealth of the Global North. Our world is still shaped by a long colonial history in which white upper class men are at the top of social hierarchy, most disciplines give disproportionate significance to the experiences, histories and achievements of this one group.

Decolonizing is about rethinking, reframing and reconstructing the current curriculum in order to make it better, and more inclusive. It is about expanding our notions of good literature so it doesn't always elevate one voice, one experience, and one way of being in the world. It is about considering how different frameworks, traditions and knowledge projects can inform each other, how multiple voices can be heard, and how new perspectives emerge from mutual learning.

Decolonizing is not just about bringing in minority ethnic writers and texts, but also how we read 'traditional mainstream' texts. Decolonizing is far more nuanced than just replacing authors, and it is more than just the topics covered in a course. It concerns not only what is taught and how it is critiqued, but how it is taught, which gives rise to an understanding of decolonization that addresses how academic literacies are experienced.

Decolonizing means identifying ways in which the university structurally reproduces colonial hierarchies; confronting, challenging and rejecting the status quo; and reimagining them and putting alternatives into practice for the benefit of our academic integrity and our social viability.

Decolonizing the curriculum means creating spaces and resources for a dialogue among all members of the university on how to imagine and envision all cultures and knowledge systems in the curriculum, and with respect to what is being taught and how it frames the world.

Decolonization is not a project over which one group can claim sole custodianship. Non-white and white academics and students are in this together. This will involve conscious, deliberate, non-hypocritical and diligent interest by both non-white and white members of the university in all knowledge systems, cultures, peoples and languages.

Decolonizing requires sustained collaboration, discussion and experimentation among groups of teachers and students, who themselves have the power to make things happen on the ground and think about what might be done differently. The change will take different forms in different universities and disciplines. There is no one-size-fits-all solution.

Decolonizing is thinking about how students experience the university differently. Race, gender, disability and class all demonstrably impact student attainment and experiences of exclusion from the university environment. These are linked to the university's historic identity and mission, as well as wider structural inequalities within society.

Decolonizing requires the courage to admit that any knowledge could and should be open to challenge and question; regardless of its original power relations. This is the only way to avoid the mere 'displacement' of one curriculum colonizer by another.

Decolonizing is about how we can ensure a system where all those who engage with the university to make their living, or to study, can do so under conditions of dignity, respect and security.

Activity 7.2 On Decolonizing the Curriculum

Based on Vignette 7.1, use any type of graphic organizer to help you visualize what decolonizing the curriculum means to you.

You will return to this graphic organizer later in the chapter.

7.2 Understanding Decolonization

In Section 7.1, we briefly mentioned the concepts of (re)colonization and decolonization. But what do they mean to language as social practice, what we may call languaging, and languages in education? Languaging, in this book, is conceptualized as a transformative practice that enables students and teachers to engage critically with dominant narratives and systemic inequities. Drawing on Halliday's (2016) conceptualization of the term, languaging can be viewed as a dynamic, socially embedded process that not only facilitates communication but also constructs and transforms knowledge and experience. Thus, languaging can be positioned as both a means of organizing thoughts and reflecting critically on social issues and a collaborative practice that fosters dialogue and mutual understanding within specific cultural and social contexts. In this landscape, languages, language (in) education and TESOL can serve as influential tools for emancipation.

When it comes to discussing what decolonizing the TESOL curriculum involves, several authors have proposed different pathways to unsettle hegemonic views of English (among other named languages) and how English could be taught. I provide a few snapshots in the following paragraphs.

In his volume about social justice, decoloniality and southern epistemologies around TESOL in Brazil, Tavares (2023) summarizes the long history of Global North knowledges in TESOL being considered the norm, which has resulted in Global South knowledges

---

Activity 7.3 Understanding Key Terms

To answer the question posed at the beginning of Section 7.2, use Figure 7.1 to access an article by Poudel et al. (2022).

Figure 7.1 QR code access to Poudel et al. (2022)

1. Now that you have accessed the article, please read the first two sections, and pay particular attention to the second as the authors discuss the concepts of colonization and decolonization in relation to language education.
2. With this knowledge, return to your answers to Activity 7.1 and reflect on any connections you see between your examples and the authors' understanding of (de)colonization.
3. Based on the knowledge gained from the two sections from Poudel et al. (2022), return to your concept map and produce an improved version that captures your understanding of what all these notions mean in relation to decolonizing the curriculum.

being othered, i.e. being treated as different, lower in status, not part of a group. However, he emphasizes that decolonizing TESOL

> does not equate to merely 'adding some perspectives from the South, or including various Southern people who are often forgotten, or incorporating geographical areas or topics occluded from analysis in Global Northern applied linguistics' (Pennycook & Makoni, 2019, p. 1). Or in the words of Lynn Mario Menezes Souza, it is not simply about bringing Southern knowledges to the table, but rather, questioning 'who owns the table?,' along with 'who does the inviting to the table?' and 'who is considered eligible to be invited?' (Menezes de Souza, 2022).
>
> (p. 2)

From that starting point, the author states:

> decolonising TESOL from a Southern perspective requires an openness to 'new' ontologies by the Global North that can hardly be considered so for Southern scholars. Decolonisation is about 'a deconstruction of how Applied Linguistics from the Global North has silenced other knowledges and many times stopped Applied Linguistics from realizing its own shortcomings' (Jordão et al., 2020, p. 841). The decolonial option is necessary for the ontologies, epistemologies, and practices of the Global South to be recognised in their own right and not in comparison to Western thought from the Global North by scholars from the North and the South alike.
>
> (Tavares, 2023, p. 2)

Tavares's (2023) words unequivocally not only seek to shake the dominant knowledges informing TESOL but also warn that decolonizing the TESOL curriculum does not mean adding a few tokenistic elements here and there. His words are an invitation to problematize and re-imagine how we understand and construct knowledges in the field. This problematization should not only occur at a curriculum level. For decolonization to be possible and sustainable, four levels or stages (Figure 7.2) may be necessary (which you could link to the ecological subsystems discussed across the chapters in this book).

The inverted pyramid (Figure 7.2) seeks to illustrate that we need to start with ourselves, and from that individual starting point, we can move into collective systems. However, you

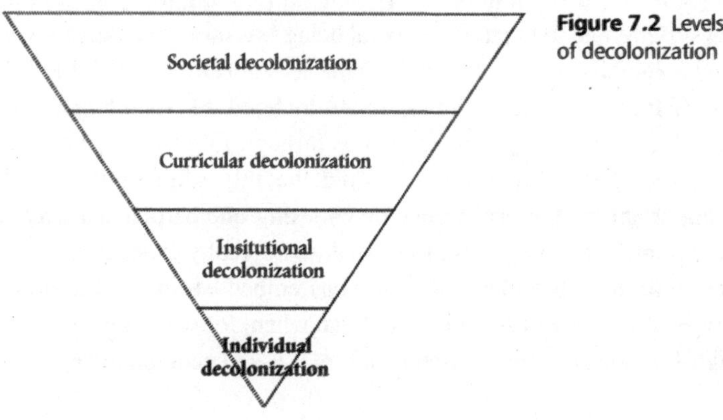

Figure 7.2 Levels of decolonization

can approach the levels by having the pyramid flipped so that individual decolonization is understood as trickling down the meso and macrosystems; or you can also have it as the basis of the pyramid.

The issues raised above may be seen as overwhelming but necessary. Where do we start, then, with decolonizing the TESOL curriculum? Let's take a look at an example. Based on a collaborative autoethnography about their attempts to decolonize the TESOL curriculum in their practices in Canada, Wilbur et al. (2024) conclude that the first step for TESOL stakeholders (including curriculum developers and teachers) is to engage in self-reflection, re-imagining current practices not just in the teachers' microsystem but also beyond and the field, and active involvement through relational approaches which prioritize harnessing teaching and learning on students' lives, being supported in powerful communities of practice. If we translate this recommendation to TESOL curriculum development, self-reflection about language, English, and the teaching of English may need to be embedded in the environment analysis stage (see Chapter 1: Section 1.4), as this stage should include an ecological understanding of stakeholders' beliefs.

Wilbur et al.'s (2024) suggestion about starting with self-reflection may make you think of the level of individual decolonization as well as the concept of *conscientização* (in Portuguese, which could be translated as conscientization). Drawing on Paulo Freire's work, Cruz (2013) defines the term as 'the active process through which a critical understanding of the social-political-economic circumstances is gained that enables one to actively change oppressive circumstances' (p. 173). The author underlines that this is not merely a process of raising awareness. It involves reflection and action, which can be subsumed under the notion of praxis.

Once reflection has been employed to question our own assumptions as educators, actions and decisions are needed to turn those reflections into change, i.e. praxis. In her chapter on decolonizing languages and the construction of language education programmes, Garcia (2019) proposes that

> taking up translanguaging, an epistemology that takes the point of view that language is what speakers do, rather than what nation-states legitimate and schools teach, could transform the present reality of language and education.

> (p. 166)

If we narrow the lens and zoom in on the TESOL curriculum, translanguaging could lead to educational systems and the sector in general being less obsessed with nativespeakerism, monolithic and colonialist notions of what 'counts as' American/British English, Received Pronunciation (RP), and instead, being more inclined to including a more diverse representation of users who negotiate meanings through English and other languages. In my experience, some TESOL educators may think that this is fine for illustrative purposes, but that it is important to show coherence by choosing one particular *variety* of English; but as we know, something like British English does not really exist, as there are variations across Great Britain due to a plethora of reasons embedded in the complex ecology of cultural practices. It is also worth pointing out that when, for whatever reason, one variety/dialect of English is selected, more often than not, it is a hegemonic type.

In the case of the TESOL curriculum, translanguaging both as everyday practice (Mazzaferro, 2018) and as a decolonizing epistemology and pedagogy (Vaish, 2020) can inform all elements of the curriculum. In the following bullet points, I include examples that I imagine as part of a TESOL curriculum in the context of state secondary schools.

- Goals: 'To enable students develop their understanding of language(s) based on their own experience and utilize their full linguistic repertoire to construct their use of English'.

- Principles: 'In this curriculum, pedagogical translanguaging informs the teaching approaches to be considered by the teachers. The curriculum prioritizes culturally-sustaining, relational approaches which are negotiated between the teacher and their students.'

- Content: 'Pronunciation from diverse speakers', 'Comprehension and production skills development through translingual practices'.

- Materials: 'Student-produced videos, podcasts, and writing pieces from regional/multilingual users of English'.

- Activities: 'Compare and contrast meanings and appropriacy across languages, users, and contexts'.

- Assessment: 'Students will develop assessment rubrics which recognize their full linguistic repertoire as part of their identities and their ways of knowing.'

In relation to decolonizing the curriculum, Baker et al.'s (2025) study on Global English and TESOL provides a helpful summary of advances and critical conversations in the field:

> [C]ore features of 'decolonial' perspectives include de-centering the NES [native English speaker] and essentialist Anglophone norms, challenging the hierarchization of languages and modes of interaction, and valuing students' communicative resources, locally relevant knowledge and pedagogies, and addressing power imbalances and unequal opportunities in education and language use. Such approaches recognize the agency that multilingual and multicultural users have in adapting English and other semiotic resources to their communicative needs. The aim is, therefore, to provide a potentially more empowering approach to English and TESOL for both students and teachers in which both their use of English and other languages/resources [what we may link to translanguaging] are valued and their role in shaping English acknowledged. Yet, the extent to which these approaches are 'empowering' students to simply participate more fully in neoliberal processes of globalization or enabling them to challenge colonialism and neoliberalism is debatable (Kubota & Takeda, 2021; O'Regan, 2021; Sayer, 2015; Tupas, 2019).
>
> (p. 285)

The issues raised in Baker et al.'s (2025) quote may resonate with different contexts. For example, Vignette 7.2 offers examples of how colonization is perpetuated (e.g. 'Western cultural norms and narratives dominate the materials') as well as how decolonization can be enacted (e.g. 'indigenous folklore and Chinese idioms into English lessons').

The quote from Baker et al. (2025) above and Vignette 7.2 just shared encapsulate some powerful messages that, I believe, can inform the overall philosophy, goals and principles of the TESOL curriculum. What is important to remember is that a TESOL curriculum could adopt a Global Englishes perspective by featuring different Englishes and by promoting their recognition and acceptance. Teachers may need to stress to their students that by fully acknowledging their existence, they are also becoming aware of ownership, i.e. of the people who use those Englishes. While it can be contended that nobody needs our acceptance to exist and use any language they wish, the TESOL curriculum cannot be an instrument that perpetuates erasure and systemic discrimination.

Vignette 7.2

Decolonization in a TESOL Curriculum from Taiwan, by Chia Sheng (Leo) Huang

The TESOL curriculum in Taiwan has long been shaped by a mixture of local educational policies and the influence of Western pedagogical frameworks. English is a mandatory subject from elementary school through senior high school, and the curriculum mainly emphasizes grammar, vocabulary, and reading comprehension, often tailored to standardized testing requirements such as the Comprehensive Assessment Programme for Junior High School Students or the General Scholastic Ability Test. These assessments tend to prioritize rote memorization and accuracy, leaving limited room for communicative competence or cultural diversity. Also, in December 2018, the president of Taiwan announced that Mandarin-only policy would be replaced by a policy aiming to turn Taiwan into a bilingual country in 2030 (Ferrer, 2021).

The TESOL curriculum reflects the colonial legacy embedded in English language teaching (ELT). Western cultural norms and narratives dominate the materials, sidelining local or non-Western perspectives. Textbooks are frequently based on foreign-authored content, which often reinforces Eurocentric ideals of modernity and progress. Teachers, under pressure to prepare students for examinations, may accidentally perpetuate these biases by focusing on content that aligns with these external benchmarks.

As a novice TESOL teacher, I believe that decolonization in this context involves rethinking the TESOL curriculum to prioritize local relevance. For instance, incorporating Taiwanese cultural elements and multilingual realities into lesson plans could help dismantle the inherent power dynamics in traditional ELT practices. An example of this is a junior high school programme that integrates indigenous folklore and Chinese idioms into English lessons. Through this initiative, students not only learn the language but also gain an appreciation of their heritage while questioning monolithic representations of culture in English materials.

Moreover, teacher training programmes in Taiwan are beginning to include modules on critical pedagogy and intercultural competence. These initiatives encourage educators to challenge the dominance of nativespeakerism and recognize the legitimacy of diverse English varieties, including Taiwanese-accented English. By shifting the focus from linguistic perfection to meaningful communication, teachers can foster a more empowering learning environment.

The path towards decolonization in Taiwan's TESOL curriculum is complex and ongoing. It requires collaboration among policymakers, educators, and communities to create a curriculum that not only equips students with global competencies but also affirms their cultural identities.

Activity 7.4 Looking Back at Your Own Experience

When you learnt English (or other languages) at school and/or university, did you experience a hegemonic/colonial or decolonial learning experience? You can place it using the continuum provided (Figure 7.3) and think of examples.

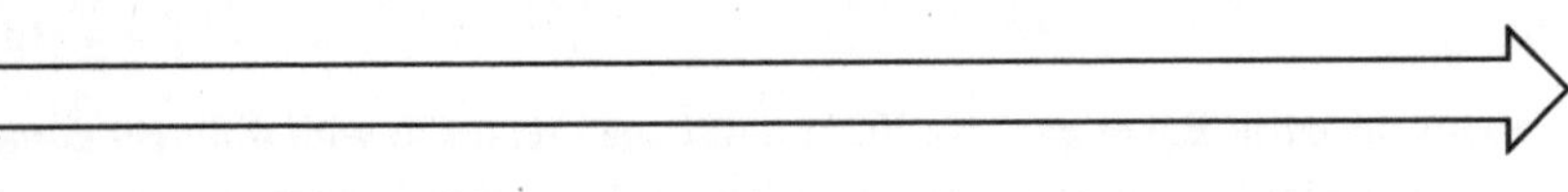

Figure 7.3 Continuum of (de)colonial experiences

Colonial experiences   Decolonial experiences

Activity 7.5 On Baker et al. (2025)

Please access the Baker et al. (2025) article using Figure 7.4.

Figure 7.4 QR code access to Baker et al. (2025)

1. Quickly read the abstract and methodology sections. With those key ideas in mind, read the Findings section, and make notes on how the findings may (not) resonate with your own views and experiences.
2. In what ways can stakeholders use these findings to decolonize the TESOL curriculum in the participants' contexts as well as your own?

Activity 7.6 A Practitioner's Suggestion

The following extract comes from Graham-Brown (2021). In the article, the author reflects on designing a training course for decolonizing the curriculum in an ESOL context. In the UK, this context usually refers to English language courses offered in the UK to people living in the UK whose dominant language is not English. Do you agree with the author's suggestion? Do you think that it responds to the main issues discussed so far in the chapter in relation to decolonizing the TESOL curriculum?

I think we need to develop awareness of our students' rights to challenge exclusionary practices, and the tools they may need to be able to do so. We should re-examine our curriculum content to see if it (a) reflects learners' real lives, and (b) adequately develops their language and knowledge to enable them to build independence to self-advocate. [...] Many of the materials related to teaching how to make appointments present language as very straightforward and non-problematic. In reality, many teachers have anecdotes of their students struggling to make appointments with GP [General Practitioner, a medical doctor who is a consultant in general practice] surgeries because of difficulty communicating with reception or surgery staff. Some say they do not understand their accents and/or present them with language that is unexpected and biased – e.g. 'That doesn't sound serious enough to see a doctor!'; 'You have to follow the procedure. All new appointments are opened at 8am daily.'; 'Have you gone online and looked at the NHS [National Health Service, in Britain] website?' More recently, our students have experienced digital exclusion. If our language lessons are to be meaningful, we should be considering the range of difficulties our students could encounter, including the potential for discriminatory practices in language and digital transactions, and what they could do in these situations, and to include these in our lessons. (p. 68)

7.3 Decolonization and Global Citizenship

Conscientização, critical thinking, and praxis are pivotal for emancipation and to interrupt globalization as another form of oppression and transform it into an opportunity to:

- Foster resistance towards monolingualism and monoculturalism imposed/promoted by policies, developed/intended curriculum and pedagogical materials.
- Advance multilingualism and multiculturalism across the globe.

With globalization came the concept of global citizenship, which we may see as an invitation to think globally and act locally. UNESCO (2015) has defined global citizenship as:

> a sense of belonging to a broader community and common humanity. It emphasizes political, economic, social, and cultural interdependency and interconnectedness between the local, the national and the global.
>
> (UNESCO, 2015, p. 14)

> [Through global citizenship education] learners learn about their identities and how they are situated within multiple relationships (for example, family, friends, school, local community, country), as a basis for understanding the global dimension of citizenship.
>
> (UNESCO, 2015, p. 23)

According to Pashby (2018), UNESCO's (2015) views on global citizenship education stress two potent notions: '(1) Everyone belongs to a human community, and (2) identities are multiple and extend from local to national to global' (p. 277). These notions, which a TESOL curriculum can take as core principles, can be channelled through a range of topics. For example, Stace (2020) suggests the following in relation to general education:

1 Social justice and equality
2 Identity and diversity
3 Globalization and interdependence
4 Peace and conflict
5 Human rights
6 Power and governance
7 Sustainable development

Some of the topics included in the list are familiar to you by now, as we have already discussed social justice (Chapter 6) and sustainability (Chapter 5). In some contexts, TESOL educators and students are not strangers to such topics (e.g. Banegas et al., 2025; López-Medina et al., 2025), and therefore, it may be a matter of (re)calibrating the TESOL curriculum so that principles such as social justice and global citizenship are consistently embedded in practice. While global citizenship education seems commendable,

Pashby (2018) warns that depending on the notions of identity, language and culture that inform the practices of global citizenship education, such practices may reinforce hegemonic and colonial systems of power. For example, students learning English in Germany may develop a project about what they can do to help people in vulnerable contexts in Nicaragua. Inadvertently, this project may perpetuate the notion of helping people *over there*. While global citizenship and social justice will promote the recognition of complicity within inequitable distribution of power and resources, a TESOL curriculum needs to embrace critical global citizenship as a tool for analysis, a tool that can help students reflect critically on the legacies of their own contexts, recognize asymmetrical globalization and power imbalance, acknowledge injustices, take responsibility for their actions, and imagine enabling frames of action for themselves and with people elsewhere. In this regard, the TESOL curriculum may use a postcolonial approach for debating and/ or promoting systemic change as students and teachers engage in learning and teaching English. As you can appreciate, social justice and global citizenship education are intertwined. I would say that critical global citizenship could be included within social justice since the latter is an ideological stance, a philosophy (of education).

From a decolonial perspective, global citizenship may be embraced in the TESOL curriculum as an opportunity to:

- Encourage the expression of multi-layered identities through activities such as students' creation of multimodal identity texts (e.g. Huang, 2022).

- Prioritize everyone's interests and potential as a way to harness the notion of the learner-centred curriculum.

- Include multiple World Englishes (Barduhn, 2018) as well as other languages, particularly those that continue to be marginalized.

Activity 7.7 Sharing Resources on Global Citizenship and TESOL

What resources from your own context are you aware of that can be used to embed critical global citizenship in the TESOL curriculum? Do you know of any TESOL curricula which include a clear critical global citizenship perspective? Have you designed materials and/or lesson plans which reflect the issues discussed so far in the chapter? Feel free to answer these questions using TESOLand (Figure 7.5).

Figure 7.5 QR code access to TESOLand

> ### Activity 7.8 On Bridge 47
>
> Bridge 47 was a project aimed at fostering global citizenship education. Use Figure 7.6 to access their website. Use the resources available to deepen your understanding of global citizenship education and think about ways in which you can transfer that knowledge to the TESOL curriculum.
>
> 
>
> **Figure 7.6** QR code access to Bridge 47

7.4 Decolonization and Intercultural Awareness

With the sociocultural turn in applied linguistics, attention to culture increased and expanded in TESOL. From a practice point of view, culture in TESOL has been traditionally associated with literature from some English-speaking countries or with knowledge about the arts and artists, usually from Europe. In textbooks for the teaching of English, culture has also been reduced to some festivals and traditions (e.g. students being asked to deliver a presentation about Diwali), stereotypes (e.g. a reading passage about five o'clock tea in England) and monolithic, essentialist, reductionist, and stereotypical views of culture which imply that there is one culture per country (e.g. a text about Australian culture) (Dasli, 2025). Now you know that, from decolonial and social justice (including epistemic justice) perspectives, culture as a social construct is much broader and more complex than that. These examples demonstrate that notions of culture and who determines what is culture and what is not, or what gets included/ excluded in a curriculum/syllabus/coursebook is a highly ideological and political act irradiating from the macrosystem of the TESOL curriculum.

At a theoretical level, the sociocultural turn brought about intercultural communicative competence (e.g. Byram, 1997) and intercultural language learning (Liddicoat, 2021). According to Porto (2023b), these two notions suggest that 'learners need intercultural awareness and competence not only to use language in appropriate ways depending on contextual elements, but also to act as intercultural speakers and/or intercultural mediators across several languages, domains, and cultures' (p. 143). As with most of the concepts we have discussed so far in the book, culture, intercultural communicative competence, and intercultural awareness can be interpreted from different lenses, and an in-depth discussion of them exceeds the scope of this chapter. Sometimes, interculturality can be again reduced in a TESOL curriculum to some unit sections just called 'culture' as I briefly exemplified in the paragraph above.

Dervin (2025) states that the term intercultural is 'polysemic and multifaceted' (p. 59) and may need to be understood as a daily phenomenon embedded in social practice. The author also suggests that in the language curriculum, intercultural awareness not only necessitates a nuanced and critical discussion of cultures, but also a recognition of plurilingualism within and beyond the very same classroom in which language teaching occurs. If interculturality is a phenomenon, then, following Liddicoat (2015), through intercultural awareness in the TESOL curriculum, learners need to be able to discuss the interpretation and creation of meanings with people (their own classmates, people represented in a coursebook) who may not share their same linguistic and cultural background to arrive at mediation and decentring of their own views and situated lives experiences. In a chapter about interculturality through the lens of critical pedagogy and (or versus) deconstruction, Dasli (2025) takes a critical angle at discussing what she calls 'the promises of interculturality' (p. 69) as she argues that interculturality tends to overlook issues of power and (lack of) agency at an individual level implicated in intercultural encounters. As you may have suspected, these discussions around interculturality can be placed in the macrosystem that might inform the TESOL curriculum. Along these lines, Soto Molina (2022) proposes that language teaching could assume a decolonial perspective by embracing bilingual intercultural citizenship with the aim of recognizing and mobilizing the multiple ways of becoming and knowing across communities.

What happens with interculturality at the micro and meso levels? In an article which discusses intercultural awareness (referred to as ICA in the quotes below), research into practice, Baker (2015) offers different avenues to explore the concept in the language teaching curriculum. Below, you will find some quotes which may help you define the concept of intercultural awareness:

> ICA focuses on the **inter** or **trans** cultural dimension where there is no clear language–culture–nation correlation, particularly in global uses of English. This also involves a move away from cross-cultural comparisons, where cultures are treated as discrete entities that can be compared with each other, e.g. 'in British culture people do … but in Italian culture people do … '.
>
> (p. 131, Baker's emphasis)

> In contrast, an intercultural approach examines communication where cultural differences, at a range of levels, may be relevant to understanding but does not make a priori assumptions about cultural difference.
>
> (p. 131)

> [A]wareness in ICA is expanded beyond its everyday usage to include knowledge, skills and attitudes and used as a more holistic alternative to intercultural competence, which avoids the problematic competence-performance distinction. [...] ICA emphasises the flexible and context specific nature of the knowledge, skills and attitudes needed.
>
> (p. 131)

Recommendations for implementing ICA in the classroom include investigating the relationships between culture, language and communication through: exploring local cultures; exploring language learning materials; exploring the media and arts both online and through more 'traditional' mediums; making use of cultural informants; and engaging in intercultural communication both face-to-face and electronically.

(p. 131)

With these basic notions, I would like you to complete the activities that bring this section to a close.

Activity 7.9 On Baker (2015)

Choose a coursebook to teach English in your context and answer these questions:

1. Is culture and/or interculturality included? If so, how? Just remember that these may not just be confined to a specific section or sections, but you can find references in the choice of texts, the types of activities, the illustrations, the characters/people represented in the book, and even the voices used for listening/pronunciation activities.
2. Are cultures treated as 'discrete entities' (Baker, 2015, p. 131)? Or can you see a more complex and decolonial problematization of cultures?
3. Can you see examples of input and/or activities that promote local cultures? If so, how are these portrayed? Is there a certain degree of decentring? Or are local cultures othered and/or assessed against hegemonic cultural norms? (For example, drinking mate could be described as an exotic infusion in a coursebook produced in the Global North, but many people from Argentina and Uruguay might simply say that that's what they drink, and it's not exotic at all in their eyes).

Activity 7.10 Intercultural Awareness in a TESOL Curriculum

Choose a TESOL curriculum or syllabus from your context.

1. Are there mentions of culture, intercultural communication or awareness? If there are, how are these presented? Are these mentioned in the principles, objectives, content, materials, activities and/or assessment elements of the document?
2. If the treatment of intercultural awareness is problematic when interpreted under the light of what we have discussed in this section, why do you think this is the case? What would you do as a teacher to contest such notions? Think of very practical ways of imbuing critical cultural awareness in the enacted TESOL curriculum? Or if you were a curriculum developer, how would you incorporate the notions discussed in this section, bearing in mind a decolonial perspective?

7.5 Decolonizing Space

So far in this book, we have discussed the whats, whens, hows and whys of the TESOL curriculum, but the wheres are just as important since the curriculum will necessitate some form(s) of space to be enacted. You may think that by default the prototypical space of the TESOL curriculum is a physical classroom, or a room used for teaching, whether this is in a school, a language teaching centre, a company or a community hub. However, we know that the spatiality (and materiality) of English language teaching and education in general is complex, as research continues to show how educational spaces influence and are influenced by social relations (e.g. Banegas, 2023a; Benson, 2021). In this section, I adopt an objects-as-space view of spatiality since the space of TESOL consists of the place(s) in which learning and teaching occur, as well as the objects present in those places to facilitate (or impede) such processes. In other words, the TESOL curriculum needs to consider the places (e.g. a classroom) as well as the objects (e.g. chairs, desks, boards, books, mats, toys, posters, tablets) present/absent in such places.

The list below, while not exhaustive, seeks to illustrate some of the spaces in which the TESOL curriculum may be enacted:

- A spacious classroom with rows of individual seats for twenty learners. The classroom has big windows, high ceilings, one big blackboard, and shelves and boxes with materials.

- A large classroom in which multi-grade teaching occurs, with groups of students of different ages and grades working on different topics on small tables.

- A small classroom with perhaps too many students.

- A small room within a children's hospital.

- Someone's home.

- A child at the kitchen table while their father is making lunch and their siblings are playing around the table.

- A café.

- A bus on which someone is doing their listening homework.

- An app (e.g. Duolingo).

- A Zoom meeting.

- A virtual classroom on Moodle for both synchronous and asynchronous learning.

- A space with a roof made of tin and wood. No walls, no tiled floor.

- A classroom and an online platform for hybrid learning.

- Students' homes and the classroom for a flipped classroom experience (Akçayır & Akçayır, 2018).

- A small classroom within a prison (Banegas, 2018a).

- A library.

You can think of a dozen more cases that can help make the list more diverse and decolonial, since TESOL can occur in so many spaces which are not those expected or recommended by experts. Such spaces or places could be anything between the physical and the virtual or digital, but all of them are 'spatially configured and entangled with the material world' (Flynn et al., 2018, p. i). Even in the digital world, learners necessitate material objects such as technological devices, a room, a headset, etc.

In their book on pluriliteracies for deeper learning, Coyle and Meyer (2021) position educators as designers of learnscapes. A learnscape is a space in which learning occurs in a highly interactive environment. The authors recognize that while learning is often associated with the physical and digital worlds, both bound to materiality, there are other spaces involved in learning such as the social and the cognitive. The organic assemblage of all these spaces may enable curriculum developers, teachers, learners, and other stakeholders to (re)imagine decolonial spaces that break the walls of the traditional classroom in whatever context to make space for other places in which learning develops in formal, informal and non-formal TESOL education.

Activity 7.11 Space in a TESOL Curriculum

Choose a TESOL curriculum or syllabus from your context. Are there mentions of space? Where is the curriculum expected to happen? What changes would you make to the curriculum so that it embraces a decolonial conception of space?

Activity 7.12 The Spatiality of the TESOL Curriculum

In Banegas (2023a), I put forward a model of the spatiality of language teacher education. You can access the open-access article using Figure 7.7. Just read the Discussion section of the article.

Figure 7.7 QR code access to Banegas (2023a)

Based on the model, your context, and your own experiences with TESOL, create your own model of the spatiality in TESOL. Then, get together with other peers and develop a model that considers different experiences and contexts from a decolonial perspective as discussed in this chapter.

7.6 The Plurilingual TESOL Curriculum

Plurilingualism is a potent construct that can help decolonize the very notion of language as conceptualized from a Western paradigm. Through a plurilingual lens, the barriers or frontiers between named languages are somehow dismantled. According to Piccardo and Capron Puozo (2015),

> plurilingualism is a unique, overarching notion, implying a subtle but profound shift in perspective, both horizontally, toward the use of multiple languages, and vertically, toward valuing even the most partial knowledge of a language (and other para- and extralinguistic resources) as tools for facilitating communication.
>
> (p. 319)

On the quote above, Piccardo and North (2020) stress that plurilingualism recognizes the complexity of languaging by paying attention to the interconnection of languages at individual as well as collective/group levels. Therefore, they make three proposals at the level of curriculum development:

- Language education should be seen in conjunction with the promotion of linguistic and cultural diversity.

- Language in the curriculum should be viewed holistically, the individual curricula for different languages coordinated and an emphasis placed on the development of an integrated repertoire with transversal competences.

- Learning experience in relation to other languages should be recognized and built on, rather than starting each time as if it were from scratch (p. 291).

The three proposals signal that language education cannot be dissected from identity, as the teaching of English can draw from learners' biographies, lived experiences and funds of knowledge and identity. They also stress that TESOL cannot be viewed from a monolingual mindset and the pernicious English-only mandate that continues to be witnessed around the world. From a curriculum standpoint, such proposals may inform the principles and aims of a TESOL curriculum, which will then impact the content, materials, activities and assessment elements.

Recent publications have shown the role which plurilingualism can have in the TESOL curriculum. In a paper on pluralistic approaches to refugees or asylum seekers in Europe, Smetanová (2025) suggests that through plurilingual and intercultural activities, teachers can enable learners to extend their language range and cultural identities and foreground the social value of linguistic and cultural diversity. In addition, the author suggests the utilization of a wide range of materials, which also underline non-verbal communication. In a similar vein, Zeaiter (2023) promotes the use of plurilingual tasks and pedagogical strategies such as translation, cross-linguistic comparisons, cross-cultural comparisons, translanguaging, and pluriliteracies to enable learners to manage their own emotional wellbeing as they engage in tasks to talk about their identities. These two publications reinforce the necessity of embedding the TESOL curriculum with inclusive, socially just-orientated educational/language teaching principles which can recognize, guarantee and maximize the diversity present inside and outside a learning environment.

Activity 7.13 Plurilingualism in a TESOL Curriculum

Choose a TESOL curriculum or syllabus from your context. Are there mentions of bilingualism, multilingualism or plurilingualism? Do the principles, aims, content, materials, or assessment suggest anything that may tell you that plurilingualism has been considered for its design and/or implementation? What changes would you make to the curriculum so that it embraces plurilingualism?

7.7 Bringing It All Together

Activity 7.14

Go back to TESOLand (Figure 7.8) and take a look at the answers that folks have left under Activity 7.7. Can you see anything which seems to illustrate a decolonial perspective?

Figure 7.8 QR code access to TESOLand

Activity 7.15

In Banegas (2023a), one of the participants drew the pizza of language teacher education space (Figure 6 in the article). How would you represent the spaces and objects present in your life as a (future) teacher of English in your context?

Activity 7.16

Return to the revised concept map you developed in Activity 7.3. Based on all the key notions discussed in the chapter, produce a final version of your concept map with the aim of having a network that connects the main issues addressed around the construct of decolonizing the TESOL curriculum.

Activity 7.17

Imagine that you are a teacher of English working in your context, and you decide to decolonize the enacted TESOL curriculum, drawing on the main topics addressed in this chapter. Create a decalogue of specific actions you would do to achieve that aim. You can use your concept map to guide you.

Activity 7.18

Now, imagine that you are a curriculum developer working for the Ministry of Education in your country and you have been tasked with leading TESOL curriculum change. What would you need in order to change the curriculum so that the decalogue (Activity 7.17) you have written as a teacher can be a possibility for your teacher self as well as other teachers?

Activity 7.19

Use Figure 7.9 to access a commentary article authored by Paul Meighan. Once you have read the article, think about the ways in which it (1) illustrates some of the points discussed in this chapter, and (2) extends the conversation by including other topics/concepts/issues.

Figure 7.9 QR code access to Meighan (2020)

7.8 Further Reading

If you wish to read about decolonization in general, language education or TESOL, you can direct yourself to these sources:

- Duvenage, A. (2024). *Roads to decolonisation: An introduction to thought from the Global South.* Routledge.
- Elledge, J. (2024). *A history of the world in 47 borders: The stories behind lines of our maps.* Hachette.

- Hird, D. (Ed.). (2023). *Critical pedagogies for modern languages education: Criticality, decolonization, and social justice*. Bloomsbury.
- Kennedy, D. (2016). *Decolonization: A very short introduction*. Oxford University Press.
- Keval, H. (2025). *Whiteness, racial trauma, and the university: Experiencing whiteness in the university*. Sage.
- Macedo, D. (Ed.). (2019). *Decolonizing foreign language education: The misteaching of English and other colonial languages*. Routledge.
- Marcus, G., & Van de Peer, S. (Eds.). (2025). *Anti-racism in education: Stories of growing activism*. Routledge.
- Ndhlovu, F., & Ndlovu-Gatsheni, S. J. (Eds.). (2024). *Language and decolonisation: An interdisciplinary approach*. Routledge.

If you would like to deepen your understanding of everything intercultural, these volumes can be a good start:

- Baker, W. (2022). *Intercultural and transcultural awareness in language teaching*. Cambridge University Press.
- Busch, D. (Ed.). (2023). *The Routledge handbook of intercultural mediation*. Routledge.
- Fäcke, C., Gao, X., & Garrett-Rucks, P. (Eds.). (2025). *The handbook of plurilingual and intercultural language learning*. Wiley.
- Guilherme, M., & Menezes de Souza, L. M. T. (Eds.). (2019). *Glocal languages and critical intercultural awareness: The south answers back*. Bloomsbury.
- Jackson, J. (Ed.). (2020). *The Routledge handbook of language and intercultural communication* (2nd ed.). Routledge.

Chapter 8
What Does Identity Mean for the TESOL Curriculum?

Summary

The aim of this chapter is to foreground the centrality that identity can play in planning, enacting and changing the TESOL curriculum. The chapter offers a discussion of identity, which is employed to introduce the notion of intersectionality. The chapter particularly attends to gender, sexuality, race, ethnicity and social class with the aim of raising awareness of how the combination of certain differences may lead to oppression and privilege. Students are made aware of who learns and teaches English as well as representation in the TESOL curriculum and teaching materials such as coursebooks. The chapter puts forward an identity-driven TESOL curriculum model. This model invites students to revisit the key concepts discussed in Chapters 1–7.

8.1 Warm-Up

Let me start by asking you some perhaps blunt questions:

Who are you?

Where are you going?

What/who has made (and continues to make) you who you are?

Does your self change according to where you are, who you are with?

Does your self change if you are being a student, or if you are being a teacher, or if you are being someone's partner, someone's relative?

When we discussed interculturality in Chapter 7, we briefly touched on the need for the TESOL curriculum to open an inclusive space for plurilingual and pluricultural students, but this openness needs to embrace the diversity that teachers bring into the spatiality of TESOL as an act of social justice (Kalaja & Melo-Pfeifer, 2025).

If our point of departure for a TESOL curriculum is learner-centredness as discussed in Chapter 2, then we need to consider the diversity of lived experiences happening at the microsystem of the ecology of the TESOL curriculum, as well as what happens outside the classroom, in learners' personal and collective lives.

Activity 8.1 Making a Podcast on Learners' Identities

With peers or on your own, create a podcast of around 10 minutes in which you reflect on what identity means to you in the context of TESOL, and what identities learners may bring, display, develop or hide in a TESOL classroom. You can use any digital tool to record it. Share your podcast with another peer/group and move on to Activity 8.2.

Activity 8.2 Listening to a Podcast on Learners' Identities

Listen to a podcast made by another peer/group and think about in what ways it can help you deepen your understanding of learners' identities and the TESOL curriculum.

8.2 Understanding Identity

As with other terms discussed in this book, identity is a complex and hard-to-define construct, and it depends on the theoretical framework or perspective we use to understand it. According to Sinha and Hanuscin (2017), identity is a fluid and social construct, a historical and dynamic composite of self-image and others' perceptions of oneself via a socio-dynamic approach. I have chosen this definition because it shows that while our individual identities could be located at the microsystem of the ecology of the TESOL curriculum, our social identities may be connected to the mesolevel, as we recognize that who we are shapes and is shaped by the sociocultural institutions and communities we are part of (Douglas Fir Group, 2016). An oft-cited definition of identity in TESOL is that proposed by Norton (2013) in which context, historicity and humans as social beings are highlighted: 'how a person understands his or her relationship to the world, how that relationship is structured across time and space, and how the person understands possibilities for the future' (p. 45). Again, this definition highlights development in context emphasizing the influence of the chronosystem on that journey.

With the same focus on the power that society has on shaping one's identity, Esteban-Guitart and Moll (2014) define identity in the plural, stating that 'identities are social products, cultural devices, a kind of box of tools which can be used to define oneself' (p. 35). This conceptualization can be helpful to recognize that, as social beings, we have multiple and transportable identities which are the product of past, present and imagined selves. While before I connected identity to the past when I used the word *historical*, it is also fair to say that how we project ourselves into the future, our imagined/future self, also contributes to how we shape our identities. As for transportable identities, it is important to acknowledge that we cannot fully depersonalize ourselves as educators or learners, and while we may develop a professional identity as teachers or curriculum developers, we cannot fully detach ourselves from our personality, our personal lives. We are one, but that *one* is composed of many selves that we take with us wherever we go, though, of course, we may choose to display or amplify some identities over others. This may also be applicable to learners. If I go down memory lane to my years as a teacher of English in Argentina, I remember, for example, learners whose motivation for English had increased because they had developed a taste for a US-based music band, or learners whose academic performance and behaviour in class was concerning because their parents were, for example, going through a divorce. These cases illustrate that these teenagers were transporting their individual selves to a context in which they would display (or be expected to display) a certain learner self. Last, this definition may help to envision and materialize how learners' and teachers' identities can be harnessed in the TESOL curriculum, for the tools to be used to define themselves can help make an identity-driven TESOL curriculum pedagogically possible and spatially viable.

While we may think that we need to pay attention to learners' identities when developing the principles of a TESOL curriculum and how these can inform all the other elements of its design and implementation, it is equally important to consider teachers' identities as well as the identities of those beyond schools, so that the TESOL curriculum is culturally responsive to the wider community. From a social justice perspective, this includes the acknowledgement of identities which are minoritized and discriminated against in the community (e.g. people with disabilities, people living in vulnerable conditions, transgendered people).

In relation to identity, it is worth including the conceptualization of possible selves into the picture as it has had a tremendous impact on the study of language teachers and learners as well as language teaching and learning processes (e.g. Al-Murtadha, 2025; Dörnyei & Ushioda, 2009). Proposed by Markus and Nurius (1986), possible selves theory

> describes the importance and dynamics of self-relevant, future-oriented self-concepts, and how these self-views relate to motivation for present and future action. These self-concepts pertain to 'how individuals think about their potential and about their future' (Markus & Nurius, 1986, p. 954), and may reflect an individual's expectations, including hopes, aspirations, fears, and threats that she or he anticipates in the near or distant future. The formation of various possible selves could include an unlimited and diverse array of future self-projections, but it is important to note that the formation of possible selves is connected with representations of the current self. That is, future selves are derived from individually salient desires, hopes, reservations, and fears, but these aspirations and fears are influenced by an individual's current (and past) specific social, cultural, and environmental experiences. Because possible selves are thought to be created within the parameters of an individual's social context, projections of the self are likely derived from what is valued, or perceived to be valued, within an individual's specific social experiences.
>
> (Hamman et al., 2010, p. 1351)

These possible selves have been usually framed around three overlapping categories, as Figure 8.1 shows.

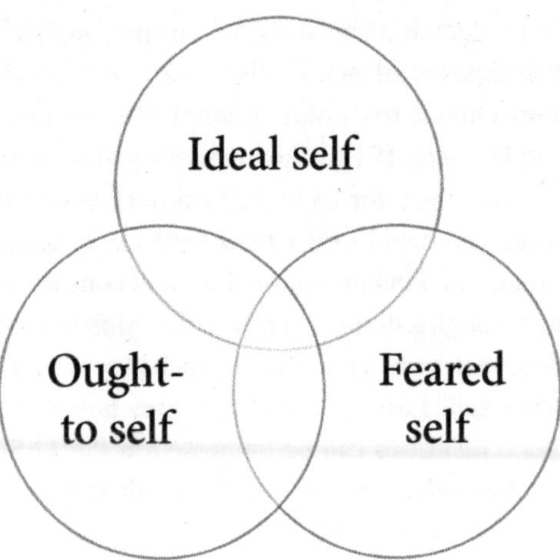

Figure 8.1 Possible selves

Applied to the field of language education, these possible selves may be described as follows:

- Ideal self: The language learner or language teacher you would like to become, with that *positive* vision increasing your motivation to learn/teach.

- Ought-to self: The language learner or language teacher you think/you are expected to become. This self is influenced by institutional expectations, family desires, etc., at the micro (in interaction with students/teachers), meso and macrosystems. This self may act as an external source of (de)motivation and/or anxiety if you believe you cannot live up to such external expectations.

- Feared self: The language learner or language teacher you are afraid of becoming when you think about examples of learners and teachers you are not comfortable with. For example, think about yourself as a teacher not wanting to become like a teacher you did not like when you were in high school. Therefore, your motivation is to avoid that self-concept.

In language education, the possible selves theory has found traction in the area of language learning motivation (e.g. Banegas & Lowe, 2021). For example, Dörnyei's (2009) L2 motivational self system is built on three dimensions: (1) the ideal L2 self, (2) the ought-to L2 self, and (3) the L2 learning experience. While the first two dimensions refer to two of the selves included in Figure 8.1, the third dimension in this model refers to 'the perceived quality of the learner's engagement with various aspects of the learning process' (Dörnyei, 2019, p. 20). This model emphasizes the interconnections between key concepts such as identity, motivation and engagement, which could be core principles in TESOL curriculum development. In their book on motivating learners and teachers, Dörnyei and Kubanyiova (2014) put forward a battery of practical activities with the dual purpose of supporting language learning and helping learners create, enhance, and sustain their vision as language learners (ideal self) as well as transform their vision into action.

Now, how can these notions inform the TESOL curriculum? If we think about principles, attention to identity can help curriculum developers and educators harness the centrality of learners in their own learning. Imagine creating a TESOL syllabus for a particular course within a secondary school setting following the principles of, for example, inquiry-based learning or task-based language teaching, in which every unit of work, which may include the language systems (e.g. vocabulary and grammar) and skills (e.g. speaking and writing), is built around learners' identities. For example, as a teacher, I would have the following aims:

1 To create a learner-centred, identity-orientated language learning environment.

2 To enable learners to construct an actionable ideal vision of their self while developing their English language proficiency.

3 To support learners in carrying out individual as well as collaborative projects to learn English meaningfully.

With those aims in mind, I would organize the course content as shown in Table 8.1.

Table 8.1

Snapshot of an Identity-Oriented TESOL Syllabus

UNIT		Language Functions	Language Systems	Language Skills in Focus
1	Who am I?	Describing myself and others	Present simple, simple past, noun phrases, verb phrases, and adjectival phrases	Listening: identifying personal characteristics Speaking: introducing myself and others
2	What defines me as a teenager?	Describing myself/others, places and activities. Expressing likes, interests and opinions. Illustrating. Arguing.	Present simple, connectors to express reasons (because), phrases to introduce examples	Listening: identifying key information, checking information Speaking: asking and answering about interests.
3	Who defines me? Who do I define?	Narrating events (e.g. telling an anecdote with a friend). Providing details about people.	Past tenses. Reported speech.	Speaking: talking about people who have influenced me. Writing: biographies and personal anecdotes.
4	How did I see myself in the past?	Narrating events. Reflecting on events.	Past tenses. Passive voice. Connectors. Textual organization.	Reading: sequencing events. Writing: a story.

UNIT	Language Functions	Language Systems	Language Skills in Focus
5 How do I see myself today?	Discussing current issues. Expressing personal views.	Perfective tenses. Connectors. Comparatives and superlatives. Modal verbs.	Reading: identifying facts and opinions. Speaking: reflecting on present identities in relation to current issues.
6 How do I see myself in a few years?	Expressing future plans. Justifying decisions.	Present and future tenses. Conditional forms.	Listening: summarizing. Speaking: interviewing/ being interviewed for a podcast.

Activity 8.3 On Your Possible Selves

Think about yourself as a teacher of English in a specific context of your choice. Complete the sentences below:

1. As a teacher, I'd like to be someone who …
2. To achieve that ideal self, I need to …
3. I can work on this ideal self by enacting a TESOL curriculum that …
4. In my context, teachers of English are expected to …
5. In relation to such expectations, I think that …
6. Based on my personal experiences, I don't want to become a teacher who …
7. To avoid that feared self, I'm planning to …

The organization sketched in Table 8.1 could lead to activities and materials in which learners can exercise their autonomy by carrying out projects through which they are also content creators. These projects could be firmly rooted in activities that enable them to create a positive, situated and doable vision of themselves. In my experience, activities which encourage learners to create an empowering vision of themselves as language learners but primarily as teenagers are of paramount importance in contexts in which learners are marginalized and the victims of systemic oppression. I remember having teenage students who could not imagine themselves in any better situation in the future because their context was so oppressive and disempowering that they had believed that they could not study or learn languages or even dream of going to university because of their socioeconomic status and/or ethnicity. In those settings, a TESOL curriculum which promotes building a positive vision and acting on it alongside the development of skills to do it is, I would say, a moral obligation.

8.3 Funds of Identity

Let's now go back to the notion of identities as a box of tools put forward by Esteban-Guitart and Moll (2014, see also Esteban-Guitart, 2014). This concept appears to give prominence to the idea that people deploy a wide range of resources to construct and display who they are to themselves and others. Based on the decolonizing construct of funds of knowledge (for a summary, see Waddington & Esteban-Guitart, 2024) or funds of knowledge*s* (Ortega & Oxford, 2025), Esteban-Guitart and Moll (2014) put forward funds of identity (FoI), which could be defined as

> the historically accumulated, culturally developed, and socially distributed resources that are essential for a person's self-definition, self-expression, and self-understanding. Funds of knowledge – bodies of knowledge and skills that are essential for the well-being of an entire household – become funds of identity when people actively use them to define themselves. From our point of view, identity is made up of cultural factors such as sociodemographic conditions, social institutions, artifacts, significant others, practices, and activities.
>
> (Esteban-Guitart & Moll, 2014, p. 31)

To examine FoI with learners and teachers, researchers have employed ethnographic and arts-based instruments such as duoethnography (Harrison et al., 2024), self-portraits, significant circles, or drawings (Subero et al., 2017), photovoice (Villacañas de Castro, 2017), teachoramas (Banegas, 2024), or mediagrams (Little & Cheng, 2024), among others. Table 8.2 summarizes the types of funds of identities often exhibited by learners and pre-service language teachers according to two publications.

FoI with Learners (Esteban-Guitart, 2014)	FoI with Pre-Service Teachers (Banegas et al., 2022)
1. social (e.g. friends, teachers) 2. institutional (e.g. schools, workplaces) 3. geographical (e.g. places, communities) 4. cultural artifacts (e.g. books) 5. practical (e.g. playing music)	1. social (e.g. classmates, family, language assistants, teacher-educators, boyfriend, students) 2. institutional (e.g. language institutes, schools, TESOL teacher education programmes) 3. geographical (e.g. Buenos Aires, schools as buildings) 4. cultural artifacts (e.g. books, TED Talks, TV programmes, coursebooks, novels, resources, coursework) 5. practical (e.g. travelling, studying, learning, journal writing) 6. valuative (e.g. reflection, justice, inclusion, God) 7. disciplinary (e.g. English language proficiency, knowledge of TESOL, knowledge of the language, teaching experience) 8. anticipatory (e.g. future colleagues, future students, professional development, notions of future/ideal selves)

Table 8.2 Funds of Identity with Learners and Teachers

Table 8.3 Find
Someone Who
Activity

Find someone who ...	Write your peers' names here
a. ... enjoys hanging out with friends.	
b. ... has a dear friend.	
c. ... enjoys coming to school.	
d. ... likes going to a local sport club/gym/ library, _________ (you can mention another institution/space)	
e. ... has a favourite place in town or elsewhere.	
f. ... has something that is special to them.	
g. ... has a hobby.	
...	
...	

Let's focus on learners' FoI. I would dare say that in TESOL, the official and/or the enacted curriculum in a given context may already include aims, activities and learning outcomes which enable learners to talk about their FoI. For example, activities such as *Find someone who ...* (Table 8.3) may be inadvertently tapping into learners' identities.

An activity such as *Find someone who* may enable learners to: (1) ask questions by turning affirmative sentences into direct questions, (2) answer a peer's questions, (3) report back on their findings to the classroom either orally or in writing, (4) use reported speech to report on their overall findings or someone in particular.

As mentioned above, the use of significant circles as part of a speaking activity may prompt learners to reflect on people, experiences, places, etc., that are meaningful to them (Figure 8.2). In my experience, I have organized this activity as part of a unit on identity and diversity with teenage or adult learners. The prompt would be as follows:

Who is important to you? What places, items, institutions, or activities/hobbies are important to you? Draw a big circle on a page, and use words to answer these questions. To show degrees of importance, place the most important/meaningful to you at or near the centre. Place, those that may be less important (but still significant) towards the margins of the circle. If you wish, you can talk about it with your peers.

Once the learners draw their significant circle, I ask them to sit down in pairs or small groups to share their circles and explain why they have included those items. As they do that, I would walk around the classroom taking notes or perhaps photos (with their permission) to then use that information to create follow-up activities that would allow me to incorporate their FoI into the enacted curriculum.

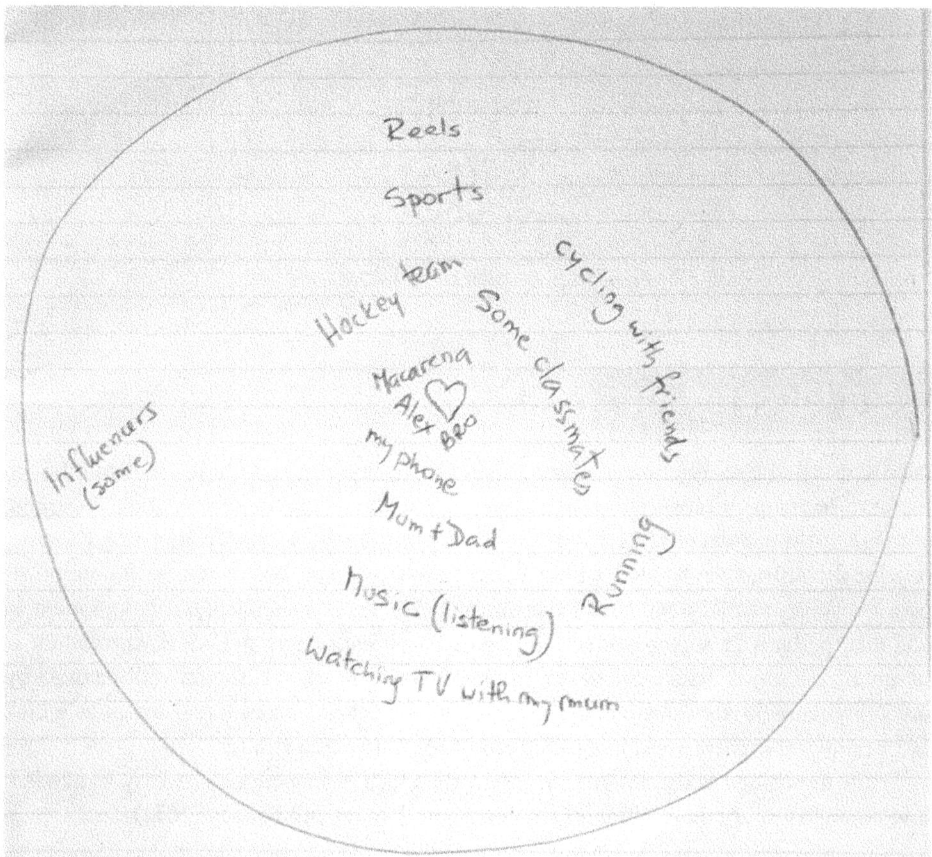

Figure 8.2
Significant circle

Activity 8.4 Identifying FoI

Look at Figure 8.2. Based on Esteban-Guitart's (2014) typology (Table 8.2), what types of FoI can you identify?

Activity 8.5 On Your FoI

Draw a circle. Who and/or what has helped you become who you are as a future/ practising TESOL teacher? You can include people, experiences, items, places, etc. Place nearer the centre those which/who are the most significant to you. To show different degrees of relevance, start placing words further out from the centre towards the margins.

If you wish, share your significant circle on TESOLand by using Figure 8.3. Look for Chapter 8:

Figure 8.3 QR code access to TESOLand

8.4 Investment

As discussed above, the aim of developing an identity-driven TESOL curriculum is to increase learners' motivation, which may contribute to memorable English language learning. In the context of TESOL, current developments approach motivation as a dynamic, relational construct embedded within complex systems and connected to the notion of possible selves as discussed above (Lamb et al., 2019; Ushioda, 2020). It is important to add that, perhaps at a deeper level, the aim of an identity-driven TESOL curriculum is to mobilize a social justice-oriented curriculum which is co-constructed with learners by involving them through democracy (participation), relevance (topics and activities which are meaningful to them), and inclusion (access to quality education).

While motivation is crucial, from a critical perspective, something else may be needed: investment. How are these different? According to Norton and Toohey (2011),

> A language learner may be highly motivated, but may nevertheless have little investment in the language practices of a given classroom or community, which may, for example, be racist, sexist, elitist, anti-immigrant, or homophobic. Alternatively, the language learner's conception of good language teaching may not be consistent with that of the teacher, compromising the learner's investment in the language practices of the classroom. Thus, the language learner, despite being highly motivated, may not be invested in the language practices of a given classroom.
>
> (p. 11)

This quote underscores the societal implications of investment and the view that language is not just 'a neutral medium of communication, language is theorized as a social practice in which speakers negotiate meaning' (Darvin & Norton, 2018, p. 1). It also highlights that whereas motivation refers to internal drives, investment is about the commitment to the goals, practices, and identities that constitute the learning process and that are continually negotiated in different social relationships and structures of power. In this view, learners can be highly motivated to learn a language, but may not necessarily be invested in the language practices of a given classroom if its practices are, for example, racist or sexist.

(Darvin & Norton, 2018, p. 2).

Thus, investment could be a powerful concept to include in the principles, aims, and other elements of the TESOL curriculum if we wish that learners become aware of issues at the macrosystem of TESOL and social life. The notion of investment can also come to support moves towards an inclusive, socially just TESOL curriculum. In this regard, we may say that social justice and investment share an interest in raising awareness around issues of power, positioning, and ideological forces around who speaks and *owns* English (Widdowson, 1998), i.e. the so-called legitimate speaker of English (Darvin & Norton, 2023).

Vignette 8.1 comes to illustrate how identity and investment could become channelled by mobilizing a TESOL curriculum with a focus on comprehensive sexuality education.

<table>
<tr><td>Vignette 8.1</td><td>**Comprehensive Sexuality Education (CSE) in a Foreign Language Primary School Curriculum, by Flavia Bonadeo**</td></tr>
</table>

In 2023, I was part of a curriculum development team that produced new curricular guidelines for primary education in my province, Santa Fe (Argentina). The primary education system in Santa Fe is organized into three cycles: the first cycle encompasses the first, second and third grades (children aged between 6 and 8); the fourth, fifth and sixth grades represent the second cycle (children aged between 9 and 11); and the seventh grade is the last cycle (children aged 12).

I specifically worked on the foreign language teaching guidelines with four other colleagues who teach English, French, Italian, German, and Portuguese. We had been invited to execute this task as members of *Docentes de Lenguas Extranjeras de Santa Fe [Foreign Language Teachers from Santa Fe]*, a grassroots movement of language practitioners that maintains that the teaching of foreign languages in state schools is an educational right. The outcome of this collective, pro-bono, effort was a school curriculum, divided into three different texts, each directed at one of the cycles. The general framework, and the specific decisions emerging from it, were based on national educational laws and policies.

One such law is the Comprehensive Sexual Education Law N° 26,150 (Congreso de la Nación Argentina, 2006a) which states that CSE must be included in the official curriculum for all educational levels; depending on the specific level, CSE can be taught in a cross-curricular fashion or become an independent subject. In the case of primary education, and these particular curricular guidelines, CSE appears both as part of the organizing principles and as specific recommendations to facilitate its integration in the foreign language classroom.

First and foremost, these curricular guidelines seek to promote an open, progressive, view of childhood, acknowledging the plural and diverse ways a child is a child, thus trying to avoid monolithic or standardized perspectives about families, provenance, upbringing, gender, cultural background, and interests, among other aspects. Secondly, and equally important, the three documents include aims, contents, and methodological suggestions involving CSE.

An example of the latter is the objectives for the learning of foreign languages in the seventh grade:

To value and use the foreign language, both orally and in writing, to learn about topics of interest and other curriculum areas, and to communicate one's knowledge, thoughts, and feelings.

To start developing critical discourse awareness, both in the foreign language and the mother tongue or language of schooling, that contributes to the construction of one's identity and the acknowledgement of others.

These objectives imbue other sections of the guidelines where specific language-related activities are suggested:

Reading in a foreign language to obtain relevant information and accomplish tasks and projects related to other curriculum areas and cross-curricular contents such as CSE.

Writing and presenting project reports related to other curriculum areas and cross-curricular contents such as CSE.

In addition, the didactic recommendations highlight the value of approaches such as project-based learning and content and language integrated learning which promote the learning of languages alongside other school content; this section in particular incorporates an example of a didactic sequence based on authentic texts, such as poems, films, and diaries, that focus on identity.

The value of these curricular guidelines resides mostly in the fact that many of the choices made were based on the views of hundreds of practitioners surveyed by our movement, especially those related to the integration of cross-curricular content, such as CSE, to the foreign language teaching agenda.

As you read it, you may want to underline how the principles and objectives coalesce to offer a framework that interweaves identity and language as social practice to interrupt inequities.

Activity 8.6 On Vignette 8.1

The vignette shows that the curriculum incorporated CSE, and therefore, an identity orientation in response to specific legislation/policy. Are there in your own context, policies which can help curriculum developers and practitioners work towards the development of an identity-driven TESOL curriculum in which learners' identities (and their funds) could be considered?

8.5 Intersectionality

As we have discussed in previous chapters, ideological forces and dominant discourses in society may create a hierarchy of identities. Paraphrasing George Orwell's (1945/2022) *Animal Farm*, all humans are equal … but some humans are more equal than others. In the case of education, you can replace *humans* with *learners*. What does this mean? It means that, unfortunately, not all learners enjoy the right to the same access, quantity and quality of education. If you think about your own context, do all learners have the same quality access to learning English? Do they all have the same material conditions? Who has the *best* teachers? Why? What learners appear to be consistently excelling others in national/international exams that measure English language proficiency? Why is that? From a social justice lens, the answers to such questions come to show that some identities are subjected to inequity and marginalization in terms of equitable access to education and meaningful learning experiences. While intersectionality is not about identity itself, this can be an entry point to discuss wider issues around discrimination and oppression.

The concept of intersectionality finds its origins in the realm of law, particularly around conversations on lack of justice and systemic discrimination against Black women, where the intersectional experience is greater than the sum of racism (Black) and sexism (women) (e.g. Crenshaw, 1991; Collins & Bilge, 2020; Marcus, 2019). Intersectionality 'challenges mainstream feminism by displacing essentialised notions of women and the universalization of white middle-class women's experiences' (Marcus, 2019, p. 108). Carbado et al. (2013) maintain that intersectionality was mobilized by Black women; the term has now moved to involve different efforts for equal change.

Intersectionality is a political challenge. It is a holistic approach to social justice and identity which problematizes entrenched inequities at the seams of key constructs in social dynamics, such as race, age, class, language(s) in use, formal education, ethnicity, citizenship status, geographical location, gender, physical abilities, qualities, sexual orientation, and spirituality/religion, among others. From this approach or lens, identity can be understood as a site of struggle in power relationships that exposes structures of privilege and marginalization (Paiz & Coda, 2021). Awareness raising around intersectionality is a good starting point, but it is not enough. According to Konstantoni and Emejulu (2017),

> [intersectionality] is a counter-hegemonic praxis that seeks to challenge and displace hegemonic whiteness in the naming and legitimating of particular kinds of politics, policymaking and knowledge production.
>
> (p. 15)

If we understand intersectionality as praxis, then we seek to transform institutions. The aim of an intersectional view is to interrupt entrenched injustices and engage in courses of civic action guided by equity. So, for example, TESOL provision in Spain may be different for a student who is a Spain-born, young man from a middle-class background, or for a refugee, young woman from a vulnerable background. In this example, even though both people are of the same age, the first person may receive (more) quality TESOL provision because of their gender, citizenship, ethnicity, *and* socioeconomic upbringing, as they may be able to pay for a private course at a language centre, whereas the second person may be taking English lessons with an organization that supports refugees. As Ortaçtepe Hart (2023) states, intersectionality denounces 'discrete forms of oppression' (p. 11) as identities intersect with each other.

Kayi-Aydar et al. (2022) remind us that

> intersectionality is not only a framework for considering identity but is also deeply connected to an orientation and understanding of justice, or what others have called intersectional justice 'as committing to consistently acknowledging and disrupting layered, interlocking inequities in the lives and communities of multiply-marginalized students' (Annamma & Winn, 2019, p. 319) as is the case with many of our English language teacher candidates and our students.
>
> (p. 2)

This quote may remind you of the concept of curricular justice addressed in Chapter 6 (Section 6.6) as intersectionality, more specifically, intersectional justice pedagogy, can contribute to creating a curriculum which is socially just for all identities, especially those that, when combined, are subjected to marginalization.

What follows is a summary (Table 8.4) of activities, placed in no particular order, based on examples or suggestions published in the language education literature. These examples show activities that learners can carry out as part of a TESOL curriculum based on principles of social justice and identity/FoI.

Table 8.4
Activities Which
Can Prompt the
Discussion of
Intersectionality

Author	Activity
Kayi-Aydar et al. (2022)	On the topic of inequities in their local area, prompt teenage/adult students to work in groups to address questions that help them identify types of inequities. Examples: What is the background of the politicians in your local area? Do they tend to belong to the same social class? Are they mostly men? Who is usually stopped by police officers in your city? What do people think of immigrants with a different set of beliefs in your area?
Bryan et al. (2022)	On the topic of (anti)racism, ask your learners to examine the ethnic diversity present in their English coursebook. They can create a table and count the number of Black, white, brown, etc. people/characters included *and* in what ways.
Ortega and Oxford (2025)	On a unit of work around funds of knowledges and identity, ask learners to form circles and share stories of their families, relatives and friends who have been displaced during a violent conflict in the country. They can also use drawings of their home-country lives and/or experiences of transit and arrival. This activity is primarily intended to be used with immigrant and refugee students.
Svarstad (2021)	On the topic of celebrities, ask students to make groups and talk about a celebrity who is vocal about gender and sexuality and/or projects a fluid, inclusive gender identity. Ask them to think about what dimensions of identity enable them to enjoy that privilege in comparison to other people. The aim is to raise awareness that socioeconomic status and their celebrity status place them in a privileged position, which many of their own fans may not enjoy.

Activity 8.7 On the Intersectionality Wheel

Go on an online search for 'intersectionality wheel' and see what images you get. What dimensions of identity are common across them? Choose any of them and see whether language(s) or multilingualism are included. Would you include such terms? Why (not)?

Activity 8.8 Intersectionality in TESOL

Design an English language learning project for a group of learners in your context with an intersectionality orientation. Think about its aims, content, and procedures and your justification for it.

8.6 Towards an Identity-Driven TESOL Curriculum

Based on the concepts and practices discussed in Chapters 6–8, I imagine a configurational shift at curriculum level so that we can see TESOL curricula which are built upon identity and intersectionality across core elements and courses (Figure 8.4). I envisage the proposed curriculum as containing five interrelated context-sensitive, research-informed elements.

This model may need to be taken as a compass, or literally *a* model, and therefore it can be modified and shaped in any way that stakeholders see fit in order to align with or disrupt broader policies and practices across the subsystems in the ecology of the TESOL curriculum. As mentioned elsewhere in this book, a TESOL curriculum needs to be envisaged and embraced as an organic entity, a living organism, which means that all elements will be interconnected, interrelated, interdependent and subject to change.

In relation to the goals, these need to consider what learning, language, language learning and language use mean when approached from a social justice lens. Therefore, the goals as well as learning outcomes will need to be developed and articulated in such a way that inclusion, democracy and relevance have been considered as central drives. In other words, these may need to be collaboratively constructed with different stakeholders with the aim of taking into account their identities in context. Such conversations will also become

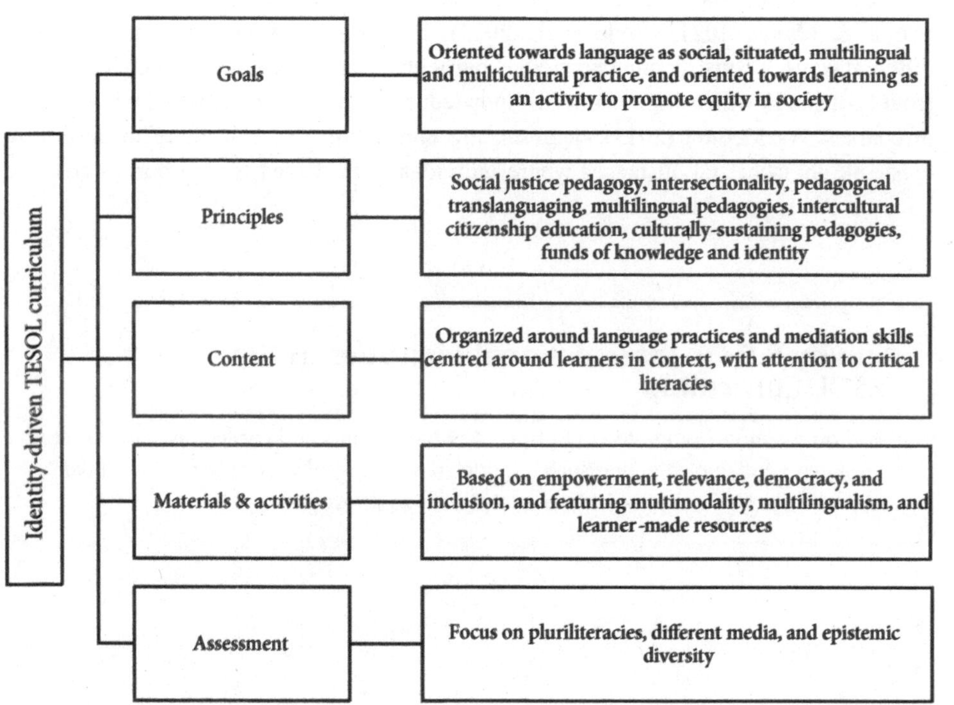

Figure 8.4 A proposed model of an identity-driven TESOL curriculum

an opportunity to agree on key principles. In Figure 8.4, I suggest principles which are compatible with the views on identity I have succinctly conveyed in this chapter. However, these principles are not being prescribed, and therefore, the curriculum may feature some of them or others not included in the list. What is central is that such principles coherently merge general educational positionings such as social justice pedagogy or culturally-sustaining pedagogies (e.g. Paris & Alim, 2017) with more language teaching-oriented perspectives such as pedagogical translanguaging (Li, 2024), which can encourage learners to mobilize their own linguistic repertoires and identities in the construction of multilingual and multicultural identities, or Porto's (2024) approach to content and language integrated learning (CLIL) from an intercultural citizenship perspective which highlights learners' and communities' identities. As Waddington (2025) suggests, embracing multilingualism and multilingual identities to create inclusive, translanguaging spaces can contribute to enhancing learners' sense of agency, self-efficacy and wellbeing as they feel they are fully recognized.

Content, materials, activities, and assessment need to be constructed in such a way that they materialize the intersecting identities focus which has been moulded in the goals and principles. It is here that different stakeholders would like to see how an identity-driven TESOL curriculum has pedagogical valency, in other words, teachability. As Figure 8.4 shows, learners must be at the centre of the learning experience, and therefore there needs to be activities that harness their funds of knowledge and identity in relation to their possible selves as language users and as individuals. As for assessment in particular, different forms of formative and summative assessment could be combined together with different media and literacies (e.g. disciplinary literacies, general academic language, interactional language in different contexts) as a way to ensure pluriliteracies (Coyle & Meyer, 2021; Coyle et al., 2023). It will also be important to recognize different ways of constructing knowledge, particularly in classes with learners who come from contexts in which what counts as knowledge is different or silenced by hegemonic discourses. As Medina (2013) suggests, the curriculum can contribute to unsettling epistemic injustice, i.e. instances where individuals are denied recognition as credible knowers due to social biases.

Activity 8.9 On Intersectional Identities in the TESOL Curriculum

Based on the model presented in Figure 8.4, what benefits and challenges can you see in designing and implementing such a model in a context of your choice? How could such challenges be overcome? Make a table to organize your answers.

8.7 Bringing It All Together

Activity 8.10

Choose a TESOL curriculum or syllabus from your context. Are there any mentions of identity and/or intersectionality? Do the principles, aims, content, materials, or assessment suggest anything that may tell you that learners' identities have been considered for its design and/or implementation? What changes would you make to the curriculum so that it embraces intersectionality and identities?

Activity 8.11

In an ethnography-based study, Ortega (2024) proposes a framework to humanize English language teaching. You can access this open-access article through this URL: https://doi.org/10.1177/13621688241262618
As you read the article,

a. Note down any key terms that are used in the article which we have covered in Chapter 8.
b. Note down any specific teaching/learning examples and think about how they can resonate with your context.
c. Create a list of bullet points as take-aways in relation to how such a study can inform aspects of the official curriculum and enacted curriculum in TESOL in a specific context of your choice.

Activity 8.12

Imagine that you would like to design an identity-oriented TESOL curriculum for the educational institutions where you work, but first, you need to convince your colleagues and other stakeholders that this is a good move. Based on the content included in this chapter, design and deliver a brief presentation to support your case.

Activity 8.13

In Vignette 8.2, the author highlights race and nativespeakerism as issues which may affect TESOL teacher education and TESOL with learners in Korea. Do some of the statements made in the vignette resonate with TESOL in your own context?

| Vignette 8.2 | **Race and/or Ethnicity in a TESOL Teacher Education Curriculum from Korea, by Ko Hye-Kyong** |

In general, the TESOL teacher education curriculum in the Korean context aims to train experienced teachers and pre-service teachers to become experts in English language teaching through English-medium instruction. Specific goals are related to developing global perspectives as well as theoretical and practical knowledge of teaching, English proficiency, and technology-mediated teaching skills. More specifically, global perspectives can foster students' awareness of English as a global language. English proficiency and technology-mediated teaching skills are incidental skills that students can build throughout the entire TESOL teacher education programme. In particular, due to the government-led curriculum in English education, American English is regarded as a model so that American accents are widespread across the Korean peninsula. In fact, all faculty consists of Americans, Canadians, and Koreans, who can speak English 'like a native speaker'. Also, all TESOL materials, which TESOL students are exposed to, are strongly associated with American English.

In this respect, monolingual norms and native speakerism are prevalent in TESOL, leading to a dichotomy of white and non-white speakers based on race and ethnicity. In other words, the EMI-centred TESOL programme in the Korean context might view predominantly white speakers' English as the legitimate English in the EFL classrooms. At the same time, the TESOL materials appear to suggest that white native speakers' norms and cultures are superior to those of non-white speakers.

On the other hand, people of colour seem not to have ownership of English in Korea, beyond the curriculum, thus non-white speakers feeling as illegitimate and underprivileged English-users in the Korean context. In this sense, in TESOL, non-white speakers' ideologies and cultures are inferior to those of white speakers. As a consequence, students can easily ignore the important roles of a variety of English in international communication. Furthermore, Korean English is classified as Konglish in response to distinct English pronunciation, resulting in self-deprecation and lack of social legitimacy (McPhail, 2018). As a result, TESOL students perceive accented English from various ethnic groups, including a Korean accent, as incorrect English. Simultaneously, TESOL students are suffering from the sense of inferiority of their accented English not only by using materials but also by being taught by white native English speaker instructors.

8.8 Further Reading

If you wish to read more about the psychology of language learning and teaching, you can explore these titles:

- Gregersen, T., & Mercer, S. (Eds.). (2022). *The Routledge handbook of the psychology of language learning and teaching*. Routledge.

- Mercer, S., & Dörnyei, Z. (2020). *Engaging language learners in contemporary classrooms*. Cambridge University Press.

If you would like to learn more about discrimination, intersectionality and feminism, these titles could be helpful:

- hooks, b. (1987). *Ain't I a woman: Black women and feminism*. Pluto Press.

- Huo, X. (2020). *Higher education internationalization and English language instruction: Intersectionality of race and language in Canadian universities*. Springer.

Chapter 9
How Can We Research the TESOL Curriculum?

Summary

The aim of this chapter is to encourage students to select a TESOL curriculum of their choice as a potent artefact to write about in their dissertation or other form of assessment as part of a degree they might be pursuing. Thus, it supports researching the TESOL curriculum by engaging in desk-based research, i.e. a systematic literature review, document analysis, or empirical research through exploratory studies (e.g. auto- and duo-ethnographies) and studies which involve different degrees of intervention, such as action research. This chapter also makes connections to Chapters 5–8, since students may wish to choose one specific element/part of the TESOL curriculum to examine from different perspectives (e.g. social justice, teacher agency, intersectionality).

9.1 Warm-Up

Perhaps you are reading this chapter as part of an undergraduate or postgraduate degree programme, or perhaps you are interested in carrying out your own research outside a degree. Curiosity is a wonderful thing!

Researching the TESOL curriculum may include curriculum analysis (i.e. using content/document analysis to look at some aspects of an official curriculum) or an examination of stakeholders' views of a curriculum (e.g. surveying teachers) and/or their practice (i.e. exploring the enacted curriculum through interviews, surveys and classroom observations). Researching the TESOL curriculum may be framed under different methodologies: interpretivist/qualitative, quantitative or mixed. This is a very crude summary of how we can research the TESOL curriculum. I must acknowledge that in this chapter, attention is given to qualitative methodologies in response to practices in the field and my own experience. If you thus think I am biased, you may be right.

You can also embark on a more focused and brief analysis of a TESOL curriculum of your choice. In this regard, you can think of all the activities included in previous chapters in which you were asked to select a curriculum and examine if, for example, it mentioned teacher agency and how. In the course on second language teaching curriculum that I lead

Activity 9.1 Identifying Information

Read the introduction to an essay and identify the element and construct selected by the student. Check your answer in Chapter 10.

> This essay aims to analyse the Critical Reading and Writing for Translators (II) syllabus from the perspective of teacher agency, focusing on the element of monitoring and assessment. This syllabus I encountered during my undergraduate study period is primarily designed for translation major students. However, it serves as a mandatory course for all first-year students to build a foundation in English writing before entering translation studies. Remarkably, this syllabus is designed and enacted by one teacher for almost 100 students across four different classes.
>
> In this essay, I will first introduce the context of this syllabus and establish a theoretical framework to conceptualize the element of monitoring and assessment, and teacher agency. Based on this prerequisite theoretical foundation, I will identify this syllabus's strengths and weaknesses before proposing corresponding changes with anticipated benefits and challenges. Lastly, I will conclude with a reflection on the discussed analysis and proposal, and make a future implication.
>
> The Critical Reading and Writing for Translators (II) syllabus is designed for the second course in a two-part sequence. Building upon the four bases of effective English writing—unity, support, coherence, and language skills—learned in the previous semester, this course, adopting a project-based writing mode, is organized in two parts during a whole semester. The first period focuses on reading monitoring, while the second concerns project-based writing assessment. The overall goal is to nurture writing as a process for improving students' writing skills and additional learning skills.

at the University of Edinburgh, students are asked, as part of their summative assessment, to do exactly that, i.e. to select a TESOL curriculum, syllabus or coursebook, then select a specific curriculum element (e.g. goals), and finally select a specific perspective or construct (e.g. sustainability).

9.2 Topics and Issues

The point of departure to narrow down the scope of researching a TESOL curriculum is to think about what you would like to scrutinize, what you aim to achieve with your research, and why you are interested in that topic. It is also worth thinking about the type of curriculum you are keen to examine: Is it the official curriculum? Is it the enacted curriculum? Is it the assessed curriculum? Is it a combination of more than one? For example, the essay

> ## Activity 9.2 Identifying Topics and Issues
>
> Go over the vignettes included in previous chapters and make a list of the topics/
> issues they address. Are any of these topics appealing to you to examine? If you have
> identified one, how would you go about investigating it?

extract included in 9.1 shows that the author was interested in analysing the assessment element of an official curriculum for TESOL. Another example could be that of Atuhura and Nambi (2024), who examined an enacted TESOL curriculum in Uganda, focusing on the challenges that teachers found as they implemented the curriculum. The sentence starters below can be helpful to limit the scope of your project. You can use them in any order you wish:

A I would like to examine a TESOL curriculum by looking into the topic or issue of …

B With my research, I would like to …

C I am interested in …

Then, it is important to be honest about what you can achieve with the resources, time and possibilities that you have. For example, if you wish to investigate the enacted curriculum, as in Atuhura and Nambi (2024), that logically entails having access to participants and classrooms, is that feasible? If your study will include human participants, have you secured ethical approval from your institution and obtained all the types of clearance required in your context? In this chapter, I briefly discuss different forms of empirical research, and for all of them, you would first need clear ethical guidelines, approval in place before you start, and an understanding of key ethical issues (De Costa et al., 2024).

9.3 Systematic Literature Review-Based Research

As mentioned in Section 9.1, the TESOL (or any language) curriculum or issues connected to the TESOL curriculum could be examined either through desk-based research and/or empirical-based research. In the former, I include systematic literature reviews as well as studies which have examined documents (e.g. official curricula, coursebooks). These are called desk-based research because the researcher can carry out their investigation without the need to leave their physical space or collect data from participants.

According to Andreini and Bettinelli (2017), a systematic literature review is

a reliable, scientific overview of extant research on a subject area or topic (Petticrew and Roberts 2006). Its purpose is to identify, appraise and synthesize all relevant studies using a transparent, replicable process (Tranfield et al. 2003). Protocols for the literature search, article admittance and exclusion, and analytical processes are explicated and provide an audit trail of the processes followed (Jones et al. 2011: 634).

(p. 3)

In connection to the quote, the aim is to examine a topic based on the published literature with certain criteria and protocols which include having a clear corpus of publications over a period of time, with a set of clear inclusion and exclusion criteria, and a rigorous process in place. Macaro (2019) adds that the main benefit of carrying out this type of research is to allow researchers and other stakeholders (e.g. policymakers) to access a synthesis of studies which can inform different courses of action.

In our case, you may not have a specific TESOL curriculum in focus, but rather a topic (e.g. the use of artificial intelligence in the language curriculum), a level of education (e.g. TESOL curriculum development in primary education), a geographical region (e.g. the TESOL curriculum in higher education in Spain), or a combination of these together with other potential aspects. For example, consider these different research questions which can be answered through systematic literature reviews:

- How do TESOL teachers grapple with curriculum change in Malaysia? (The researcher will collect empirical articles and book chapters published in the last ten years.)

- In what ways has the curriculum been decolonized in TESOL programmes in the UK?

- What are the trends about the TESOL curriculum in the last five years in the three most reputable journals in the field of language education?

- How do language textbooks represent foreign culture? (Canale, 2016)

In Vignette 9.1, you will find an example of a systematic literature review on the use of films in the TESOL classroom (Sánchez-Auñón et al., 2023), which could be considered part of curriculum elements such as materials and activities. You can use Figure 9.1 to access the article.

Figure 9.1 QR code access to Sánchez-Auñón et al. (2023)

In Vignette 9.2, you will find another example of a systematic literature review. In this case, the article was not published in a language educational journal but in a journal on health and communication. In this case, the article is not open access, and therefore, there is no QR code to access it.

You may have noted that both systematic reviews followed similar procedures and shared key elements such as the use of specific databases or the delineation of inclusion/exclusion criteria to make their search and scrutiny robust. This is to stress that desk-based research should be as transparent, clear and rigorous as any other type of research. I would say that the benefit of it is that you do not depend on accessing participants to gather data. That said, you still depend on having full access to the publications that you identify for your review. If you embark on this type of research, do examine the relevant literature to develop your understanding of principles, models and procedures that can help you conduct a robust systematic literature review.

Vignette 9.1

On Sánchez-Auñón et al. (2023)

In their article, the authors set out three research questions: (1) What pedagogical guidelines does available scholarship offer EFL teachers to implement films in class?, (2) What are the perceptions of EFL teachers and learners on the educational use of films?, and (3) How does cinema-based EFL impact students' learning?

To answer those research questions, they carried out a systematic literature review according to the guideline of Preferred Reporting Items for Systematic Reviews and Meta-Analyses (PRISMA). The literature search included the use of five databases (see, it is not just a Google search!) with a clear search strategy to identify key words from titles and abstracts. They also established a set of inclusion/exclusion criteria, namely: (1) journal papers written in English, (2) peer-reviewed, and (3) published in open-access journals. Of the 416 sources the authors had identified, only 44 journal papers were included as they scrutinized the sources in more detail.

Vignette 9.2

On Chen et al. (2015)

In the context of health literacy in the US, Chen et al. (2015) set out six research questions: (1) What theories have been used to guide English as second language (ESL) health literacy curriculum development?, (2) What activities and resources have been used to design these curricula?, (3) What classroom activities are included in these curricula?, (4) Which population groups do these curricula target?, (5) What are the goals and health topics of these curricula?, and (6) How effective are these curricula in improving participants' health literacy?

To answer their research questions, they started with a search of the online databases of ERIC, Sage, Springer, PubMed, Medline, and Scopus to identify potential publications. They agreed on a set of key terms to guide their search. Their inclusion criteria were: (1) be peer-reviewed journal articles, (2) be published in English, and (3) describe a curriculum and its design/development procedures. Because their review focused on language curricula for health consumers, curricula for health care providers were excluded. They also did a full review of each item to ensure they aligned with their research questions. They explain that

> 95 articles were identified in the electronic search, and we conducted full-text reviews of 22 articles after excluding 73 that did not meet our criteria. We further excluded eight articles after reviewing the full texts of the 22 articles, and we retrieved another four articles from reference lists that did not appear in the results of the automatic search. A total of 18 articles describing and evaluating seven health-based ESL curricula were reviewed and composed our final sample (p. 103).

Activity 9.3 Topics and Research Questions

Based on the research questions included in Vignettes 9.1 and 9.2, think about a topic, an aim, and one or two research questions you would like to answer by means of a systematic literature review. You could be more inclusive and perhaps even consider including publications in more than one language if you are multilingual, since, as you may have noted, a limitation in both studies is that the authors only included publications in English.

9.4 Document Analysis

By document analysis, I mean research or analysis-based essays that examine, for example, a TESOL curriculum in particular, a coursebook or a set of documents with a common denominator. You can also compare, for instance, different TESOL curricula for primary education in your country, or compare a current TESOL curriculum and its previous version.

As part of their summative assessment in the course on language curriculum I lead, students have to write an essay in which they analyse one TESOL curriculum of their choice. Vignette 9.3 includes the assignment instructions. The aim of this vignette is to illustrate how a TESOL curriculum, syllabus or coursebook could be analysed considering the TESOL curriculum elements addressed in Chapter 3 and those key concepts and

---

Vignette 9.3

Assignment Instructions

1. You will write a 3,000-word essay (NOTE: 10 per cent less or more, range 2,700–3,300 words) in which you will describe and evaluate a part of a TESOL/EFL curriculum that you have experience of as student or as a teacher from one of the perspectives covered in the course.
2. You need to choose a specific English language teaching context, such as an EFL course in a primary or secondary school, university, or adult classes in an independent private school. You may also choose a national or state curriculum. Our advice is – choose a real situation that you have experienced or know about, as a teacher or a student. You will have more concrete and specific sources of information, which tends to increase the quality of the assignment.
3. If you choose to make use of a coursebook (just one coursebook from a series) that you brought from home when you came to Edinburgh or that you used as a student or a teacher, make sure that you know the policy documents, education ideology, the history of TESOL in the teaching context, the needs analysis, objectives, assessment and evaluation that exist around the course book. Remember that the coursebook contains materials and tasks that reflect parts of the syllabus and the methodology, but the coursebook does not usually contain the entire curriculum. The curriculum includes the objectives, the syllabus, the methodology and the assessment.
4. The first step is for you to choose one curriculum/syllabus/coursebook. Read it carefully and take notes of any element (e.g. aims, principles, assessment) of curriculum development that could be improved. As you think about it, consider the role that you as a teacher can play in curriculum improvement.
5. Your second step is to choose a perspective from which you will analyse that element/part chosen. By perspective we mean: social justice, curricular justice, teacher agency, sustainability, decolonization, and intersectionality. So, for example, you could choose the EFL curriculum for primary school learners in Japan, and from there analyse content (element) from the perspective of social justice.
6. This is the structure you need to follow for writing your essay. You MUST use the headings in bold below:

Title (make sure the title you write at the beginning of your essay is a fair reflection of what your essay specifically discusses)

Introduction. Around 250 words. Introduce the topic/issue of your essay. State the aim of your essay, use the aim to mention the specific element/part of the curriculum you will address and the perspective selected. Briefly justify why you think this aim is important to you, and describe the context of the curriculum you will analyse. For the context part, these questions can guide you: Who's the curriculum for? What specific context (School? Country? Programme?) is it for? What are the goals/aims/learning outcomes? How is it organized?

Conceptual framework. Around 700 words. Conceptualize the specific element of curriculum you will address, keep it focused, but do make critical links to relevant concepts, topics, and authors discussed in the course and beyond. Then, conceptualize the perspective you are analysing the element from. Make sure that you show more than one view when conceptualizing the element and the perspective.

Analysis. Around 850 words. Analyse the curriculum through the element of your choice by identifying strengths and, in particular, problems, which you will later address in the next section. Include examples from the curriculum to support your analysis. Refer back to the concepts and authors included in your conceptual framework.

Proposal for change. Around 1,000 words. Suggest a doable and context-sensitive way in which that element of curriculum development can be improved in the curriculum of your choice from the perspective chosen as well as others. Discuss the role that teachers can have to make those changes. Support your suggestions for change by making reference to authors and concepts discussed in your conceptual framework and empirical articles. Evaluate the changes recommended in terms of benefits as well as challenges, and how the latter could be overcome.

Conclusion. Around 200 words. Reflect on the ways in which the analysis and proposal can help you strengthen your agency and practice as a teacher. We strongly encourage you to use I-statements.

References. Not included in the word count. Use APA 7th ed., at least 12 quality and updated references, at least 4 of these must be from the course.

perspectives included in Chapters 5–8. You (and your instructor) can adapt them or create an entirely new set of instructions.

In the published literature, you can also find articles which are based on the thorough analysis of curricula and/or coursebooks (e.g. Canale, 2016). Vignette 9.4 includes the abstracts from different articles with a shared interest: representations of culture(s) in coursebooks. As you read the vignette, think about whether you would like to conduct similar studies with your context in mind. In the vignette, I have italicized those phrases that indicate the type of analysis conducted by the authors.

Activity 9.4 Essays Including Document Analysis

Use Figure 9.2 to access five essays (anonymized for ethical reasons).

1. Your first task is to identify how each author (student) analysed the curriculum element and perspective/key concept of their choice. Please, DO NOT take these essays as models or perfect examples. They are just samples, and I am sure there is plenty of room for improvement in them.

2. The folder also includes the feedback the essays received for contextual purposes (I am sure that you may have different views on the feedback, but again, worry not). Your second task is to match the essays with the feedback. See Chapter 10 for the answer to this second task.

Figure 9.2 QR code access to essays and feedback

Vignette 9.4	**Abstracts from Coursebook Analysis-Based Studies**

Abstract 1: 'Adopting the Common European Framework Reference in ELT led the Malaysian Ministry of Education to replace locally developed textbooks with imported (global) coursebooks. Given the Malaysian English curriculum emphasis on learners' intercultural skills, the question that arises is whether imported coursebooks meet local learners' needs. The current study addresses this based on an *analysis of the cultural content* in English Form 1, a locally developed textbook, and Pulse 2, an imported coursebook. The study employed Byram's Intercultural Communicative Competence (ICC) framework to capture intercultural content and measured the spectrum of cultures (source, target and other cultures) in each book. The intercultural content and the cultural spectrum in the local textbook are found to be wider and more in keeping with ICC objectives than the imported book. Replacing a local textbook with an imported coursebook, therefore, may not necessarily be in the best interest of the country's English language agenda.' (Rahim & Jalalian Daghigh, 2020, p. 317)

Abstract 2: 'Neoliberal ideologies, evidenced in locally developed and internationally published imported English Language Teaching (ELT) textbooks, are compared in the context of Malaysia, an outer circle country. Historically, locally developed ELT textbooks have been used to teach English but recently imported books have been prescribed following the adoption of the Common European Framework Reference (CEFR). This move has met with criticisms from many who are concerned with the culture and ideologies reproduced in imported texts. The current study addresses this concern through the *thematic content analysis* of locally developed and imported textbooks used in Malaysian classrooms. It is found that the neoliberal values demonstrated in imported textbooks outweigh those in locally published ones. This necessitates a critical reading of imported ELT textbooks by local educational authorities before they are prescribed for use. This is particularly important in outer- and expanding-circle countries where local cultural values and beliefs may be different from the Western, neoliberal values reproduced in imported materials.' (Jalalian Daghigh, & Abdul Rahim, 2021, p. 493)

Abstract 3: This study examines the representation of cultures across three sets of national English textbooks currently used in China by conducting a *synchronic content analysis* to explore what and how cultures are represented in the textbooks. Data analysis was conducted based on a newly constructed framework focusing on the content (countries and categories) and forms of cultural representation. Our findings mainly indicated that American and British culture dominated in the culture of inner circle countries and international culture was represented the least in all three textbooks, while Chinese culture was represented more than the cultures of inner circle countries in two sets of textbooks. As for cultural categories, the representation of cultural products was the most, and cultural perspectives and cultural communities were represented the least in all three sets of textbooks. Regarding the form of cultural representation, the cultural representation in implicit forms was, to varying degrees, more than that in explicit forms. Based on the findings, suggestions for English as a foreign language (EFL) textbook writers, EFL teachers and textbook researchers are provided. (Zhang et al., 2024, p. 3394).

Activity 9.5 On Content Analysis

1. Do a quality search to learn more about content analysis, what it means and how it can be carried out. Prepare a summary and share it with a peer.
2. With your peer, record a brief presentation that brings together what you have understood. Include references where appropriate. You can share your presentation via TESOLand (Figure 9.3):

Figure 9.3 QR code access to TESOLand

As highlighted in the vignettes, the authors employed different forms of content analysis. According to Selvi (2019), this research technique or method can help us understand a phenomenon (e.g. how inclusive a TESOL curriculum is) by analysing 'the presence of meaning and relationships through various forms of human activity and communications' (p. 440). As with a systematic literature review, content analysis requires a clear set of steps and procedures for the preparation, organization and reporting of our results in relation to our research question(s) and aim(s). It usually involves the quantification of occurrences, for example, the number of times that the word 'culture' appears in a curriculum. However, it is not just counting occurrences; it is also about how and where these are placed and what they mean in context.

9.5 Ethnographies, Case Studies, and Mixed Methods

In the area of language curriculum research, scholars have not only paid attention to documents (curricula, coursebooks, etc.) but also to them in relation to practices and perceptions with the aim of understanding what happens at the level of the enacted curriculum.

As a research methodology, ethnography is characterized by direct observation of and interaction with a given community to understand their situated (place and time-bound) practices from the perspective of the ethnographer (Chawla & Mercado Jones, 2017; McGranahan, 2018). Usual ethnographic instruments are participant observation, fieldwork notes, interviews and the use of videos, audios and photos to capture different practices. The writings (or other outputs) coming from ethnographic work seek to offer a thick description and interpretation, i.e. a detailed account, of what has been observed (Wei, 2019). While ethnography could be, in principle, associated with anthropology and related fields, it has found its place in education (e.g. Beach et al., 2018) as well as applied linguistics and language education (e.g. Wang & Canagarajah, 2024).

I use the term ethnographies to acknowledge the different types you may find depending on focus/field (e.g. linguistic ethnography), approach (e.g. critical ethnography), instrument(s) (visual ethnography), space (e.g. digital ethnography), or people doing the ethnography (e.g. autoethnography). While a description of all these forms exceeds the scope of this chapter, Table 9.1 provides illustrative and fictitious examples of potential projects you may wish to consider to conduct an ethnographic examination of a TESOL curriculum from your context. Please be aware that the projects are varied to recognize the different pathways that ethnographic research may take. Also, bear in mind that for all these projects, ethical clearance is a core step to include before data collection/generation starts.

Table 9.1 only provides some fabricated situations, but you can certainly consider different forms of ethnography to conduct research yourself or with others. Sometimes, ethnographic research begins with a very broad aim, and researchers may not even have research questions. These may be asked after data sets have been gathered and scrutinized to identify any patterns or interesting phenomena.

Within an interpretivist paradigm, case studies are also employed to investigate language curriculum development. A case study could be understood as the detailed examination of a single example either because it may be seen as representative/prototypical of a larger class/group, or because it is distinctly different from the rest in one way or another (Flyvbjerg, 2011; Yin, 2018). It should be noted that 'single' does not just mean one person/individual. You can also find studies of multiple case studies, such as a study with more than one teacher (as Vignette 9.5 illustrates). A case could also be a school or a community, i.e. it could be a larger group that is bound together for different circumstances. For example, in Atuhura and Nambi's (2024) study about the challenges that Ugandan teachers of English encounter when implementing a 2020 language competence-based curriculum, they collected data from sixty-nine in-service teachers and two specialists. The authors argue that they conducted a case study because the participants were bound by the context (Uganda) and the curriculum under scrutiny.

Vignette 9.5 not only shows that the authors' methodological framework included four participants as cases embedded in a university, but it also shows that, as noted in ethnography, they combined instruments such as observation, semi-structured interviews and journals. While in this case, the study is interpretivist and therefore associated with qualitative methodologies, the authors utilized different instruments to enhance the

Type of Ethnography	Potential Project
Autoethnography (e.g. Canagarajah, 2012; Yazan, 2019)	Research question: In what ways does the enacted curriculum respond to a group of learners' needs? As a teacher of English in a primary school in your city, you set out to write a journal for one school year about the curricular changes you enact in relation to content and skills in order to respond to your learners' needs. You then use your journal as data and examine it through thematic analysis.
Duoethnography (e.g. Banegas & Gerlach, 2021; Sawyer & Norris, 2013)	Aim: To explore the assessed TESOL curriculum in my programme through conversation with a colleague. With a colleague, we decide to meet on Microsoft Teams (the meetings get recorded) once a week for a whole term to share our views and practices on how we assess our students, and how our assessment practices may align or not with how assessment has been laid out in the TESOL curriculum. As the meetings progress, we realize that in practice we pay attention to ensuring that assessment is inclusive of learners' strengths, identities, adaptations and needs. Therefore, we decide to continue our meetings with a more specific question: How do we make assessment inclusive? To engage in thematic analysis, we use the automatic transcription of Microsoft Teams.
Multimodal ethnography (e.g. Canale & Fernández Fasciolo, 2022; Dicks et al., 2006)	You have been invited to join a team of stakeholders whose task is to write a new TESOL curriculum for secondary education in their country. The task involves having meetings online and in person, as well as having a shared online space in which people can write collaboratively, and hold discussions on forums and more informal chats. You would like to take this opportunity to understand how the development of a new official curriculum is negotiated and constructed. You thus decide to keep notes of the online and in-person meetings for analysis as well as collect evidence of what happens on the shared online space particularly with a focus on how decisions are made, and what/whose ideas are included/excluded as the official curriculum begins to take shape.

Activity 9.6 Using Ethnography

Do a search on different types of ethnographies. Choose one you would feel comfortable with using to examine a TESOL curriculum, syllabus or coursebook. Think about how you would use it. Share your plan with a peer.

<table>
<tr><td>Vignette 9.5</td><td>On Yang et al. (2022), by Kyung-Eun Kwak</td></tr>
</table>

The study conducted by Yang et al. (2022) sought to find out the relationship between emotion work and emotion capital through the exploration of teacher engagement. It aimed to discover how emotions that the observed teachers felt while implementing a curriculum reform could impact on their teacher engagement and the way they form their identities as educators. Therefore, the main research question was: What roles did emotion work play in EFL teachers' engagement in curriculum implement over one academic year?

The study was conducted with four participants who were EFL teachers in a public Chinese university. Therefore, there were four teachers as individual cases, but the authors also framed the chosen university as their case.

This research mostly utilized qualitative methods based on one-year longitudinal observation within a specific context in which teachers were supposed to keep the curriculum reform issued by Chinese MOE in 2019. The four participants also participated in semi-structured interviews and were asked to keep a journal.

The authors concluded that high teacher engagement was interrelated to teachers' self-efficacy and the definite understanding of the teachers' role, claiming that the teachers with positive thinking were more likely to have higher resilience when navigating curriculum change.

Activity 9.7 On Mixed Methods

Access an article by Andreani and McKinley (2025) using QR code 9.4.

1. Read the abstract and the methodology section. What makes the study mixed-methods suitable?
2. Read the results section. How were the quantitative and qualitative data integrated to answer the research questions?

Figure 9.4 QR code access to Andreani and McKinley (2025)

robustness of their study. In research, there are other combinations, particularly when researchers decide to integrate quantitative and qualitative research methodologies, which is often labelled as mixed methods.

According to Brown (2014), mixed-methods research strategically integrates qualitative and quantitative features, data collection instruments, forms of analysis and the context in which the research develops. For example, if you wish to examine an official TESOL curriculum in a region, you can first design and implement an online survey consisting mostly of closed-ended items so that the results can be quantified. You could then use those results to identify some initial patterns or trends (e.g. those who find the curriculum detached from reality, those who find it helpful), and therefore, you decide to select some participants representing those patterns to carry out interviews with the aim of digging deeper into their responses and views. This survey, followed by an interview design, is what is usually called sequential mixed methods. Methods can also be used simultaneously. In either case, what is important to highlight is that there must be some sort of connection/relationship/interaction between the methods.

You may have noted that the research methodologies briefly discussed above may often be used to describe a phenomenon, to understand what, for example, TESOL teachers and students think about and do in relation to the TESOL curriculum. Broadly speaking, we can subsume them under the notions of descriptive research. This type of research seeks to understand a phenomenon in a given context as is, i.e. without manipulating the environment. That said, case studies, for instance, can be used as exploratory research in preparation for a larger study. For example, you may conduct a case study with one class at a local school to explore what happens when students are given more participation in assessment. Based on the findings, you may wish to devise a plan to be implemented by the whole school.

9.6 Interventionist Research and Action Research

There is another type of research in which the researchers and/or participants introduce a change to the TESOL curriculum and observe what the effects of that change are. In other words, the study itself intervenes in the regular dynamics of teaching and learning. This is what we call intervention or interventionist research (Mahali & Swartz, 2018; Penuel, 2014). The aim of interventionist research is to enhance practice through the planned and informed use of educational techniques/approaches/methods situated in the context where the intervention takes place. Interventionist research may not always take place within a regular TESOL course. In this regard, interventionist research may be classified as explanatory research for it seeks to establish (degrees of) causality between variables (e.g. whether learners' English language proficiency improves when the curriculum allows for more learner agency). Interventions may seem quasi-experimental at times since researchers may select a handful of learners from a larger cohort and implement the intervention as an extra activity. For example, Vignette 9.6 summarizes a study carried out by Lo (2025) at a secondary school in Southeast China. Although the researcher was not one of the teachers involved in the intervention, there seems to have been some sort of collaboration, even though this is not clearly described in the article.

Vignette 9.6 shows that in interventionist research, data collection is often integrated into the pedagogical intervention itself. While there can be, for example, surveys and interviews/focus groups pre- and post-intervention, gathering data through less intrusive instruments during the intervention could prove extremely helpful to understand the whole process, not just the end results. You can access Lo (2025) using Figure 9.5 to read the full study and what the findings were.

Figure 9.5 QR code access to Lo (2025)

Other intervention-based studies may include treatment and control groups to measure the effectiveness of an intervention by comparing two groups of students, one which *received* the intervention (treatment group) with one which did not (control group). For example, Brown and Lally (2019) carried out an interventionist study for fifteen weeks at a US university to examine whether an immersive (L2 English only) or non-immersive approach (L2 + other languages) approach facilitated English language development more effectively. Vignette 9.7 is a section from the article so that you can have an example of interventionist research with treatment and control groups.

Vignette 9.6

On Lo (2025)

In this study, the researcher sought to investigate pedagogical relationships between digital multimodal composing, transculturality, English as multilingua franca and general English with secondary school students. Thus, the study introduced digital multimodal composing as a pedagogical approach.

The intervention was framed as a *Global Englishes ambassador* four-week programme designed to introduce a few selected students to diverse varieties of English and their global use. The programme was delivered after exams as an extra-curricular activity. In other words, while it was part of the enacted curriculum for the participating students, it was not part of the official curriculum or the curriculum that every student was navigating. According to the author:

> In this programme, students assume the role of GE ambassadors. Their primary task is to create a digital multimodal poster that promotes GE. This culminates in a group project, where each group selects and represents digitally a specific variety of English based on a recommended list of English varieties from Galloway and Rose (op.cit.) but is encouraged to expose other Englishes except the commonly exposed British and American Englishes (see Figure 2 for their selections). Platforms such as Canva (www.canva.com) are recommended for creating the poster, although students are free to choose other suitable digital tools. (p. 5)

In terms of data collection,

> sources included written reflections and DMC artefacts, serving both pedagogical and research purposes. To minimize language barriers, students could write their reflections in either English or Chinese. A total of fifty-three reflective entries were collected and converted into electronic files, with Chinese entries translated into English and proofread for accuracy. In addition, fourteen DMC artefacts were collected, with five representative artefacts selected from different geographic variations of English to provide a comprehensive view of students' work and perspectives. (p. 7)

Vignette 9.7

On Brown and Lally (2019)

All the sections included in this vignette have been copied and pasted from Brown and Lally (2019), pages 608–611, with only a table having been removed from the original. Some sentences are in bold to draw your attention on the role that a teacher-researcher had and the integration of different types of data collection instruments.

Participants
Sixty-six international undergraduate students and one graduate student at a large university in the northeastern United States initially participated in this study. Students were enrolled in four intact classes at two proficiency levels. The low-intermediate students were approximately B1 on the Common European Framework of Reference for Languages (CEFR) global scale1 as rated by the instructor, and those at the high-intermediate level ranged from B2 to C1 on the same scale. Several nationalities and L1s were represented among the participants, but the majority were from China.

A researcher-practitioner also participated in the study, serving simultaneously as the teacher of all four courses. The researcher-practitioner possessed a CEFR B2 proficiency level in Spanish and 25 years of domestic and international TESOL experience, including 8 years teaching courses of the type involved in this study, with training in communicative language teaching and task-based learning and teaching. Although acknowledging the potential weaknesses of a researcher-practitioner role, ensuring the same instructor for all four classes minimized the risk of instructor variation as an explanatory variable, critical for the professional judgments typically employed in implementing L1 use (Macaro, 2009). Furthermore, the data gathered from the researcher-practitioner in the form of a reflective journal helped demonstrate fidelity to the condition.

Treatment and Control Groups

Student participants were dispersed across four academic writing courses for second language users of English. The four courses comprised two proficiency levels in English: low-intermediate (CEFR B1) and high-intermediate (CEFR B2-C1). All courses were taught in a student-centered CLT environment, with frequent use of inductive focus-on-form and content (writing)-based activities and considerable student-to-student interaction. One course at each level was designated the treatment group and the other the control group, and the form of instruction was systematically varied between the two. In the longitudinal design, data were collected at regular intervals throughout the 15-week semester.

In the control groups, a statement reflecting the standard policy of English-only featured prominently on the syllabi. The policy was enforced in the classroom by the researcher-practitioner, and also by some of the students, through frequent reminders. The researcher-practitioner sought maximum student comfort in the English-only environment, with ample positive reinforcement and instructional assistance offered in negotiation of meaning when needed. No penalties were enforced after L1 use; students were simply politely asked to continue their discussions in English.

In the treatment groups, there was no syllabus statement requiring English only. In addition, in line with Moore (2013) and Macaro (2009), during frequent specific instructional activities based on the researcher-practitioner's professional judgment, students were encouraged to communicate in whichever language they felt comfortable using. They typically switched between L1 and L2 when they worked with classmates with whom they shared an L1 and utilized their L2 when communicating with others, including the teacher, who did not share their L1. Inspiration for classroom activities such as prewriting and project preparation were drawn from resources such as Celic and Seltzer (2012). However, the researcher-practitioner stopped short of permitting translingual products for assessment, because institutional grading polices for these courses required that all final assignments be submitted in English (see J. W. Lee, 2016, for a discussion of the implications of translingual writing on assessment).

Tasks for Analysis

Data collected from the students included quantitative measures of class performance with analyses of final grades and a selection of standard assignments from each of the courses. In the low-intermediate classes, scores from seven paragraph assignments and three exams were targeted. Assignments were preceded by draft submissions, and final graded versions demonstrated student proficiency in various rhetorical patterns: narrative, compare and contrast, cause and effect, descriptive, process, and definition writing. Three exams given at 5-week intervals measured the students' proficiency with course content in writing (specific rhetorical patterns), vocabulary (taken from stories assigned for reading comprehension and lexical development), and grammar (tenses and time shifts, modals, nouns and determiners, passive voice, adjective and adverb clauses, and conditionals).

In the high-intermediate classes, five genre-based writing assignments (summary, critique, explanatory synthesis, argument synthesis, and a literature review/research paper) and two speaking tasks (group and individual presentations) were examined. Writing assignments were preceded by draft submissions, and final versions demonstrated mastery of genre-specific writing as well as grammatical and lexical accuracy. Speaking assignments were graded on five presentation criteria: organization and content, delivery and speaker presence, slide quality, time management, and handling of questions.

A second window on the student perspective at both proficiency levels came from their evaluations of the courses, assessed quantitatively using standardized course evaluation rating formats. These included sections on the instructor, the course, the student, and course outcomes, all measured on a Likert scale. Importantly, with the required use of standardized formats, none of the evaluative items specifically touched on issues of language policy and use in the class. Thus, with the understanding that associative and not causal claims could be made, particular items most closely related to the study were selected for analysis, namely (1) whether the instructor encouraged class discussion, (2) the level of comfort and associated student participation, (3) self-perceptions of improvements in writing, and (4) self-perceptions of improvements in reading.

A final source of qualitative data came from the researcher-practitioner. During and at the end of each class period, the instructor took field notes for later consultation, which culminated in a 15-week reflective journal. This journal served two purposes: documenting evidence of fidelity to condition and contributing a qualitative, observer perspective on classroom interactions. The researcher-practitioner reported on the amount of L2 versus other languages used during the lesson in both open class and group/pair work, the pedagogical content of each class, his observations of student performance generally in relation to speed and accuracy, and his observations of student reactions to tasks and language use.

The intervention reported in Brown and Lally (2019) demonstrated no statistically significant differences between the academic performance of the treatment and control groups. However, we need to be particularly cautious with the ethics surrounding treatment and control groups. What would have happened if the intervention had proved to be effective? Does that mean that the students in the control groups were disadvantaged and received less quality teaching for fifteen weeks?

Another form of research that involves intervention is action research. According to Banegas and Güngör (2025), action research

Activity 9.8 Ethical Issues with Intervention Research

Imagine that you are carrying out longitudinal research with two classes during their English language lessons for a whole school year; that is to say, your research is directly intervening in the TESOL curriculum. You are examining the effects of one specific teaching strategy to teach vocabulary. Class A is your treatment group and Class B is your control group. After a term, you begin to notice that the findings indicate that Class A's performance and attitude towards learning English is significantly improving. What would you do? Would you maintain the study going as is until the end of the school year? Should Class B be brought up to speed so as not to be left behind?

is a transformative, reflexive, and situated form of inquiry which reconciles two core concepts: action and research. Placed within an interpretivist paradigm, the juxtaposition and order of these items, at least in English, exhibit the objective of integrating research rigor with the practical imperatives demanded from social practice. In this sense, research as action is carried out to transform reality. In other words, AR [action research] is a political act for curricular justice and societal change.

(p. 1)

In this case, the pedagogical intervention is designed and implemented, solo or collaboratively, by the teacher in their identity as teacher-researcher, their learners and sometimes a researcher supporting the teacher. Because of the people involved and how they are involved, some forms of action research are called collaborative action research or participatory action research.

The main feature of action research is that it is done by teachers for teachers with the aim of improving their situated practice. Therefore, it is highly contextual and culturally sustaining, and it is not aimed, in principle, at producing original research for the academic community. AR is, by definition, small in scale, and it is ecological as it happens alongside teaching and learning. In other words, teaching and learning are action research and vice versa (Banegas & Consoli, 2020; Burns & Dikilitaş, 2025). Thus, action research contains elements of descriptive and exploratory research, and while it may uncover causal insights, its primary goal is local and participatory intervention to improve practice.

Another distinctive feature of action research is that it is often organized in stages and cycles, with the idea that the end of a cycle may lead to another cycle. Table 9.2 illustrates what the architecture of action research may look like in practice.

The fabricated example included in Table 9.2 illustrates the typical four stages of an action research cycle. It also shows the role of reflection as another stage, going across the other stages. You may have noted that the teachers collected data from various sources: students' self-reported needs, teaching materials, students' coursework, classroom observations (teachers' notes), reflective journals and a student survey.

Table 9.2 An Example of Action Research

Context: A group of three teachers teaching courses on English for specific purposes at a university in Egypt have noted that while the official curriculum is clear about the prevalence of reading comprehension over other skills, their practices in Term 1 seem not to be supporting their students judging by their academic performance in exams. Therefore, they have set out to investigate what the issue seems to be and how it can be addressed in Terms 2 and 3 of the academic year.

	Stage	Activities
Cycle 1	Explore	At the end of a session, each teacher asks their students to take a piece of paper and anonymously write down in Arabic, the students' L1, what kind of needs and/or activities they would like to do more of to improve their reading comprehension skills.
		They collect their responses and find out that most of the students would like to do more pre-reading activities aimed at vocabulary learning. The teachers decide to go online and create a list of vocabulary learning strategies that seem to work in other contexts, and with learners who are speakers of Arabic. They also take a look at a few books on vocabulary learning.
		They create a shared folder on Google Drive to keep the students' responses, their search results, and everything else that may be relevant as the project unfolds, with the aim of documenting and reflecting on every stage.
	Plan	Based on their search, the teachers work together to create lesson plans containing activities for vocabulary learning. Their plan is to have at least one vocabulary activity in every lesson and ask students to do one more activity outside of classroom time. The lesson plans, activities and materials they develop or adapt are all uploaded on their shared folder. They have also started individual journal-like documents they use to reflect on the planning.
	Implement	They individually implement the lesson plans during Term 2. At the end of each lesson, they verbally ask the students to share their views on the vocabulary activities included. The teachers note down the students' views and upload them on the shared folder. They also keep track of students' progress via formative and summative assessment tasks. In some cases, with the students' permission, they scan students' answers to some of the new activities. All this data is uploaded too. They carry on journaling their reflections.
	Evaluate	At the end of the term, they design and give their students an online survey (in Arabic) asking them to rate the changes introduced. They then go through all the evidence gathered and their own reflections and note that while there has been an improvement, this comes from the activities completed in class, not from those assigned as homework. This poses a new question, which triggers a second cycle of action research for Term 3: How can we create vocabulary activities that students do want to complete outside of classroom time?

Activity 9.9 Understanding Action Research in Practice

Read the following abstracts. All of them have a sentence missing. Use the sentences below to complete them. Then, see if you can identify any of the action research features mentioned in this chapter. Check the answers in Chapter 10.

Sentence 1: The study involved a lecturer-researcher, four instructors and eight university students in second language learning settings in a Turkish university; it aimed to improve our social practices and enable the teacher-students and student-teachers to reflect on the current content of the standard curriculum and to produce a critical syllabus for a listening-speaking class.

Sentence 2: Data were collected through a survey, group and individual interviews, reflective journals and whole class discussions.

Sentence 3: Therefore, an AR methodology of two cycles was employed with two different groups of English majors throughout two successive semesters during the academic year 2012/13.

Abstract A (Abdallah, 2017)

Action research (AR) – as a participatory, problem-oriented methodology – has been employed recently in Egypt to resolve complicated classroom and learning problems, and provide context-based solutions. Simultaneously, new 'special education' courses have been included recently in the university bylaws of Egyptian colleges of education. This imposes challenges, especially on course design and content selection. The present study therefore aimed at negotiating and improving the structure and delivery of a new special education language-learning course entitled 'TESOL/TEFL for Special Needs' taught to English majors (English as a foreign language [EFL] student-teachers) at Assiut University College of Education, and reaching a final framework. [SENTENCE MISSING NUMBER ___]. The first group included 106 junior general-section EFL student-teachers (first semester, 2012); and the second group consisted of 51 senior primary-stage EFL student-teachers (second semester, 2013). Data collection tools were used for both formative and summative evaluation purposes, and thus varied both at the initial stage and during iterations. They included questionnaires, online diaries, semi-structured interviews, final feedback reports and follow-up logs. The two AR cycles resulted in a final framework of course structure/content along with some suggestions and guidelines on how to deliver it. Moreover, some implications for teaching EFL to students with special educational needs as well as some conclusions related to using AR in Egypt to resolve many teaching/learning problems were presented.

Abstract B (Ordem, 2023)

The use of a participatory approach may entail taking risks in certain contexts. It involves discussing socio-political issues that aim to challenge the discourse of those in power representing neoliberal ideology. Critical pedagogy and the participatory approach oppose political and neoliberal power relations in educational settings that determine the content of the curriculum and syllabus. This study is a personal reflection on a participatory research activity to create meaningful change through reflection and action. [SENTENCE MISSING NUMBER ___]. The findings show that the participants and the researcher were anxious about articulating their radical ideas because of the current political atmosphere. Meanwhile, they reported having developed a positive attitude towards the preparation of a critical syllabus. Besides, the participants and the researcher produced a six-stage recommendation for teachers and learners to use a participatory approach. By doing so, we could help one another develop critical perspectives and take action by producing an action plan in classrooms.

Abstract C (Banegas, 2019)
This article describes part of a larger action research study carried out in 2018 with secondary school learners and teachers of English in southern Argentina. The study was guided by two aims: (1) improving English language learner motivation, and (2) transforming the English as a foreign language (EFL) curriculum through teacher and learner engagement. The project also sought to help teachers develop professionally and exercise they agency as curriculum makers and developers through the support of teacher research. The study involved the participation of 920 learners in the design and implementation of EFL lessons which responded to their beliefs, expectations, and experiences. [SENTENCE MISSING NUMBER ___]. Drawing on thematic analysis and descriptive statistics, findings also show that learners moved from demotivation to motivation as they noted that they could contribute to curriculum enactment and transformation through active participation in teachers' pedagogical decisions. Findings also reveal that the enactment of a context-responsive and bottom-up curriculum led to motivational synergy, and teachers' agency enhancement through collaborative lesson planning, materials development, and research engagement for professional development. However, teachers experienced lack of confidence regarding teacher-made materials.

9.7 Putting It All Together

Activity 9.10

Read Vignette 9.8. Write a list of questions you would like to discuss with its author in relation to the methodology employed.

<table>
<tr><td>Vignette
9.8</td><td>

Extracurricular Activities in English: Their Impact on Motivation and the Development of Situated Practices in University Students, by Sandra Cabrera

</td></tr>
</table>

The main objective of this research was to determine how extracurricular activities (EAs) can influence both the motivation of students and the development of their language practices in learning English as a foreign language (EFL). The study aimed to explore the effectiveness of various EAs in enhancing student engagement and language skills.

Several authors have discussed the importance of extracurricular activities in language learning. For example, Deci and Ryan (2000) highlight the role of motivation in learning, suggesting that engaging in enjoyable activities can foster intrinsic motivation, which is crucial for language acquisition. Furthermore, Dörnyei (2014) points out that motivation is a key factor in successful language learning, and extracurricular activities can be used as a motivational tool.

The research utilized a mixed explanatory design and it was conducted in two phases (two semesters), each lasting 10 weeks. The participants included 50 students in the first phase and 42 students in the second phase, all of whom were EFL learners at the second (A2-) and third (A2) levels at the Institute of Languages of the University of Cuenca, Ecuador. Four specific extracurricular activities were organized: a conversation club, a WhatsApp interaction group, music in English, and a cinema forum. The promotion of these activities relied heavily on word of mouth to attract participants. The study assessed the initial and final performance of both the intervened groups (those participating in EAs) and the control groups (those not participating) to evaluate the impact of the activities on their language skills.

The results indicated that the extracurricular activities had a positive influence on the students' performance in both phases of the study. Specifically, the grade point averages of the intervened groups improved significantly, while the control group only showed improvement in the first phase and was outperformed by the intervened group in the second phase. Although there was no consistent pattern in the increase of basic language skills, the most notable improvement in the intervened group was observed in their use of language, which increased by 0.35 points in each phase.

Qualitative feedback from both tutors and students revealed that participation in these activities significantly boosted students' motivation to learn EFL. The activities were found to be effective in reinforcing motivation, particularly when they aligned with students' interests in the target language. Overall, the study concluded that extracurricular activities play a crucial role in enhancing both the motivation and language skills of EFL learners, highlighting the importance of integrating such activities into the educational framework of public universities in Ecuador.

Activity 9.11

Go on an engine search and type 'Champion Teachers: stories of exploratory action research edited by Paula Rebolledo, Richard Smith and Deborah Bullock'. You should be able to access a free book in PDF format. The book contains nine stories of English language teachers carrying out exploratory action research in Chile. Choose three of the chapters and complete Table 9.3.

Table 9.3 Examples of Exploratory Action Research

Questions	Chapter Number:	Chapter Number:	Chapter Number:
What issue/puzzle triggered the action research?			
What steps/stages did the action research include?			
How did the teacher gather data?			
What did the action research experience lead to?			

Activity 9.12

Scan the article by Waluyo et al. (2025), which you can access through Figure 9.6, and complete Table 9.4.

Figure 9.6 QR code access to Waluyo et al. (2025)

Table 9.4 On Waluyo et al.

Title
Aim(s)
Aspects/elements/types of the TESOL curriculum investigated
Research question(s)
Key concepts informing the theoretical framework
Context
Research methodology
Participants
Data collection instruments
Data analysis
Ethical issues

Activity 9.13

Think about an empirical study you would like to carry out around a TESOL curriculum of your choice. Use Table 9.5 to help you organize your ideas. You can complete the table in any order and way you wish. You can even add or delete rows.

Table 9.5 Planning an Empirical Study

Title
Aim(s)
Aspects/elements/types of the TESOL curriculum to be investigated
Research question(s)
Key concepts informing your theoretical framework
Context
Research methodology
Participants
Data collection instruments
Data analysis
Time frame to conduct your study
Ethical issues

Activity 9.14

How would you report and disseminate the findings of your TESOL curriculum research so that they reach the most diverse range of stakeholders possible? What kinds of outputs/media/languages/spaces would you use? Where? When? Who with?

9.8 Further Reading

Here are two seminal books on curriculum research.

- McKernan, J. (1996). *Curriculum action research: A handbook of methods and resources for the reflective practitioner* (2nd ed.). Routledge.

- Stenhouse, L. (1975). *An introduction to curriculum research and development.* Heinemann.

If you would like to know more about research methods in (language) education, you can familiarize yourself with these titles.

- Coe, R., Waring, M., Hedges, L. V., & Day Ashley, L. (Eds.). (2025). *Research methods and methodologies in education* (4th ed.). Sage.

- Cohen, L., Manion, L., & Morrison, K. (2018). *Research methods in education* (8th ed.). Routledge.

- Dikilitas, K., & Mastruserio Reynolds, K. (Eds.). (2022). *Research methods in language teaching and learning: A practical guide.* Wiley Blackwell.

- King, K. A., Lai, Y.-J., & May, S. (Eds.). (2017). *Research methods in language and education* (3rd ed.). Springer.

Chapter 10
Answers

Chapter 1, Activity 1.3

1 b (The specialist only had to comply with high-level guidelines and organization, but she had the freedom to select the goals, content, principles, etc. of what the TESOL curriculum would have).

2 all the options (She worked individually and only received feedback from the national Ministry of Education).

3 b and c (The provincial Ministry of Education solely relied on the specialist. This could be a sign of full trust and support but also a sign of lack of engagement with the actual curriculum).

Chapter 4, Activity 4.12

(a) information, (b) judgements, (c) uses, (d) change, (e) needs

Chapter 5, Activity 5.6

Abstract 1: The authors seem to be adopting a sociocultural perspective as they emphasize mediation and development.

Abstract 2: The authors appear to have adopted a poststructuralist perspective as they have paid attention to the influence of power individual, institutional and societal factors in curriculum change.

Chapter 9, Activity 9.1

Element: monitoring and assessment. Note: These are curriculum elements included in the Macalister and Nation (2020) model of curriculum design.

Perspective: teacher agency

Chapter 9, Activity 9.4

Essay 1: Feedback B
Essay 2: Feedback C
Essay 3: Feedback D
Essay 4: Feedback A
Essay 5: Feedback E

Chapter 9, Activity 9.9

Abstract A: Sentence 3
Abstract B: Sentence 1
Abstract C: Sentence 2

References

Abbasi, B. N., Wu, Y., & Luo, Z. (2025). Exploring the impact of artificial intelligence on curriculum development in global higher education institutions. *Education and Information Technologies, 30*, 547–581. https://doi.org/10.1007/s10639-024-13113-z

Abdallah, M. M. S. (2017). Towards improving content and instruction of the 'TESOL/TEFL for Special Needs' course: An action research study. *Educational Action Research, 25*(3), 420–437. https://doi.org/10.1080/09650792.2016.1173567

Administración Nacional de Educación Pública (2023a). Programa de educación básica integrada: Inglés.

Administración Nacional de Educación Pública (2023b). Programa de educación básica integrada: Inglés: Tramo 6, Grado 9.

Akçayır, G., & Akçayır, M. (2018). The flipped classroom: A review of its advantages and challenges. *Computers & Education, 126*, 334–345. https://doi.org/10.1016/j.compedu.2018.07.021

Al-Murtadha, M. (2025). Motivating second language learners with a possible selves intervention program. *Journal of Language, Identity & Education, 24*(1), 43–56. https://doi.org/10.1080/15348458.2022.2075874

Altay, M. (2025). The intersection of human capital and linguistic protectionism. *Journal of English-Medium Instruction, 4*(1), 74–98. https://doi.org/10.1075/jemi.24002.alt

Andreani, C., & McKinley, J. (2025). Global Englishes teaching in secondary schools in Italy. *ELT Journal*, ccaf010. https://doi.org/10.1093/elt/ccaf010

Andreini, D., & Bettinelli, C. (2017). *Business model innovation: From systematic literature review to future research directions.* Springer.

Aneja, G. A. (2016). (Non) native speakered: Rethinking (non) nativeness and teacher identity in TESOL teacher education. *TESOL Quarterly, 50*(3), 572–596. https://doi.org/10.1002/tesq.315

Ansarian, L., & Teoh, M. L. (2018). *Problem-based language learning and teaching: An innovative approach to learn a new language.* Springer.

Apple, M. W. (2018). *Ideology and curriculum* (4th ed.). Routledge.

Ashbee, R. (2021). *Curriculum: Theory, culture, and subject specialisms.* Routledge.

Atuhura, D., & Nambi, R. (2024). Competence-based language curricula: Implementation challenges in Africa. *ELT Journal, 78*(3), 245–254. https://doi.org/10.1093/elt/ccae003

Baker, W. (2015). Research into practice: Cultural and intercultural awareness. *Language Teaching, 48*(1), 130–141. https://doi.org/10.1017/S0261444814000287

Baker, W., Morán Panero, S., Álvarez Valencia, J. A., Alhasnawi, S., Boonsuk, Y., Ngo, P. L. H., Martínez-Sánchez, M. M., Miranda, N., & Ronzón-Montiel, G. J. (2025). Decolonizing English in higher education: Global Englishes and TESOL as opportunities or barriers. *TESOL Quarterly, 59*(1), 281–309. https://doi.org/10.1002/tesq.3317

Ball, S. (1993). What is policy? Texts, trajectories and toolboxes. *Discourse: Studies in the Cultural Politics of Education, 13*, 10–17. https://doi.org/10.1080/0159630930130203

Ballester Almagro, M., García-Pastor, M., & Rodríguez-Gonzalo, C. (2024). Enseñanza gramatical, reflexión metalingüística y transferencia interlingüística en los libros de texto de inglés de Educación Primaria. *Didacticae, 15*, 1–22. https://doi.org/10.1344/did.43086

Banegas, D. L. (2011). Teachers as reform-doers: Developing a participatory curriculum to teach English as a foreign language. *Educational Action Research, 19*(4), 417–432. https://doi.org/10.1080/09650792.2011.625654

Banegas, D. L. (2018a). 'I want to make the invisible visible': Teacher motivation in Argentinian prison education. In K. Kuchah & F. Shamim (Eds.), *International perspectives on teaching English in difficult circumstances: Contexts, challenges and possibilities* (pp. 133–154). Palgrave.

Banegas, D. L. (2018b). Learning subject-specific content through ESP in a Geography teaching programme: An action research story in Argentina. *English for Specific Purposes, 50*(1), 1–13. https://doi.org/10.1016/j.esp.2017.11.001

Banegas, D. L. (2019). Language curriculum transformation and motivation through action research. *The Curriculum Journal, 30*(4), 422–440. https://doi.org/10.1080/09585176.2019.1646145

Banegas, D. L. (2023a). 'What if it's been space all this time?': Understanding the spatiality of language teacher education. *System, 113*, 102978. https://doi.org/10.1016/j.system.2022.102978

Banegas, D. L. (2023b). Four spheres of student-teachers' professional identity formation through learning about curriculum development. *Journal of Education for Teaching, 49*(3), 370–383. https://doi.org/10.1080/02607476.2022.2105644

Banegas, D. L. (2024). The spatiality of pre-service language teachers' funds of professional identity. *Innovation in Language Learning and Teaching, 18*(3), 253–268. https://doi.org/10.1080/17501229.2023.2209546

Banegas, D. L., & Consoli, S. (2020). Action research in language education. In J. McKinley & H. Rose (Eds.), *The Routledge handbook of research methods in applied linguistics* (pp. 176–187). Routledge.

Banegas, D. L., & Gerlach, D. (2021). Critical language teacher education: A duoethnography of teacher educators' identities and agency. *System, 98*, 102474. https://doi.org/10.1016/j.system.2021.102474

Banegas, D. L., & Glatigny, R. (2021). The *ateneo* as an effective model of continuing professional development: Findings from southern Argentina. *Pedagogies: An International Journal, 16*(4), 363–377. https://doi.org/10.1080/1554480X.2021.1897012

Banegas, D. L., & Güngör, M. N. (2025). Action research. In C. A. Chapelle & K. Toohey (Eds.), *The encyclopedia of applied linguistics*. Wiley. https://doi.org/10.1002/9781405198431.wbeal20086

Banegas, D. L., & Lowe, R. J. (2021). Creative writing for publication: An action research study of motivation, engagement, and language development in Argentinian secondary schools. *Studies in Second Language Learning and Teaching, 11*(3), 401–421. https://doi.org/10.14746/ssllt.2021.11.3.5

Banegas, D. L., & Sanchez, H. S. (2024). Editorial: Social justice and language teacher education from Latin America. *Teachers and Teaching, 30*(2), 131–138. https://doi.org/10.1080/13540602.2023.2169669

Banegas, D. L., & Velázquez, A. (2014). Enacting a people-centred curriculum in ELT with teenage learners. *Profile: Issues in Teachers' Professional Development, 16*(2), 199–205. https://doi.org/10.15446/profile.v16n2.40902

Banegas, D. L., & Zappa-Hollman, S. (Eds.). (2023). *The Routledge handbook of content and language integrated learning*. Routledge.

Banegas, D. L., Beacon, G., & Perez Berbain, M. (Eds.). (2021). *International perspectives on diversity in ELT*. Palgrave Macmillan.

Banegas, D. L., Corrales, K., & Poole, P. (2020). Can engaging L2 teachers as material designers contribute to their professional development? Findings from Colombia. *System, 91*, 102265. https://doi.org/10.1016/j.system.2020.102265

Banegas, D. L., Pinner, R. S., & Larrondo, I. D. (2022). Funds of professional identity in language teacher education: A longitudinal study on student-teachers. *TESOL Quarterly, 56*(2), 445–473. https://doi.org/10.1002/tesq.3060

Banegas, D. L., Sacchi, F., San Martín, M. G., & Porto, M. (2025). Teachers' and student teachers' conceptualisations and enactment of social justice in English language teaching: A case in Argentinian secondary schools. *Teachers and Teaching, 31*(8), 1377–1395. https://doi.org/10.10 80/13540602.2024.2411957

Barduhn, S. (2018). World Englishes. In J. Liontas (Ed.), *The TESOL encyclopedia of English language teaching*. Wiley. https://doi.org/10.1002/9781118784235.eelt0641

Beach, D., Bagley, C., & Marques da Silva, S. (Eds.). (2018). *The Wiley handbook of ethnography of education*. Wiley.

Benson, P. (2021). *Language learning environments: Spatial perspectives on SLA*. Multilingual Matters.

Bierce, A. (1911). *The devil's dictionary*. Arthur Bird.

Biggs, J., & Tang, C. (2007). *Teaching for quality learning at university*. Open University Press.

Bland, J. (Ed.). (2015). *Teaching English to young learners: Critical issues in language teaching with 3-12 year olds*. Bloomsbury.

Blume, C. (2021). Inclusive digital games in the transcultural communicative classroom. *ELT Journal, 75*(2), 181–192. https://doi.org/10.1093/elt/ccaa084

Bonacina-Pugh, F. (2012). Researching 'practiced language policies': Insights from conversation analysis. *Language Policy, 11*, 213–234. https://doi.org/10.1007/s10993-012-9243-x

Bonacina-Pugh, F. (2020). Legitimizing multilingual practices in the classroom: The role of the 'practiced language policy'. *International Journal of Bilingual Education and Bilingualism, 23*(4), 434–448. https://doi.org/10.1080/13670050.2017.1372359

Bonacina-Pugh, F. (Ed.). (2024). *Language policy as practice: Advancing the empirical turn in language policy research*. Palgrave Macmillan.

Borg, S. (2019). Language teacher cognition: Perspectives and debates. In X. Gao (Ed.), *Second handbook of English language teaching* (pp. 1149–1170). Springer.

British Council (2015). *English in Colombia: An examination of policies, perceptions and influencing factors*. British Council. https://www.teachingenglish.org.uk/sites/teacheng/files/ English%20in%20Colombia.pdf

British Council (2023). *English without borders*. https://inglessinfronteras.co/LEE (2023). Inglés, el factor de competitividad pendiente en Colombia. Report No. 69. British Council. https://lee. javeriana.edu.co/-/lee-informe-69

Bronfenbrenner, U. (1979). *The ecology of human development*. Harvard University Press.

Brown, A., & Lally, R. (2019). Immersive versus nonimmersive approaches to TESOL: A classroom-based intervention study. *TESOL Quarterly, 53*(3), 603–629. https://doi.org/10.1002/ tesq.499

Brown, J. (2014). *Mixed methods research for TESOL*. Edinburgh University Press.

Bryan, K., Romney-Schaab, M., & Cooper, A. (2022). The illusion of inclusion: Blackness in ELT. *CATESOL Journal, 3*(1), 1–13.

Burns, A., & Dikilitaş, K. (Eds.). (2025). *The Routledge handbook of language teacher action research*. Routledge.

Byram, M. (1997). *Teaching and assessing intercultural communicative competence*. Multilingual matters.

Canagarajah, A. S. (2012). Teacher development in a global profession: An autoethnography. *TESOL Quarterly, 46*(2), 258–279. https://doi.org/10.1002/tesq.18

Canale, G. (2016). (Re)Searching culture in foreign language textbooks, or the politics of hide and seek. *Language, Culture and Curriculum, 29*(2), 225–243. https://doi.org/10.1080/07908318.20 16.1144764

Canale, G., & Fernández Fasciolo, M. (2022). Multimodality, ethnography and the English language teaching textbook: Negotiating heteronormativity in visual representations. In T. Xiong, D. Feng & G. Hu (Eds.), *Cultural knowledge and values in English language teaching materials* (pp. 163–181). Springer.

Cantoni, D., Chen, Y., Yang, D. Y., Yuchtman, N., & Zhang, J. (2017). Curriculum and ideology. *Journal of Political Economy, 125*(2), 338–392. https://doi.org/10.1086/690951

Caraballo, L., Lozenski, B. D., Lyiscott, J. J., & Morrell, E. (2017). YPAR and critical epistemologies: Rethinking education research. *Review of Research in Education, 41*(1), 311–336. https://doi.org/10.3102/0091732X16686948

Carbado, D. W., Crenshaw, K. W., Mays, V. M., & Tomlinson, B. (2013). Intersectionality: Mapping the movements of a theory. *Du Bois Review: Social Science Research on Race, 10*(2), 303–312. https://doi.org/10.1017/S1742058X13000349

Caruso, M. (2023). The coming of 'age': Educational and bureaucratic dimensions of the classification of children in elementary schools (Western Europe, 19th century). *European Educational Research Journal, 22*(3), 394–412. https://doi.org/10.1177/14749041211062017

Cenoz, J., & Gorter, D. (2021). *Pedagogical translanguaging.* Cambridge University Press.

Chang, B. (2018). Social justice. In J. Liontas (Ed.), *The TESOL encyclopedia of English language teaching.* Wiley. https://doi.org/10.1002/9781118784235.eelt0137

Chapelle, C. (2021). Language programme evaluation. In C. Chapelle (Ed.), *The encyclopedia of applied linguistics* (pp. 1–7). Wiley.

Châteaureynaud, M.-A. (2022). *Sociodidactique du plurilinguisme et de l'altérité inclusive: Des langues régionales aux langues des migrants.* Peter Lang.

Chawla, D., & Mercado Jones, R. (2017). Ethnography/Ethnographic methods. In J. Matthes, C. S. Davis & R. F. Potter (Eds.), *The international encyclopedia of communication research methods.* Wiley. https://doi.org/10.1002/9781118901731.iecrm0090

Chen, X., Goodson, P., & Acosta, S. (2015). Blending health literacy with an English as a second language curriculum: A systematic literature review. *Journal of Health Communication, 20*(sup2), 101–111. https://doi.org/10.1080/10810730.2015.1066467

Chevallard, Y. (1985). *La transposition didactique: Du savoir savant au* savoir enseigné (1st ed.). La Pensée Sauvage.

Chevallard, Y., & Bosch, M. (2014). Didactic transposition in mathematics education. In S. Lerman (Ed.), *Encyclopedia of mathematics education* (pp. 170–174). Springer.

Chong, S. W., & Reinders, H. (Eds.). (2024). *Innovation in language learning and teaching: The case of England, Northern Ireland, Scotland, and Wales.* Palgrave.

Cirocki, A., & Farrell, T. S. C. (2019). Professional development of secondary school EFL teachers: Voices from Indonesia. *System, 85,* 102111. https://doi.org/10.1016/j.system.2019.102111

Cirocki, A., Farrelly, R., & Buchanan, H. (Eds.). (2023). *Continuing professional development of TESOL practitioners: A global landscape.* Springer.

College of International Studies (2019). Six major programs at the School of Foreign Languages-深圳大学外国语学院. https://sfl.szu.edu.cn/info/1199/4029.htm

Collins, P., & Bilge, S. (2020). *Intersectionality* (2nd ed.). Polity Press.

Congreso de la Nación Argentina (2006a). *Ley 26.150: Programa Nacional de Educación Sexual Integral.* Buenos Aires.

Congreso de la Nación Argentina (2006b). Ley de Educación Nacional 26.206.

Cook, V. (2013). What are the goals of language teaching? *Iranian Journal of Language Teaching Research, 1*(1), 44–56.

Cook, V., & Singleton, D. (2014). *Key topics in second language acquisition.* Multilingual Matters.

Cope, B., & Kalantzis, M. (Eds.). (2015). *A pedagogy of multiliteracies: Learning by design.* Palgrave.

Copland, F., Garton, S., & Barnett, C. (2024). *Global practices in teaching English to young learners: Ten years on.* British Council. https://doi.org/10.57884/JHCP-DS26

Council of Europe (2020). Common European framework of reference for languages: Learning, teaching, assessment – Companion volume. Council of Europe Publishing. Available at www. coe.int/lang-cefr.

Coyle, D., & Meyer, O. (2021). *Beyond CLIL: Pluriliteracies teaching for deeper learning.* Cambridge University Press.

Coyle, D., Hood, P., & Marsh, D. (2010). *Content and language integrated learning.* Cambridge University Press.

Coyle, D., Meyer, O., & Staschen-Dielmann, S. (Eds.). (2023). *A deeper learning companion for CLIL: Putting pluriliteracies into practice.* Cambridge University Press.

Crenshaw K. (1991). Mapping the margins: Intersectionality, identity politics, and violence against women of color. *Stanford Law Review, 43*(6), 1241–1299. https://doi.org/10.2307/1229039

Crites, K., & Rye, E. (2020). Innovating language curriculum design through design thinking: A case study of a blended learning course at a Colombian university. *System, 94,* 102334. https://doi.org/10.1016/j.system.2020.102334

Cruz, A. L. (2013). Paulo Freire's concept of conscientização. In R. Lake & T. Kress (Eds.), *Paulo Freire's intellectual roots; toward historicity in praxis* (pp. 169–182). Bloomsbury.

Curriculum Development Council (2001). *Learning to learn – the way forward in curriculum.* HKSAR Government Printing Department.

Darvin, R., & Norton, B. (2018). Identity, investment, and TESOL. In J. I. Liontas (Ed.), *The TESOL encyclopedia of English language teaching.* Wiley. https://doi.org/10.1002/9781118784235.eelt0802

Darvin, R., & Norton, B. (2023). Investment and motivation in language learning: What's the difference? *Language Teaching, 56*(1), 29–40. https://doi.org/10.1017/S0261444821000057

Dasli, M. (2025). Critical pedagogy, deconstruction, and the promises of interculturality. In F. Dervin (Ed.), *The Routledge handbook of critical interculturality in communication and education* (pp. 69–82). Routledge.

De Costa, P. I., Rabie-Ahmed, A., & Cinaglia, C. (Eds.). (2024). *Ethical issues in applied linguistics scholarship.* John Benjamins.

de Oliveira, L. C., Willging, T., & Beatty, J. (2024). Developing curriculum materials integrating language and social studies: Implementing a functional approach to language development. In K. Mastruserio Reynolds & K.-D. Kuttig (Eds.), *K-12 classroom research in language teaching and learning: Narratives for understanding and engaging in teacher research* (pp. 127–145). Routledge.

Deci, E. L., & Ryan, R. M. (2000). The 'what' and 'why' of goal pursuits: Human needs and the self-determination of behavior. *Psychological Inquiry, 11*(4), 227–268. https://doi.org/10.1207/S15327965PLI1104_01

Dervin, F. (2025). Critical interculturality in language learning: Plurilingualism for problematising and enriching the notion. In C. Fäcke, X. Gao & P. Garrett-Rucks (Eds.), *The handbook of plurilingual and intercultural language learning* (pp. 59–70). Wiley.

Dewey, J. (1916/1966). *Democracy in education.* Free Press.

Dewey, J. (1929). *The sources of a science of education.* H. Liverright.

Dewey, J. (2008a/1900). *The school and society.* In J. A. Boydston (Ed.), *The middle works of John Dewey, Vol. 1* (pp. 1–112). Southern Illinois University Press.

Dewey, J. (2008b/1902). *The child and the curriculum.* In J. A. Boydston (Ed.), *The middle works of John Dewey, Vol. 2* (pp. 271–292). Southern Illinois University Press.

Dewey, J. (2008c/1916). *Democracy and education.* In J. A. Boydston (Ed.), *The middle works of John Dewey, Vol. 9* (pp. 1–370). Southern Illinois University Press.

Dewey, J. (2008d/1928). Philosophies of freedom. In J. A. Boydston (Ed.), *The later works of John Dewey, Vol. 3* (pp. 291–303). Southern Illinois University Press.

Díaz Maggioli, G. (2023). *Initial language teacher education.* Routledge.

Dicks, B., Soyinka, B., & Coffey, A. (2006). Multimodal ethnography. *Qualitative Research*, *6*(1), 77–96. https://doi.org/10.1177/1468794106058876

Dörnyei, Z. (2009). The L2 motivational self system. In Z. Dörnyei & E. Ushioda (Eds.), *Motivation, language identity and the L2 self* (pp. 9–42). Multilingual Matters.

Dörnyei, Z. (2014). *The psychology of the language learner: Individual differences in second language acquisition*. Routledge.

Dörnyei, Z. (2019). Towards a better understanding of the L2 learning experience, the Cinderella of the L2 motivational self system. *Studies in Second Language Learning and Teaching*, *9*(1), 19–30. https://doi.org/10.14746/ssllt.2019.9.1.2

Dörnyei, Z., & Kubanyiova, M. (2014). *Motivating learners, motivating teachers: Building vision in the language classroom*. Cambridge University Press.

Dörnyei, Z., & Ushioda, E. (Eds.). (2009). *Motivation, language identity and the L2 self*. Multilingual Matters.

Dörnyei, Z., & Ushioda, E. (2021). Teaching and researching motivation (3rd ed.). Routledge.

Douglas Fir Group (2016). A transdisciplinary framework for SLA in a multilingual world. *Modern Language Journal*, *100*(Supplement 2016), 19–47. https://doi.org/10.1111/modl.12301

Eagleman, D. (2015). *The brain: The history of you*. Canongate.

Ellis, R. (2003). *Task-based language learning and teaching*. Oxford University Press.

Esteban-Guitart, M. (2014). Funds of identity. In T. Teo (Ed.), *Encyclopedia of critical psychology* (pp. 752–757). Springer.

Esteban-Guitart, M., & Moll, L. C. (2014). Funds of identity: A new concept based on the funds of knowledge approach. *Culture & Psychology*, *20*(1), 31–48. https://doi.org/10.1177/1354067X1351593

Fang, Y., & Liu, X. (2023). Urban higher education development with Chinese characteristics: The case of Shenzhen. *International Journal of Chinese Education*, *12*(1), 1–18. https://doi.org/10.1177/2212585X221144731

Farr, F., & Farrell, A. (2023). *The reflective cycle of the teaching practicum*. Equinox.

Ferrer, A., & Lin, T. B. (2021). Official bilingualism in a multilingual nation: A study of the 2030 bilingual nation policy in Taiwan. *Journal of Multilingual and Multicultural Development*, *45*(2), 551–563. https://doi.org/10.1080/01434632.2021.1909054

Flynn, P., Thompson, K., & Goodyear, P. (2018). Designing, using and evaluating learning spaces: The generation of actionable knowledge. *Australasian Journal of Educational Technology*, *34*(6), i–v. https://doi.org/10.14742/ajet.5091

Flyvbjerg, B. (2011). What is a case study? In N. K. Denzin & Y. S. Lincoln (Eds.), *The Sage handbook of qualitative research* (pp. 301–316). Sage.

Fraser, N. (2009). *Scales of justice: Reimagining political space in a globalizing world*. Columbia University Press.

Freire, P. (2000). *Pedagogy of the oppressed*. Continuum.

Gao, X., & Tao, J. (2017). Teacher agency and identity commitment in curricular reform. *Teaching and Teacher Education*, *63*, 346–355. https://doi.org/10.1016/j.tate.2017.01.010

Garcia, O. (2019). Decolonizing foreign, second, heritage, and first languages: Implications for education. In D. Macedo (Ed.), *Decolonizing foreign language education: The misteaching of English and other colonial languages* (pp. 152–168). Routledge.

Giroux, H. A. (2010). Paulo Freire and the crisis of the political. *Power and Education*, *2*(3), 335–340. https://doi.org/10.2304/power.2010.2.3.335

Goodwin, S., & Proctor, H. (2019). Introduction: Social justice talk and social justice practices in the contemporary university. In K. Freebody, S. Goodwin & H. Proctor (Eds.), *Higher education, pedagogy and social justice: Politics and practice* (pp. 1–20). Palgrave.

Goulah, J., & Kantunich, J. (Eds.). (2020). *TESOL and sustainability: English language teaching in the anthropocene era*. Bloomsbury.

Graham-Brown, N. (2021). Making it inclusive: Reflections on designing a training session for 'decolonising' the curriculum. *NYS TESOL Journal, 8*(2), 66–71.

Graves, K. (2008). The language curriculum: A social contextual perspective. *Language Teaching, 41*(2), 147–181. https://doi.org/10.1017/S0261444807004867

Graves, K. (2016). Language curriculum design: Possibilities and realities. In G. Hall (Ed.), *The Routledge handbook of English language teaching* (pp. 79–93). Routledge.

Graves, K. (2023). Mind the gap: A tale of two curriculum fallacies. *Language Teaching, 56*(2), 197–209. https://doi.org/10.1017/S0261444821000148

Hall, C. (2016). A short introduction to social justice and ELT. In C. Hastings (Ed.), *Social justice in English language teaching* (pp. 3–10). TESOL Press.

Hall, G., & Cook, G. (2014). Own language use in ELT: Exploring global practices and attitudes. *Language Issues: The ESOL Journal, 25*(1), 35–43.

Halliday, M. A. K. (2016). *Aspects of language and learning*. Springer.

Hamman, D., Gosselin, K., Romano, J., & Bunuan, R. (2010). Using possible-selves theory to understand the identity development of new teachers. *Teaching and Teacher Education, 26*(7), 1349–1361. https://doi.org/10.1016/j.tate.2010.03.005

Harrison, T., Ledezma, K., Morgan, M., & Morgan, J. (2024). The language of submission: A four-way duoethnography exploring translanguaging pedagogy with carceral students' funds of knowledge and funds of identity. *Innovation in Language Learning and Teaching, 18*(3), 237–252. https://doi.org/10.1080/17501229.2024.2311840

Hauser, R. (1998). Should we end social promotion? Truth and consequences. Paper delivered at the conference of the Harvard Civil Rights Project on Civil Rights and High Stakes Testing, Columbia University, December 1998. Available at https://files.eric.ed.gov/fulltext/ED445015.pdf

Hobbs, G. B., & Mourão, S. (2025). Take-home tests as an assessment for learning strategy. *ELT Journal, 79*(1), 22–34. https://doi.org/10.1093/elt/ccae023

Hoffmann, L. (2016). Nation, nationalism, curriculum, and the making of citizens. In M. A. Peters (Ed.), *Encyclopedia of educational philosophy and theory* (pp. 1–6). Springer.

Huang, S.-Y. (2022). Multimodal and critical representations of gender and sexuality. In D. L. Banegas & N. Govender (Eds.), *Gender diversity and sexuality in English language education: Transnational perspectives* (pp. 123–140). Bloomsbury.

Jalalian Daghigh, A., & Abdul Rahim, H. (2021). Neoliberalism in ELT textbooks: An analysis of locally developed and imported textbooks used in Malaysia. *Pedagogy, Culture & Society, 29*(3), 493–512. https://doi.org/10.1080/14681366.2020.1755888

Jørgensen, M., & Phillips, L. J. (2002). *Discourse analysis as theory and method*. SAGE Publications.

Kalaja, P., & Melo-Pfeifer, S. (Eds.). (2025). *Visualising language students and teachers as multilinguals: Advancing social justice in education*. Multilingual Matters.

Kanno, Y., Rios-Aguilar, C., & Bunch, G. C. (2024). English learners? Emergent bilinguals? Multilingual learners?: Goals, contexts, and consequences in labeling learners. *TESOL Journal, 15*(3), e797. https://doi.org/10.1002/tesj.797

Karataş, F., Eriçok, B., & Tanrikulu, L. (2025). Reshaping curriculum adaptation in the age of artificial intelligence: Mapping teachers' AI-driven curriculum adaptation patterns. *British Educational Research Journal, 51*(1), 154–180. https://doi.org/10.1002/berj.4068

Karimpour, S., De Costa, P. I., Ranjbar, M., & Nazari, M. (2025). An ecological exploration of the intersection between English language teachers' agency and social justice instruction. *Language Teaching Research, 0*(0). https://doi.org/10.1177/13621688251314484

Kartal, G. (2023). *From digital literacy to AI literacy in language teaching: Embracing the artificial intelligence age*. IGI Global.

Kayi-Aydar, H. (2019). Language teacher agency: Major theoretical considerations, conceptualizations and methodological choices. In H. X. G. Kayi-Aydar, E. R. Miller, M. Varghese & G. Vitanova (Eds.), *Theorizing and analyzing language teacher agency* (pp. 10–21). Multilingual Matters.

Kayi-Aydar, H., Varghese, M., & Vitanova, G., (2022). Intersectionality for TESOL education: Connecting theory and justice pedagogy. *CATESOL Journal, 33*(1), 1–10.

Keele University (no date). Keele's manifesto for decolonising the curriculum. Available on 15 January 2025 at https://www.keele.ac.uk/equalitydiversity/equalityframeworksandactivities/equalityawardsandreports/equalityawards/raceequalitycharter/kdnmanifestofordecolonising/

Kelly, A. V. (2009). *The curriculum: Theory and practice* (6th ed.). Sage.

Kiczkowiak, M., & Lowe, R. J. (2019). *Teaching English as a lingua franca: The journey from EFL to ELF*. Delta Publishing.

Kleckova, G., & Dalle, T. (2018). Working with a course book and the curriculum. In J. I. Liontas (Ed.), *The TESOL encyclopedia of English language teaching* (pp. 1–6). Wiley. https://doi.org/10.1002/9781118784235.eelt0208

Konstantoni, K., & Emejulu, A. (2017). When intersectionality met childhood studies: The dilemmas of a travelling concept. *Children's Geographies, 15*(1), 6–22. https://doi.org/10.1080/14733285.2016.1249824

Konttinen, M. (2022). Towards more learning-centred English-medium education: Promoting the combination of backward design and community of practice in teacher training. *Innovation in Language Learning and Teaching, 16*(4–5), 381–391. https://doi.org/10.1080/17501229.2022.2064469

Krashen, S. (1981). *Second language acquisition and second language learning*. Prentice Hall.

Krippendorff, K. (2019). *Content analysis: An introduction to its methodology* (4th ed.). SAGE Publications.

Lamb, M., Csizér, K., Henry, A., & Ryan, S. (Eds.). (2019). *The Palgrave handbook of motivation for language learning*. Palgrave.

Lamb, T., Hatoss, A., & O'Neill, S. (2019). Challenging social injustice in superdiverse contexts through activist languages education. In R. Papa (Ed.), *Handbook on promoting social justice in education* (pp. 1–38). Palgrave.

Lanver, U., & Hultgren, A. K. (2018). The Englishization of European education. *European Journal of Language Policy, 10*(1), 1–11. https://doi.org/10.3828/ejlp.2018.1

Larsen-Freeman, D. (2019). On language learner agency: A complex dynamic systems theory perspective. *Modern Language Journal, 103*(Supplement 2019), 61–79. https://doi.org/10.1111/modl.12536

Lee, C. C., & Low, M. Y. H. (2024). Using GenAI in education: The case for critical thinking. *Frontiers in Artificial Intelligence, 7*, 1452131. https://doi.org/10.3389/frai.2024.1452131

Ley de Educación Nacional 26,206 (2006). Congreso de la Nación Argentina.

Li, W. (2024). Transformative pedagogy for inclusion and social justice through translanguaging, co-learning, and transpositioning. *Language Teaching, 57*(2), 203–214. https://doi.org/10.1017/S0261444823000186

Liddicoat, A. J. (2015). Interculturality. In K. Tracy, T. Sandel & C. Ilie (Eds.), *The international encyclopedia of language and social interaction*. Wiley.

Liddicoat, A. J. (2021). Teaching languages from an intercultural perspective. Rethinking the nature of learning. In R. Arber, M. Weinmann & J. Blackmore (Eds.), *Rethinking languages education: Directions, challenges, and innovations* (pp. 224–241). Routledge.

Lipponen, L., & Kumpulainen, K. (2011). Acting as accountable authors: Creating interactional spaces for agency work in teacher education. *Teaching and Teacher Education, 27*(5), 812–819. https://doi.org/10.1016/j.tate.2011.01.001

Little, S., & Cheng, K. (2024). Digital funds of identity: Understanding a young child's plurilingual development through mediagrams. *Innovation in Language Learning and Teaching, 18*(3), 208–222. https://doi.org/10.1080/17501229.2023.2276952

Liu, J., & Xu, Y. (2017). Assessment for learning in English language classrooms in China: Contexts, problems, and solutions. In H. Reinders, D. Nunan & B. Zou (Eds.), *Innovation in language learning and teaching: The case of China* (pp. 17–37). Palgrave Macmillan.

Llurda, E., & Calvet-Terré, J. (2024). Native-speakerism and non-native second language teachers: A research agenda. *Language Teaching, 57*(2), 229–245. https://doi.org/10.1017/S0261444822000271

Lo, A. W. T. (2025). A digital pedagogy for transculturing ELT through global Englishes. *ELT Journal*, ccaf011. https://doi.org/10.1093/elt/ccaf011

Long, M. H. (2009). Methodological principles for language teaching. In M. H. Long & C. J. Doughty (Eds.), *The handbook of language teaching* (pp. 373–394). Wiley-Blackwell.

López-Gopar, M. E., & Nava, D. I. P. (2025). One morning at a public elementary school in Mexico: A decolonial/critical perspective of ELT. *TESOL Quarterly, 59*(1), 552–564. https://doi.org/10.1002/tesq.3264

López-Medina, E., Beacon, G., Quinterno, M., & Sotelo, X. (Eds.). (2025). *Queer studies in English language education.* Brill.

Lu, D., & Xie, Y. N. (2022). Critical thinking cultivation in TESOL with ICT tools: A systematic review. *Computer Assisted Language Learning, 37*(1–2), 222–242. https://doi.org/10.1080/09588221.2022.2033788

Luckett, K., & Shay, S. (2020). Reframing the curriculum: A transformative approach. *Critical Studies in Education, 61*(1), 50–65. https://doi.org/10.1080/17508487.2017.1356341

Ludlow, A., & Gutierrez, R. (2014). *Developmental psychology.* Bloomsbury.

Macalister, & Nation, I. S. P. (2020). *Language curriculum design* (2nd ed.). Routledge.

Macaro, E. (2019). Systematic reviews in applied linguistics. In J. McKinley & H. Rose (Eds.), *The Routledge handbook of research methods in applied linguistics* (pp. 230–239). Routledge.

Macedo, D. P. (Ed.). (2019). *Decolonizing foreign language education: The misteaching of English and other colonial languages.* Routledge.

Mahali, A., & Swartz, S. (2018). Using qualitative tools as interventionist research strategies for emancipation. *International Journal of Qualitative Methods, 17*(1), 1–10. https://doi.org/10.1177/1609406918799573

Mahboob, A. (2020). World Englishes and culture wars. In A. Kirkpatrick (Ed.), *Routledge handbook of world Englishes* (2nd ed., pp. 447–471). Routledge.

Maley, A., & Peachey, N. (Eds.). (2017). *Integrating global issues in the creative English language classroom: With reference to the United Nations Sustainable Development Goals.* British Council. Available at https://www.teachingenglish.org.uk/sites/teacheng/files/PUB_29200_Creativity_UN_SDG_v4S_WEB.pdf

Mambu, J. E. (2022). Co-constructing a critical ELT curriculum: A case study in an Indonesian-based English language teacher education program. *TESOL Journal, 13*(3), e667. https://doi.org/10.1002/tesj.667

Manan, S. A., Tajik, M. A., Hajar, A., & Amin, M. (2024). From colonial celebration to postcolonial performativity: 'Guilty multilingualism' and 'performative agency' in the English Medium Instruction (EMI) context. *Critical Inquiry in Language Studies, 21*(3), 307–334. https://doi.org/10.1080/15427587.2023.2242989

Mann, S., & Walsh, S. (2017). *Reflective practice in English language teaching: Research-based principles and practices.* Routledge.

Marcus, G. (2019). *Gypsy and traveller girls: Silence, agency and power.* Springer.

Markee, N. (2013). Contexts of change. In K. Hyland & L. Wong (Eds.), *Innovation and change in English language education* (pp. 28–43). Routledge.

Markus, H., & Nurius, P. (1986). Possible selves. *American Psychologist, 41*(9), 954–969.

Mayhew, K., & Edwards, A. C. (1936). *The Dewey school: The laboratory school of the University of Chicago, 1896–1903*. Transaction Publishers.

Mazzaferro, G. (Ed.). (2018). *Translanguaging as everyday practice*. Springer.

McCarthy, M., & O'Dell, F. (2008). *Academic vocabulary in use*. Cambridge University Press.

McGranahan, C. (2018). Ethnography. In H. Callan (Ed.), *The international encyclopedia of anthropology*. Wiley. https://doi.org/10.1002/9781118924396.wbiea2262

McPhail, S. A. (2018). South Korea's linguistic tangle: English vs. Korean vs. Konglish: A study of the relative status of Konglish and its parent languages in South Korea. *English Today, 34*(1), 45–51. https://doi.org/10.1017/S0266078417000244

Meddings, L., & Thornbury, S. (2009). *Teaching unplugged: Dogme in English language teaching*. Delta Publishing.

Medina, J. (2013). *The epistemology of resistance: Gender and racial oppression, epistemic injustice, and the social imagination*. Oxford University Press.

Meighan, P. J. (2020). A case for decolonizing English language instruction. *ELT Journal, 74*(1), 83–85. https://doi.org/10.1093/elt/ccz055

Melles, G., Howard, Z., & Thompson-Whiteside, S. (2012). Teaching design thinking: Expanding horizons in design education. *Procedia - Social and Behavioral Sciences, 31*, 162–166. https://doi.org/10.1016/j.sbspro.2011.12.035

Mercer, S. (2011a). The beliefs of two expert EFL learners. *The Language Learning Journal, 39*(1), 57–74. https://doi.org/10.1080/09571736.2010.521571

Mercer, S. (2011b). Understanding learner agency as a complex dynamic system. *System, 39*(4), 427–436. https://doi.org/10.1016/j.system.2011.08.001

Mercer, S. (2012). The complexity of learner agency. *Apples – Journal of Applied Language Studies, 6*(2), 41–59.

Mideros, D., Roberts, N., Carter, B., & Reinders, H. (Eds.). (2023). *Innovation in language learning and teaching: The case of the Southern Caribbean*. Palgrave.

Mills, M., Riddle, S., McGregor, G., & Howell, A. (2022). Towards an understanding of curricular justice and democratic schooling. *Journal of Educational Administration and History, 54*(3), 345–356. https://doi.org/10.1080/00220620.2021.1977262

Ministerio de Educación Nacional, MEN (2006). *Serie Guías 22. Estándares básicos de competencias en lenguas extranjeras: inglés. Formar en lenguas extranjeras: ¡el reto! Lo que necesitamos saber y saber hacer*. Bogotá: MEN.

Ministerio de Educación Nacional, MEN (2016a). *Mallas de aprendizaje de inglés para transición a 5° de primaria*. https://eco.colombiaaprende.edu.co/2021/10/29/mallas-de-aprendizaje-de-ingles-para-transicion-a-5-de-primaria/

Ministerio de Educación Nacional, MEN (2016b). *Orientaciones y principios pedagógicos. Currículo Sugerido De Inglés Grados 6° a 11°: English for diversity and equity*. https://eco.colombiaaprende.edu.co/2021/09/07/orientaciones-y-principios-pedagogicos-curriculo-sugerido-de-ingles/

Ministerio de Educación Nacional, MEN (January 9, 2018). *Lengua extranjera*. Ministerio de Educación Nacional. https://www.mineducacion.gov.co/portal/micrositios-preescolar-basica-y-media/Educacion-Privada/Calidad/364450:Lengua-Extranjera

Mirhosseini, S.-A. (2018). Issues of ideology in English language education worldwide: An overview. *Pedagogy, Culture & Society, 26*(1), 19–33. https://doi.org/10.1080/14681366.2017.1318415

Mishan, F., & Timmis, I. (2015). *Materials development for TESOL*. Edinburgh University Press.

Mortenson, L. (2021). White TESOL instructors' engagement with social justice content in an EAP program: Teacher neutrality as a tool of white supremacy. *BC TEAL Journal, 6*(1), 106–131. https://doi.org/10.14288/bctj.v6i1.422

Mortenson, L. (2022). Integrating social justice-oriented content into English for Academic Purposes (EAP) instruction: A case study. *English for Specific Purposes, 65*, 1–14. https://doi.org/10.1016/j.esp.2021.08.002

Murray, J. (2021). Good teachers are always learning. *International Journal of Early Years Education, 29*(3), 229–235. https://doi.org/10.1080/09669760.2021.1955478

Nazari, M., De Costa, P. I., & Karimpour, S. (2023). The role of institutional policy in English language teacher autonomy, agency, and identity: A poststructural perspective. *Language Teaching Research, 30*(2), 885–907. https://doi.org/10.1177/13621688221143476

Nguyen, M. H. (2019). *English language teacher education: A sociocultural perspective on preservice teachers' learning in the professional experience.* Springer.

Niemi, H. (2024). AI in education and learning: Perspectives on the education ecosystem. In M. Streit-Bianchi & V. Gorini (Eds.), *New frontiers in science in the era of AI* (pp. 169–194). Springer.

Norton, B. (2013). *Identity and language learning: Extending the conversation* (2nd ed.). Multilingual Matters.

Norton, B., & Toohey, K. (2011). Identity, language learning, and social change. *Language Teaching, 44*(4), 412–446. https://doi.org/10.1017/S0261444811000309

Nozaki, Y., & Apple, M. W. (2002). Ideology and curriculum. In D. Levinson, P. Cookson & A. Sadovnik (Eds.), *Education and sociology: An encyclopedia* (pp. 381–386). Routledge.

Nunan, D. (1988). *The learner-centred curriculum: A study in second language teaching.* Cambridge University Press.

Ojha, L. P., Devkota, K. R., & Dawadi, S. (2024). Schools as sites for the reproduction of inequalities? Neoliberalism, dual-medium instruction and social (in)justice. In R. A. Giri, A. Padwad, A. & M. N. N. Kabir (Eds.), *Equity, social justice, and English medium instruction* (pp. 107–125). Springer.

Okan, Z. (2019). Language and social justice. In R. Papa (Ed.), *Handbook on promoting social justice in education* (pp. 1–14). Springer.

Ordem, E. (2023). Participatory action research in a listening-speaking class in second language teaching: Towards a critical syllabus. *Educational Action Research, 31*(1), 4–20. https://doi.org/10.1080/09650792.2021.1898431

Ortaçtepe Hart, D. (2023). *Social justice and the language classroom: Reflection, action, and transformation.* Edinburgh University Press.

Ortega, Y. (2024). 'Un futuro mejor para todos': Towards a critical humanizing English language teaching. *Language Teaching Research, 0*(0). https://doi.org/10.1177/13621688241262618

Ortega, Y., & Oxford, R. (2025). Immigrants' and refugees' 'funds of knowledge(s)' on the path to intercultural competence. *Journal of Multilingual and Multicultural Development, 46*(9), 2648–2659. https://doi.org/10.1080/01434632.2023.2170389

Orwell, G. (1945/2022). *Animal farm.* Polygon.

Paiz, J., & Coda, J. (Eds.). (2021). *Intersectional perspectives on LGBTQ+ issues in modern language teaching and learning.* Palgrave.

Paris, D., & Alim, H. S. (Eds.). (2017). *Culturally sustaining pedagogies: Teaching and learning for justice in a changing world.* Teachers College Press.

Pashby, K. (2018). Identity, belonging and diversity in education for global citizenship: Multiplying, intersecting, transforming, and engaging lived realities. In I. Davies, L. Ho, D. Kiwan, C. L. Peck, A. Peterson, E. Sant & Y. Waghid (Eds.), *The Palgrave handbook of global citizenship and education* (pp. 277–293). Palgrave.

Pedaste, M., Mäeots, M., Siiman, L. A., De Jong, T., Van Riesen, S. A., Kamp, E. T., & Tsourlidaki, E. (2015). Phases of inquiry-based learning: Definitions and the inquiry cycle. *Educational Research Review, 14*, 47–61. https://doi.org/10.1016/j.edurev.2015.02.003

Penuel, W. R. (2014). Emerging forms of formative intervention research in education. *Mind, Culture, and Activity, 21*(2), 97–117. https://doi.org/10.1080/10749039.2014.884137

Pérez Berbain, M., Payaslian, L., Sauer Rosas, A., García, B., & La Porta, A. (2023). The impact of mentoring on English language teachers: A case from Argentina. *Profile: Issues in Teachers' Professional Development, 25*(1), 49–64. https://doi.org/10.15446/profile.v25n1.101711

Peterson, E., & Beers, K. F. (Eds.). (2023). *English in the Nordic countries: Connections, tensions, and everyday realities*. Routledge.

Phillipson, R. (2010). *Linguistic imperialism continued*. Routledge.

Phung, L., Reinders, H., & Pham, V. (Eds.). (2024). *Innovation in language learning and teaching: The case of Vietnam and Cambodia*. Palgrave.

Piccardo, E., & Capron Puozzo, I. (2015). Introduction. From second language pedagogy to the pedagogy of 'plurilingualism': A possible paradigm shift?/De la didactique des langues à la didactique du plurilinguisme: Un changement de paradigme possible? *The Canadian Modern Language Review/La revue canadienne des langues vivantes, 71*(4), 317–323.

Piccardo, E., & North, B. (2020). The dynamic nature of plurilingualism: Creating and validating CEFR descriptors for mediation, plurilingualism and pluricultural competence. In S. M. C. Lau & S. Van Viegen (Eds.), *Plurilingual pedagogies: Critical and creative endeavors for equitable language in education* (pp. 279–302). Springer.

Pillemer, D. B., & White, S. H. (Eds.). (2005). *Developmental psychology and social change: Research, history, and policy*. Cambridge University Press.

Pinter, A. (2011). *Children learning second languages*. Palgrave Macmillan.

Porto, M. (2023a). Experientially grounded praxis of social justice language education: Pre-service teachers of English engage in field work in an Argentine NGO. *Teaching Education, 34*(2), 225–245. https://doi.org/10.1080/10476210.2022.2078299

Porto, M. (2023b). Intercultural citizenship as CLIL in foreign language education. In D. L. Banegas & S. Zappa-Hollman (Eds.), *The Routledge handbook of content and language integrated learning (*pp. 141–159). Routledge.

Porto, M. (2024). Intercultural citizenship as CLIL in foreign language education. In D. L. Banegas & S. Zappa-Hollman (Eds.), *The Routledge handbook of content and language integrated learning* (pp. 141–159). Routledge.

Posner, G. (2004). *Analyzing the curriculum*. McGraw Hill.

Poudel, P. P., Jackson, L., & Choi, T.-H. (2022). Decolonisation of curriculum: The case of language education policy in Nepal. *London Review of Education, 20*(1), 1–15. https://doi.org/10.14324/LRE.20.1.13

Rahim, H., & Jalalian Daghigh, A. (2020). Locally-developed vs. global textbooks: An evaluation of cultural content in textbooks used in ELT in Malaysia. *Asian Englishes, 22*(3), 317–331. https://doi.org/10.1080/13488678.2019.1669301

Raza, K., & Eslami, Z. (2024). Intersectional lens to the study of racism in TESOL leadership: A narrative inquiry of a Nonnative English-speaking leader (NNESL) exposing epistemological and institutional racism. *TESOL Journal, 15*, e803. https://doi.org/10.1002/tesj.803

Richards, J. C. (2013). Curriculum approaches in language teaching: Forward, central, and backward design. *RELC Journal, 44*(1), 5–33. https://doi.org/10.1177/0033688212473293

Richards, J. C. (2016). Assessment and evaluation. Last accessed 11 October 2024 from https://www.professorjackrichards.com/assessment-and-evaluation/

Rodríguez Mejía, S., Quiroz, R. E., & Díaz, A. E. (2019). ¿Existen relaciones entre la formación ciudadana y la justicia social en la educación? *De Prácticas Y Discursos, 8*(11), 71–90. https://doi.org/10.30972/dpd.8113825

Sadeghi, K., & Richards, J. C. (2021). Professional development among English language teachers: Challenges and recommendations for practice. *Heliyon, 7*(9), e08053. https://doi.org/10.1016/j.heliyon.2021.e08053

Sampaio, M., & Leite, C. (2017). From curricular justice to educational improvement: What is the role of schools' self-evaluation? *Improving Schools, 20*(1), 62–75. https://doi.org/10.1177/1365480216688553

Sánchez-Auñón, E., Férez-Mora, P. A., & Monroy-Hernández, F. (2023). The use of films in the teaching of English as a foreign language: A systematic literature review. *Asian-Pacific Journal of Second and Foreign Language Education, 8*, Article 10. https://doi.org/10.1186/s40862-022-00183-0

Sawyer, R. D., & Norris, J. (2013). *Duoethnography*. Oxford University Press.

Schiro, M. S. (2012). *Curriculum theory: Conflicting visions and enduring concerns* (2nd ed.). Sage.

Schurz, A., & Sundqvist, P. (2022). Connecting extramural English with ELT: Teacher reports from Austria, Finland, France, and Sweden. *Applied Linguistics, 43*(5), 934–957. https://doi.org/10.1093/applin/amac013

Seltzer, K. (2022). Enacting a critical translingual approach in teacher preparation: Disrupting oppressive language ideologies and fostering the personal, political, and pedagogical stances of preservice teachers of English. *TESOL Journal, 13*(2), e649. https://doi.org/10.1002/tesj.649

Selvi, A. F. (2019). Qualitative content analysis. In J. McKinley & H. Rose (Eds.), *The Routledge handbook of research methods in applied linguistics* (pp. 440–452). Routledge.

Shor, I. (1993). Education is politics: Paulo Freire's critical pedagogy. In P. Leonard & P. McLaren (Eds.), *Paulo Freire: A critical encounter* (pp. 24–35). Routledge.

Sinha, S., & Hanuscin, D. L. (2017). Development of teacher leadership identity: A multiple case study. *Teaching and Teacher Education, 63*, 356–371. https://doi.org/10.1016/j.tate.2017.01.004

Smetanová, E. (2025). Pluralistic approaches to refugees or asylum seekers in Europe — Language and identity. In J. I. Liontas (Ed.), *The TESOL encyclopedia of English language teaching*. Wiley. https://doi.org/10.1002/9781118784235.eelt0847.pub2

Soto Molina, J. E. (2022). *Clave decolonial para la enseñanza de las lenguas: Hacia una ciudadanía intercultural bilingüe*. Caimán Editores.

Spada, N. (2015). SLA research and L2 pedagogy: Misapplications and questions of relevance. *Language Teaching, 48*(1), 69–81. https://doi.org/10.1017/S026144481200050X

Spolsky, B. (2004). *Language policy*. Cambridge University Press.

Stace, C. (2020). Teaching students to become global citizens. Available at https://blog.pearsoninternationalschools.com/teaching-students-to-become-global-citizens/ (Last accessed 30 January 2025)

Subero, D., Vujasinović, E., & Esteban-Guitart, M. (2017). Mobilising funds of identity in and out of school. *Cambridge Journal of Education, 47*(2), 247–263. https://doi.org/10.1080/0305764X.2016.1148116

Svarstad, L. K. (2021). Cultural studies and intersectionality in English language education: Exploring students' engagement in issues of celebrity, identity, gender and sexuality. *Language Learning Journal, 49*(6), 740–752. https://doi.org/10.1080/09571736.2019.1709885

Tao, J., & Gao, X. (2021). *Language teacher agency*. Cambridge University Press.

Tavares, V. (Ed.). (2023). *Social justice, decoloniality, and southern epistemologies within language education: Theories, knowledges, and practices on TESOL from Brazil*. Routledge.

Terán Ñacato, M. F., Naranjo Vaca, D., & Maliza Muñoz, W. (2024). Gamificación como estrategia didáctica en el proceso de enseñanza del idioma inglés en el bachillerato general unificado. *Uniandes Episteme, 11*(2), 189–202. https://doi.org/10.61154/rue.v11i2.3489

The Douglas Fir Group (2016). A transdisciplinary framework for SLA in a multilingual world. *Modern Language Journal, 100*(S1), 19–47. https://doi.org/10.1111/modl.12301

Tikly, L., & Barrett, A. M. (2011). Social justice, capabilities and the quality of education in low-income countries. *International Journal of Educational Development, 31*(1), 3–14. https://doi.org/10.1016/j.ijedudev.2010.06.001

Tomlinson, B. (Ed.). (2011). *Materials development in language teaching* (2nd ed.). Cambridge University Press.

Tomlinson, B., & Masuhara, H. (2018). *The complete guide to the theory and practice of materials development for language learning*. Wiley.

UK Government (2024). School admissions. Retrieved from https://www.gov.uk/schools-admissions/school-starting-ageon 5 April 2024.

UK National Curriculum (2024). The national curriculum. Retrieved from https://www.gov.uk/national-curriculum on 5 April 2024.

United Nations (2024). Sustainable development goals. Available at https://sdgs.un.org/goals

United Nations Educational, Scientific and Cultural Organization (UNESCO) (2015). Global citizenship education: Topics and learning objectives. Retrieved from http://unesdoc.unesco.org/images/0023/002329/232993e.pdf

Ushioda, E. (2020). *Language learning motivation: An ethical agenda for research.* Oxford University Press.

Vaish, V. (2020). *Translanguaging in multilingual English classrooms: An Asian perspective and contexts.* Springer.

van Lier, L. (2004). *The ecology and semiotics of language learning: A sociocultural perspective.* Kluwer Academic Publishers.

van Lier, L. (2011). Language learning: An ecological–semiotic approach. In E. Hinkel (Ed.), *Handbook of research in second language teaching and learning* (Vol. 2, pp. 383–394). Routledge.

Vettorel, P. (2018). ELF and communication strategies: Are they taken into account in ELT materials? *RELC Journal, 49*(1), 58–73. https://doi.org/10.1177/0033688217746204

Vilches, M. L. C. (2018). Involving teachers in the change process: One English language teacher's account of implementing curricular change in Philippine basic education. In M. Wedell & L. Grassick (Eds.), *International perspectives on teachers living with curriculum change* (pp. 15–37). Palgrave.

Villacañas de Castro, L. S. (2017). 'We are more than EFL teachers – we are educators': Emancipating EFL student-teachers through photovoice. *Educational Action Research, 25*(4), 610–629. https://doi.org/10.1080/09650792.2016.1215930

Waddington, J. (2025). *Questioning the native speaker construct in teacher education: Enabling multilingual identities and decolonial language pedagogies.* Routledge.

Waddington, J., & Esteban-Guitart, M. (2024). Funds of knowledge and identity in language learning and teaching. *Innovation in Language Learning and Teaching, 18*(3), 201–207. https://doi.org/10.1080/17501229.2024.2328306

Waluyo, B., Zahabi, A., & Panmei, B. (2025). Examining the correlates and components of English test anxiety in EFL students: A quantitative study. *MEXTESOL Journal, 49*(1), 1–16. https://doi.org/10.61871/mj.v49n1-2

Wang, C., & Canagarajah, S. (2024). Postdigital ethnography in applied linguistics: Beyond the online and offline in language learning. *Research Methods in Applied Linguistics, 3*(2), 100111. https://doi.org/10.1016/j.rmal.2024.100111

Wang, L. (2022). English language teacher agency in response to curriculum reform in China: An ecological approach. *Frontiers in Psychology, 13*, 935038. https://doi.org/10.3389/fpsyg.2022.935038

Wang, Y., & Jiang, D. (2025). Investment, linguistic capital and identity in Chinese university students' EMI experience. *Language and Education, 39*(1), 252–269. https://doi.org/10.1080/09500782.2024.2314136

Wedell, M., & Grassick, L. (Eds.). (2018). *International perspectives on teachers living with curriculum change.* Palgrave.

Wei, L. (2019). Ethnography: Origins, features, accountability, and criticality. In J. McKinley & H. Rose (Eds.), *The Routledge handbook of research methods in applied linguistics* (pp. 154–164). Routledge.

Wei, L. (2024). Transformative pedagogy for inclusion and social justice through translanguaging, co-learning, and transpositioning. *Language Teaching, 57*(2), 203–214. https://doi.org/10.1017/S0261444823000186

Wicaksono, R. (2020). Native and non-native speakers of English in TESOL. In C. Hall & R. Wicaksono (Eds.), *Ontologies of English: Conceptualising the language for learning, teaching, and assessment* (pp. 80–98). Cambridge University Press.

Widdowson, H. (1998). The ownership of English. In V. Zamel & R. Spack (Eds.), *Negotiating academic literacies: Teaching and learning across languages and cultures* (pp. 237–248). Routledge.

Wilbur, A., Damji, T., & Cowie, T. (2024). The challenges and opportunities for decolonizing TESOL in the Canadian context. In D. Rashed & D. Suarez (Eds.), *Female leadership identity in English language teaching: Autoethnographies of global perspectives* (pp. 193–210). Brill.

Wiliam, D. (2011). What is assessment for learning? *Studies in Educational Evaluation, 37*(1), 3–14. https://doi.org/10.1016/j.stueduc.2011.03.001

Willis, J., & Willis, D. (2013). *Doing task-based teaching* (Kindle ed.). Oxford University Press.

Xiao, J. (2014). Learner agency in language learning: The story of a distance learner of EFL in China. *Distance Education, 35*(1), 4–17. https://doi.org/10.1080/01587919.2014.891429

Yazan B. (2019). Toward identity-oriented teacher education: Critical autoethnographic narrative. *TESOL Journal, 10*(1), 10:e388. https://doi.org/10.1002/tesj.388

Yin, R. (2018). *Case study research and applications: Design and methods* (6th ed.). Sage.

Young, M. (2014). What is a curriculum and what can it do? *The Curriculum Journal, 25*(1), 7–13. https://doi.org/10.1080/09585176.2014.902526

Yuen, S., Boulton, H., & Byrom, T. (2018). School-based curriculum development as reflective practice: A case study in Hong Kong. *Curriculum Perspectives, 38*, 15–25. https://doi.org/10.1007/s41297-017-0032-8

Zeaiter, L. F. (2023). Plurilingual tasks in TESOL: Improving learners' emotionality. In K. Raza, D. Reynolds & C. Coombe (Eds.), *Handbook of multilingual TESOL in practice* (pp. 281–294). Springer.

Zhang, H., Li, X., & Chang, W. (2024). Representation of cultures in national English textbooks in China: A synchronic content analysis. *Journal of Multilingual and Multicultural Development, 45*(8), 3394–3414. https://doi.org/10.1080/01434632.2022.2099406

Zhong, Y., Tan, H., & Peng, Y. (2019). Curriculum 2.0 and student content-based language pedagogy. *System, 84*, 76–86. https://doi.org/10.1016/j.system.2019.06.001

Zolin Vesz, F., Banegas, D. L., & C. de Oliveira, L. (Eds.). (2024). *Language teacher education beyond borders: Multilingualism, transculturalism, and critical approaches*. Bloomsbury.

Index